The Environment, Public Health, and Human Ecology

Considerations for Economic Development

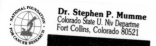

Dr. Stephen P. Mumme
Colorado State U. Niv Departme
Fort Collins, Colorado 80521

The Environment, Public Health, and Human Ecology

*Considerations for
Economic Development*

James A. Lee

Published for The World Bank
THE JOHNS HOPKINS UNIVERSITY PRESS
Baltimore and London

The Johns Hopkins University Press
Baltimore, Maryland 21211, U.S.A.

First printing December 1985

Library of Congress Cataloging-in-Publication Data
Main entry under title:

The Environment, public health, and human ecology.

  Bibliography: p.
  1. Environmental policy.   2. Environmental protection.   3. Human ecology.   I. Lee, James A. II. International Bank for Reconstruction and Development.
HC79.E5E574   333.7   82-6574
ISBN 0-8018-2911-9

Foreword

The collective actions of a world population rapidly approaching five billion are seriously affecting natural systems and their ability to support economic growth and development. Environmental constraints are becoming increasingly critical to the sustained development of many of The World Bank's developing member countries.

As part of its continuing efforts to identify and remedy environmental problems likely to be associated with development projects, the Bank produces a broad array of guidelines, manuals, handbooks, and associated specialized aids.

The Bank is pleased to make available this comprehensive handbook to assist those concerned with the development process in avoiding threats to the environment, health, and social welfare.

S. Shahid Husain
Vice President, Operations Policy
The World Bank

July 1985

Contents

Preface

The quest by developing nations to achieve higher standards of living involves deliberate modification of the natural environment to reach economic objectives. The construction of dams, irrigation systems, industrial facilities, and power plants and the process of implementing agricultural and rural development schemes can result in the degradation and destruction of life-supporting ecological systems and of natural resources. Associated with these unwanted impacts are threats to human health and to important sociocultural values. These effects vary widely in magnitude. They may be felt over the short or medium term, or they may end in irreversible damage. Unwanted environmental impacts may result from inadequate attention to environmental consequences at the project planning and design stages or from lack of the knowledge and information necessary to predict them. Even when undesirable effects are foreseen and acknowledged, planners may not be aware of cost-effective preventive or mitigating measures or may not have considered alternative project designs or locations.

Untoward environmental consequences (even if they go unmeasured) increase the true costs of development. Often a higher price must be paid to remedy the situation at a later stage of development—if, indeed, remedial action is possible.

It is important, therefore, that all those involved in a proposed development scheme—planners, political decisionmakers, engineers, financing institutions, government officials, and consultants—have a clear understanding of the potential environmental, health, and human ecological consequences. Conversely, those aspects of the scheme that enhance environmental values should also be noted and understood, and the full range of likely consequences should be ascertained at an early stage of planning. With such knowledge it may be possible to avoid or mitigate serious unwanted impacts or to promote positive consequences by incorporating appropriate measures into the project, by redesigning or relocating it, or in extreme cases by abandoning it.

This handbook is designed to provide guidance in the detection, identification, assessment, and measurement of environmental and related human ecological effects. It offers to a broad readership interested in public affairs an overview of the implications of economic development projects for natural resources, environmental systems, public and occupational health, and human ecology. It is not intended to substitute for highly specific guidelines and instructions of the kind needed by engineers and other specialists; these can be found in the World Bank's environmental and occupational health and safety guidelines for the industrial sector, which are listed in the bibliography.

The antecedents of this book go back to 1971, when the World Bank published the first such handbook ever to be prepared by a development finance institution. An expanded version, issued in 1974, proved to be popular around the world and useful in a great variety of situations. This book builds on the Bank's history of promoting awareness of the environmental consequences of development.

The book has benefited from the contributions of many individuals who provided material or reviewed and commented critically on the drafts. Among them are staff members of the Bank's Office of Environmental and Scientific Affairs, including Bernard Baratz, Robert Goodland, Ragnar Overby, and Jean Tixhon, as well as John Courtney, Anthony Pelligrini, David Williams, and others from elsewhere in the Bank. Consultants who participated in the preparation include George Darnell, Martha Dosa, Jochen Eigen, James Hughes, Irwin Karp, Donald R. King, Ralph Palange, David Pimentel, and Marvin Singer.

Manuscript preparation benefited from the work of Mary Ann Dement, Betty Luke, Olivia McNeal, Sheila Mulvihill, and Olive I. Nash.

The Environment, Public Health, and Human Ecology

Considerations for
Economic Development

Introduction

Development projects require the deliberate modification of the environment. As a result, any new development project or expansion of an existing facility poses the threat of environmental degradation and adverse effects on public health. Too often, projects have been implemented without adequate regard for their ecological consequences, for the health of local residents and workers, and for the sociocultural well-being of the community. After a project is completed, it may be extremely expensive or difficult, if not impossible, to remedy its negative effects.

The adverse consequences of development projects most often occur because they have not been anticipated in the planning and design phases. With the current state of knowledge of environmental systems and human health hazards in the environment, major negative effects can be prevented if planners anticipate them and provide for mitigating measures. All those involved in a proposed development project—planners, political decisionmakers, engineers, consultants, and financial institutions—must therefore help identify threats to the environment and the public health and take steps to prevent or control them at the earliest feasible stage of planning and preparation.

More than a hundred nations now have an environmental ministry or similar governmental organization, which strengthens their capacity to assess environmental impacts and to enforce measures for the protection and management of natural resources. In 1980 the major multilateral development assistance institutions signed a Declaration of Environmental Policies and Procedures, which commits them to ensuring, as far as possible, the environmental soundness of projects they finance. Similar actions have been taken by the principal bilateral development aid agencies. The World Bank, together with other international and national organizations, is at present using and developing improved detailed environmental, health, and human ecological criteria and guidelines in the assessment of development projects.

Since 1971 the World Bank has sought systematically to identify likely environmental problems in the early stages of project formulation and has incorporated preventive or mitigating measures into the design and implementation of projects. The Bank's Office of Environmental and Scientific Affairs provides guidance to other institutions and governments on procedures for ensuring proper consideration of environmental and health impacts of development projects. The focus is on "sustainable development," which requires careful attention in development projects to maintaining the environmental and human resource base that is essential for continued long-term economic growth.

Developing countries are expected to continue looking to the Bank for guidance on the balance between economic development and a healthy environment to sustain that development. At the same time, it is hoped that developing countries will develop their own capacity to achieve that balance.

To that end, this handbook, the first edition of which appeared in 1973, is designed to provide guidance in the identification, detection, measurement, and control of adverse environmental effects. It is intended for a wide array of users. As such, it is a general survey of the environmental, health, and human ecological impacts of development projects in sectors such as agriculture, industry, energy, and urban development (including water supply, sanitation, and transportation). The handbook is not a manual for the environmental engineer who is faced with a detailed problem of controlling environmental pollution in a specific development project. Nor is it a substitute for experts or consultants. It is intended primarily as a primer for the nonexpert to highlight the major environmental, public health, and sociocultural impacts of economic development projects. Project planners, government policymakers, economists, lending officers in financial institutions—all should find this book helpful.

The information presented here will enable individuals and institutions involved in economic development to recognize potential problems at the outset and appropriately address those problems at the earliest stages of project planning. The handbook is organized so that a reader with either a general interest in basic environmental, public health, or sociocultural impacts or a specific interest in one sector can readily locate the requisite information. But this book is merely a starting point—it calls attention to a host of issues that need to be considered in the context of an actual development project. For a list of reports, manuals, and guidelines that address specific project concerns in greater detail, see the bibliography at the back of this book.

Chapter 1 describes the World Bank's policy of "sustainable development," which tries to ensure that the environmental and human resources necessary to sustain economic growth in developing nations are not adversely affected. The Bank's project cycle is discussed, along with opportunities for environmental input in that cycle. The role of cost-benefit assessments and the difficulties of quantifying the benefits of environmental protection measures are then briefly considered. In view of past failures of project developers properly to consider environmental impacts, the Bank's policy of providing assistance to remedy existing pollution problems is discussed and relevant examples are provided.

Chapter 2 examines four environmental problems caused primarily by industrial and energy-related development projects: air pollution, water pollution, solid waste disposal, and noise pollution. The timely issue of exposure to toxic contaminants is addressed in the discussions on air and water pollution, and handling of hazardous wastes is considered in the section on waste disposal.

In addition to pollution, development projects may also create or intensify health problems by the way they affect disease transmission, housing, medical care, water supplies, and sanitation facilities. Chapter 3 focuses on direct and indirect health risks to both the inhabitants and the migrant workers in the project area and provides a comprehensive planning guide for dealing with such impacts.

As the world population continues to increase and local per capita food supplies dwindle, agricultural development becomes even more essential. Nonetheless, projects to increase the world's food supply may have severe environmental consequences if soil and water resources are not managed in a sustainable manner. Chapter 4 discusses some possible adverse effects of tropical agricultural development and ways to mitigate them. The discussion includes issues related to farming, forestry, and the production of livestock and fish.

Chapter 5 provides a framework for analyzing the environmental impacts associated with a wide variety of industrial development projects in developing nations. Problems arising from project design, site selection, and project operations are considered, along with appropriate measures to alleviate them.

Chapter 6, on energy, first discusses the environmental damage and possible mitigating measures associated with the exploration, mining, and development of traditional fossil fuels such as oil, natural gas, and coal. It then examines the effects of electric power projects and addresses ways to control the impacts of fossil-fuel generating plants, large-scale hydroelectric projects, and renewable sources of energy (such as wind, biomass, solar energy, and small hydropower).

The final chapter discusses the planning tools available for managing urban and regional development. Urban infrastructure, with emphasis on water supply and waste disposal systems, is considered, along with the potential adverse impacts of transportation projects—the development of highways, airports, and ports.

The handbook concludes with two appendixes—a checklist of environmental considerations for project analysis, and a section on information and data resources for development projects—and a bibliography.

1
Environmental Policies
of the World Bank

Recognizing the requirements both for continued worldwide economic development and for maintenance of the integrity of the environment to support development, the World Bank has, for more than a decade, addressed environmental concerns as part of its economic assistance programs. As former Bank President Robert S. McNamara stated in 1970:

> The problem facing development finance institutions, including the World Bank, is whether and how we can help the developing countries to avoid or mitigate some of the damage economic development can do to the environment, without at the same time slowing down the pace of economic progress. It is clear that the costs resulting from adverse environmental change can be tremendous. . . . It is equally clear that, in many cases, a small investment in prevention could be worth many times over what would have to be expended to repair the damage.[1]

Sustainable Development: The Overriding Objective

Since President McNamara's address, the World Bank's overriding objective has been the achievement of sustainable development. Projects that seriously degrade the environment also threaten the essential resource base upon which national economic growth depends. The Bank's vast experience with development projects and its increased funding of environmental clean-up projects demonstrate that it is far more economical to safeguard the environment by building measures into project planning and design than to attempt to cure the problems once damage has been done. Since developing countries can ill afford an expensive curative approach to environmental degradation, many are adopting the more efficient approach of preventive management. There is an increasing awareness that environmental precautions are essential for continued economic development over the long run. Thus, the goal of sustained and healthy economic growth inherently requires careful attention to the environment.

Ten years after President McNamara's statement, his successor President A. W. Clausen reaffirmed that the Bank is "convinced that it is less expensive to incorporate the environmental dimensions into project planning than to ignore them and pay the penalties at some future time."[2]

In its review of the environmental impacts of proposed development projects, the Bank is concerned with issues outside the traditional definition of environment. In addition to the effects of development on the natural or physical environment (air, water, soil, forests, wildlife, marine life, and so on), the Bank is attentive to the impacts on public health, occupational health and safety, and social welfare and cultural values.

The Bank's Office of Environmental and Scientific Affairs ensures that consideration is given to the environmental, health, and social consequences of every development project proposed for financing and that potentially adverse impacts are avoided or mitigated. The key to the successful incorporation of appropriate mitigating measures into project plans has been the Bank's insistence on a pragmatic approach. It tailors measures to local circumstances, rather than uniformly applying rigid environmental standards in all cases.

As a matter of policy, the World Bank will not finance a project that seriously compromises public health or safety, causes severe or irreversible environmental deterioration, displaces people without adequate provision for resettlement,[3] or has important transnational environmental implications. This policy is enforced by the Office of Environmental and Scientific Affairs through the Bank's project cycle.

The World Bank's Project Cycle

Since 1971, the Bank has sought to identify likely environmental problems early in the formulation of projects. Each Bank-assisted development project passes through a cycle of internal review by the Bank's project staff. The steps in the cycle are: identification, preparation, appraisal, negotiation, implementation and supervision, and evaluation. There is an opportunity for consideration of environmental impacts at each stage of the project cycle.

Identification

In the first stage of the project cycle, bank planners help ensure that a proposed project fits into a coherent strategy for sectoral development and meets the objectives of the country in question. Once identified, projects are incorporated into a multiyear lending program that forms the basis for the Bank's future work in that country. Key environmental issues are highlighted and natural resources are assessed in these country lending programs.

Preparation

While formal responsibility for preparation rests with the borrower at this phase, the Bank plays an active role. World Bank staff prepare a project brief, which must cover the full range of technical, institutional, and economic conditions and assistance necessary to achieve the project's objectives. The preparation stage includes feasibility studies that identify major environmental impacts and resettlement issues and compare the costs and benefits of alternative measures to control and mitigate any negative effects the project might have.

Appraisal

The third step in the project cycle constitutes the Bank staff's comprehensive review of the project. Four aspects of the project design are considered: technical, institutional, economic, and financial. As part of the technical appraisal, staff analyze the potential impact of the project on the human and physical environment and recommend alternative designs for the project or measures to control or mitigate adverse environmental effects. The Bank does not necessarily look for a solution that is the most technologically advanced, but rather for one that is most appropriate to the country's resource base and stage of development. In this regard, environmental measures and control technologies are subject to a detailed cost-benefit analysis at the project appraisal stage.

Negotiation

During the negotiation stage, the Bank and the borrower attempt to agree on the measures necessary to assure the success of the project. The Bank may propose conditions in the loan agreement to resolve the principal environmental issues raised during the project appraisal. These conditions are not established according to any predetermined criteria; rather they are set case by case, depending on what can reasonably be accomplished in the country and in the setting of the project. The Bank's approach is based on professional advice and worldwide experience.

Implementation and Supervision

Implementation of the environmental protection measures is the responsibility of the borrower, assisted by appropriate experts. The Bank's role is to supervise the project to ensure that such measures function adequately. All projects will face implementation problems, some of which cannot be foreseen at the time of formulation and design. Thus, one of the main purposes of supervision is to help achieve the development objectives of the project. In this phase of the project cycle, which is primarily an exercise in collective problem-solving, the Bank can provide effective technical assistance to its member countries. If impacts are more serious than initially anticipated, Bank staff will help incorporate modified control procedures into the project design. A Project Completion Report then addresses environmental, health, sociological, and human ecological issues, where appropriate, as well as any changes in the project design.

Evaluation

In 1970 a limited environmental evaluation system was established as the final stage in the project cycle. All Bank-assisted projects are now subject to a postimplementation audit, which can provide valuable information for the design and preparation of future projects. These ex post audits are conducted by the Operations Evaluation Department of the Bank and help determine the accuracy of ecological, health, and sociocultural predictions, the efficacy of control measures, and the adequacy of project supervision.

Environmental Costs and Benefits

A useful way to incorporate environmental considerations into project planning is through the cost-benefit assessment. This analysis enables both project planners and World Bank evaluators to understand better the feasibility and desirability of a particular development project.

Traditionally, cost-benefit assessments have been expressed in purely economic terms. The costs of a particular development project have included materials, labor, interest on borrowed capital, and other easily quantifiable items. Benefits typically have included the stream of revenues generated by the project. It has become increasingly clear, however, that this type of analysis is too parochial; it does not account for the costs and benefits of the project which might accrue to society as a whole. In particular, the costs and benefits associated with a project's environmental impacts must be taken into account. It has proved difficult, however, to isolate the costs and benefits of alternative ways of dealing with environmental impacts, because the World Bank integrates environmental considerations into overall development strategy and action.

In principle, the methodologies and criteria of evaluating projects with environmental aspects are similar to those applied to other kinds of projects: the benefits (broadly considered) that can be expected from incremental environmental expenditures should be greater than those that flow from the best alternative use of the resources involved. Troublesome aspects of measuring and quantifying environmental benefits, however, make the application of such a concept more of an art than a science.

Measurement Difficulties

When the extent and character of environmental change can be predicted, existing markets sometimes provide a measure of the monetary value of some of the effects. For example, the value of fish protein gained or lost through a change in water quality can usually be measured in this way, as can the costs of repairing physical structures subject to air or water pollution or siltation from deforestation upstream. Many environmental effects are "public goods," however; as such, they do not have directly measurable market values. For example, a change in the level of air pollution or the quality of drinking water may affect health in ways that are unlikely to be adequately reflected in the marketplace. Hospital data and physicians' fees capture some of the additional costs, and those able to relocate may choose to do so at a measurable cost. But it is not possible to measure all of these costs.

Another measurement problem concerns the valuation of intergenerational costs and benefits. Because of its short time horizon and its discounting of future benefits to net present value, cost-benefit analysis inherently undervalues or completely ignores many environmental functions and services. Since many of the most significant benefits of environmental management accrue to future generations, they may not even be perceptible until after the date at which cost-benefit analysis discounts completely all future benefits. This so-called intergenerational problem is, in effect, one of long-term intertemporal inefficiency, since in a timeless world future generations would presumably pay or persuade present users of the natural environment to conserve more of it. It must therefore be acknowledged that the high discount rates currently (and arbitrarily) employed in cost-benefit analyses discourage investments with long-term benefits, while promoting projects with long-term costs.

A final measurement problem associated with cost-benefit analysis is its inability to evaluate properly the costs of irreversible damage to the environment and of foreclosing future options. Many complex natural habitats (such as tropical rain forests and coral reefs) and their ecological services are now thought to be basically nonrenewable, at least within the life span of human civilizations. The world's wildlands contain millions of as yet unstudied species whose potential uses are unknown and whose evolutionary processes may offer unpredictable benefits. It is therefore impossible to estimate the value of maintaining representative samples of these systems to preserve the scientific and economic options they guard for the future. This concern is particularly urgent in the tropics where species diversity is greatest and scientific knowledge is poorest.

Willingness to Pay

Cost-benefit analyses are usually based on the marginal utility theory of value, which is embodied in the concept of "willingness to pay." In applying this concept, the analyst should of course include the value of benefits that actually accrue to individuals, whether or not the recipients are directly charged with their costs. Since willingness to pay for alternatives is a function of resource endowment (that is, national or individual wealth) and of cultural preferences and tastes, different countries (or individuals) will make different monetary choices between environmental protection and other benefits. If the benefits of environmental management (such as watershed protection) are poorly understood, countries (or individuals) will underinvest in environmental protection, to their ultimate detriment.

Willingness to pay may also involve the factor of marginal benefits, depending on available options. For example, the value of cleaning a particular river or stream will depend on the number and availability of other clean bodies of water nearby. Willingness to pay is also based on what costs will be. Individuals may not wish or be able to invest disproportionately in improvements which must be communitywide, as in the case of urban water systems that serve the poor who pay little or nothing as well as those who pay most of the costs.

Approaches to Project Analysis

A "least-cost" project figure is derived by carefully analyzing alternative proposals for achieving a particular goal so that relevant tradeoffs can be evaluated. Where some, but not all, benefits are quantifiable, least-cost analysis can be supplemented by the "switching value" approach to answer the question, How large would the value of residual environmental benefits (those not quantified) have to be to justify the project? Assuming the cost stream, discount rate, and value of directly quantifiable benefits are all known, it is possible to calculate what value the residual benefits must have in order to equalize the stream of total costs and total benefits. (Since the benefits involved usually occur over many years, future residual benefits must be expressed as a function of first-year benefits.) After obtaining a value for what the first-year benefit would have to be to justify the project, the decision whether to proceed would be based on this computed value of first-year benefits, which serves as a switching value. If a higher amount is ascribed to actual willingness to pay for these benefits, the project should be accepted; if willingness to pay is lower, the project should be rejected. The greater the difference, of course, the greater the confidence with which a project can be accepted or rejected.

This kind of analysis also has been used to deal with intangible gains or losses, including aesthetic values and recreational activities. Such analysis is therefore relevant to problems involving losses of unique natural or cultural assets, since the fact of uniqueness will, of itself, make any kind of market pricing difficult, if not impossible.

Use of Qualitative or Descriptive Analyses

If the environmental effects are significant and cannot be quantified solely in monetary terms, it is possible to describe the effects of alternative courses of action in qualitative or noneconomic terms. In fact, qualitative, logical analysis is basic; quantification should be seen as a useful supplement, rather than vice versa.

A decision on project acceptability will be easier if, for example, in a project involving air pollution, a statement describing the benefits (or costs) of reducing (or increasing) the level of sulfur dioxide in a section of an industrial city accompanies the quantification of the costs and benefits in monetary terms. The description should cover all effects of the pollutants—on sight, smell, taste, health, corrosion, recreation, attitudes, and animal and plant life. In a qualitative presentation, as in a quantitative one, it is important to show the difference between the cases with and without the negative effects or ameliorating measures, as well as the differences among project alternatives.

In addition to the standard economic cost-benefit analysis (modified to reflect all readily quantifiable environmental benefits and costs), development projects should undergo the scrutiny of "safe minimum standard" (sms) analysis. This is a time-tested standard operating procedure widely used in engineering design and elsewhere. For example, a bridge is commonly designed with a safety factor of two or three—that is, it can bear two or three times the expected load—to accommodate the unforeseen and unknown. An sms is any noneconomic criterion which a project must meet to be environmentally or socially acceptable. The main reason for using an sms is that economic cost-benefit analysis, no matter how sophisticated, cannot adequately measure and weigh all of the environmental or social costs or benefits of a proposed project, program, or policy. The costs of modifying a project so that it meets all sms criteria are accepted as normal project costs. As noted above, these costs are usually relatively low, except for human resettlement. In the event that a proposed project cannot be modified to meet sms criteria, it should be abandoned in favor of a more environmentally or socially acceptable alternative investment.

Regulatory Strategies for Reducing Pollution

Of the many national or regional strategies that have been proposed for reducing pollution, the most common are subsidies, regulations, or charges, discussed briefly here. Specific regulatory mechanisms adopted by particular nations are described in chapter 2.

Subsidies

Subsidies are often used to encourage polluters to install control equipment or to compensate them for increased costs imposed by government standards. But if improperly applied, subsidies are often to blame for inefficient investment decisions. One problem is that the regulatory agency must isolate the costs incurred by firms for purely environmental purposes from those costs that would be incurred routinely to increase production or improve efficiency. Not surprisingly, firms have an incentive to claim subsidies for investments that, strictly speaking, are not for pollution control. Furthermore, businesses may be encouraged to invest in "end-of-pipe" treatment facilities, rather than to carry out a less expensive change in internal processes, because the former can more easily be demonstrated to be an antipollution device and hence qualify for a subsidy.

Despite its well-known distorting effects, subsidization of investment in pollution control equipment is commonplace. It is sometimes justified on the grounds that industry might not otherwise cooperate in achieving environmental goals. Although enforcement of pollution control standards may make the difference between a firm's success or failure, this argument is not in itself a reason for subsidizing pollution control. When the environmental costs of pollution are internalized by businesses, pollution control becomes another cost of production, just like wages and interest. The viability of any firm whose product cannot command a price that covers the true and complete opportunity cost of resources used should be questioned and the rationale for its existence closely examined.

Regulations, Standards, and Permits

Environmental problems, particularly those caused by harmful effluents, may be addressed through regulatory mechanisms, such as permits, that allow a given volume and concentration of effluent discharge per unit of time, establish minimum standards of water or air quality, or specify the treatment equipment to be used.

The easiest type of regulation to draw up and, in theory, to enforce is one that is applied uniformly. Although a national or regional requirement that all effluents be of a specific quality is the least difficult administratively, its advantage may sometimes be outweighed by the economic inefficiences that can result. Uniform effluent standards do not take advantage of local absorptive or regenerative capacities or of variations in the costs of pollution at different sites. Furthermore, they do not account for the difference in marginal costs faced by different businesses in adjusting the quantity or quality of their effluents. Nonetheless, in many situations, uniform standards are desirable because they place the smallest burden on scarce administrative resources.

Alternatively, it is possible to adopt effluent standards that can be individually tailored to each firm. Using this system, a governmental body can appraise each firm and issue regulations specific to that firm. They would require that pollution be reduced to the point at which either the marginal cost of an additional unit reduction among all firms is equalized or the desired level of total regionwide reduction is achieved. The costs of obtaining the information to institute such a system are often excessive, however, in light of developing countries' limited administrative resources. Furthermore, the potential for delay or inaction through appeals, litigation, or bribes—a disadvantage of uniform standards—may be even greater when individual standards are set for each business. Notwithstanding these drawbacks, the World Bank has often used individually adjusted standards, tailored to specific project circumstances and conditions, in its projects.

Effluent Charges

A final technique for reducing pollution is a system of effluent charges. The amount of the fee is usually based on the total load of the harmful discharge—for example, a given level of effluents into the air or a particular watershed. A well-calculated unit charge may reduce the amount of effluents to the desired level by calling into play the self-interest of individual firms. To maximize profits, firms may invest in process changes or effluent treatment up to the point at which the cost of a unit reduction in effluent is equal to the amount of the charge. Businesses with different cost characteristics are therefore likely to respond differently.

Because environmental absorptive or regenerative capacities, and therefore the harm caused, will vary for different airsheds or watersheds, effluent charges should be set on a regional basis. The charge should be equal to the estimated cost to society of an additional unit of pollution discharged.

The question naturally arises whether an inexact effluent charge is more or less acceptable than an inexact effluent discharge standard. Where environmental pollution is excessive and the first steps at improvement are being taken, there may be no great difference in results between a system of individually specified standards and a system of effluent charges. As the desired level of environmental improvement rises, however, marginal costs typically increase in a sharply nonlinear fashion, and the case for a rigorous system of charges becomes stronger. Other nonoptimal approaches, such as "emissions trading" (trade-offs between contributing sources of emissions) may be better than charges in certain cases.

Bank-Assisted Environmental Projects

In addition to ensuring that environmental considerations are addressed in new development projects, the World Bank is funding an increasing number of projects to rectify environmental degradation caused by inadequate attention to environmental concerns in the past. Many of the large urban centers of developing countries are now experiencing major health and environmental problems as a result of increased industrialization and rapid population growth. Air and water pollution, poor sanitation, increased accumulation of solid waste, congestion, and noise are some of the pressing concerns. The Bank has therefore increased lending for projects such as reforestation and erosion control, water supply, sewage collection and treatment, solid waste management, and air and water pollution control.

For example, the Bank is working with the Mexican government to clean up air and water pollution in Mexico City. A wildlife management project has been financed in Kenya, and Nepal has received assistance in dealing with its deforestation and soil erosion problems. In the Sahel region the Bank has financed a number of projects designed to halt the expansion of the desert and to reclaim desertified land by providing shelter belts of restored forest cover.

Some of the more prominent and successful World Bank environmental projects are described here.

Sarajevo, Yugoslavia: Air and Water Pollution

The Bank's first comprehensive urban environmental control project was the rehabilitation of the city of Sarajevo, Yugoslavia.

Sarajevo had long had a high level of air pollution because of its location (deep in a valley surrounded by high mountains subject to extended periods of temperature inversions) and its reliance on lignite with a high sulfur content for heating. In addition, the city suffered from an ancient and neglected water supply system which was so inadequate that it could supply water for only six hours a day. Often, when there was no water, sewage spilled from broken sewer pipes was back-siphoned into the city's water supply system. The Bank's loan assured a reliable and safe water supply and sewage collection system, including a new treatment plant, a sanitary landfill system for solid wastes, and significant abatement of the air pollution problem by piping in a supply of clean-burning natural gas. In addition, a completely new traffic system was established, which routes vehicles around the narrow city.

São Paulo, Brazil: Air and Water Pollution

In the greater metropolitan area of São Paulo, Brazil, which contains more than 11 million people, air and water pollution reached alarming proportions because of heavy industrialization and rapid population growth. Air pollution episodes were frequent, and increased cardiovascular and pulmonary complications were the result. In addition, the city's surface and ground water was extremely polluted; approximately 96 percent of the city's sewage was being dumped untreated into rivers and waterways.

The contamination of the city's water supply as a result of inadequate sanitation led to a high incidence of infant deaths and a rise in intestinal and other viral diseases. As an additional complication, the local industries were releasing heavy metal compounds into the city's water supply sources. The World Bank reached an agreement with local pollution control agencies to focus on several hundred of the major industrial polluters and require them to apply the best available air and water pollution control technology to meet specified standards. Compliance was to be enforced through a system of fines and penalties. A reduction of pollution levels in São Paulo has become noticeable as a result of these efforts.

Titovska Mitrovica, Yugoslavia: Lead Contamination

This city in southern Yugoslavia contained a battery factory, a sulfuric acid plant, a zinc electrolysis plant, a phosphate fertilizer industry, and one of the largest lead smelters in Europe. Researchers found that the vast majority of people living near the smelter had high levels of lead in their blood. Because medical treatment would have been fruitless until the cause of the lead poisoning was controlled, the World Bank loaned funds for a pollution control system at the smelter to reduce significantly the lead emissions.

Finland: Water Pollution

The World Bank funded a ten-year program to clean up water pollution in Finland. The objective was to reduce industrial waste discharges by 1980 to approximately 50 percent of the amount discharged into the water in 1970. Among the methods employed were improved monitoring of water pollution and a review and upgrading of Finland's system of licenses and subsidies.

Tunis, Tunisia: Sewage Treatment

Greater Tunis suffered from inadequate, overburdened sewage treatment facilities. In the First Urban Sewerage Project the World Bank provided a loan to improve those facilities. An existing treatment plant was renovated and expanded, and two new plants were built. In addition, the existing sewer network was renovated and expanded, and new collector sewers were constructed.

Conclusion

Unless carefully conceived and implemented, economic development projects in developing countries can contribute to environmental deterioration. And a degraded environment cannot sustain continued growth and undermines the entire development effort. Thus, the World Bank requires that economic development be coupled with sound environmental management. By giving early and thorough consideration to environmental, health, and sociocultural impacts and incorporating preventive and mitigating measures into project planning and design, developing countries will not need to rectify mistakes in the future. The remainder of this book discusses these impacts in a systematic way, sector by sector, and suggests ways planners can accomplish this goal.

Notes

1. Robert S. McNamara, "Speech to the United Nations Economic and Social Council" (New York, 1970).

2. A. W. Clausen, *Sustainable Development: The Global Imperative*, Fairfield Osborn Memorial Lecture (Washington, D.C.: Conservation Foundation, November 21, 1981), p. 12.

3. World Bank, "Social Issues Associated with Involuntary Resettlement in Bank-Financed Projects," Operational Manual Statement 2.33 (Washington, D.C., February 1980).

2
Economic Development and Pollution Control

For effective management of the environment, contamination of the air, water, and land resources must be kept low enough to avoid deleterious effects on human health and welfare. Increasingly, in many locations the natural media are no longer capable of assimilating or neutralizing all of the wastes produced by human activities. Population growth, widespread industrialization, agricultural development, the spread of urban areas, and other factors have overloaded the environment. Although pollution has always existed, it is no longer a small or even moderate concern. Its effects are now serious and worldwide.

Virtually all development projects may be expected to release some pollutants into the environment. The purpose of this chapter is to provide an overview of the wide range of pollutants that might be associated with World Bank–assisted development projects. Ways to reduce the level of pollution and to minimize its impacts are discussed in subsequent chapters.

This chapter examines four broad categories of environmental pollution: air pollution, water pollution, solid waste disposal (land pollution), and noise pollution. Within each category both acute and chronic effects should be anticipated. Acute impacts are usually severe and occur quickly. For example, toxic gas (hydrogen sulfide) released from a sulfur recovery plant in the town of Poza Rica, Mexico, caused the death of 22 persons and the illness of some 300 others.[1] In Japan more than 200 cases of mercury poisoning (Minamata disease) resulted from the consumption of fish contaminated by effluent from a chemical plant that processed vinyl chloride.[2]

In contrast, chronic impacts are the result of continued exposure to pollutants over a relatively long period. Although often less well documented than the acute effects, chronic effects can be equally severe. It is believed, for example, that sustained exposure to certain toxic chemicals will sharply increase the likelihood of cancer in humans. Certain pollutants, such as fluoride emissions, have been shown to contaminate vegetation and thus endanger the health of livestock feeding on it.[3]

For each category of pollution (air, water, land, noise) this chapter presents a three-part discussion: an overview of the principal pollutants, regulatory alternatives, and additional considerations. The subsections on principal pollutants describe the main sources of each pollutant and the primary effects on human health and welfare. Government actions to restrict the discharge of these pollutants into the various environmental media are discussed in the subsections on regulatory alternatives. Each final subsection includes additional considerations that are germane to the pollution category under discussion.

Air Pollution

The four major sources of air pollution are:

- Industrial operations
- Combustion of fuels for heating and energy production
- Solid waste disposal facilities
- Motor vehicles and other mobile sources.

There are a large number and variety of air pollutants in each category. Although some widespread pollutants are emitted from a large number of sources, other less common pollutants are confined to a few sources but may be particularly hazardous (or even toxic) to individuals living near the source of emission.

Principal Pollutants

The most widespread pollutants, and those which have received the most attention in developed nations, are carbon monoxide, hydrocarbons, lead, nitrogen oxides, particulate matter, photochemical oxidants, sulfates, and sulfur oxides. Most (such as carbon monoxide, hydrocarbons, lead, and sulfur oxides) are emitted from a particular source; others (such as oxidants and sulfates) are not emitted directly but are the result of chemical reactions among other contaminants (precursors) already in the atmosphere. Still others (such as particulate matter) can be either emitted directly or formed from precursors.

Air pollution can have a wide variety of adverse environmental impacts. Chronic exposure may increase the incidence of respiratory and cardiovascular ailments in humans, severely damage many types of vegetation, corrode buildings and monuments, and cause unpleasant odors and appearances. The characteristics, principal sources, and major health effects of each of these common pollutants are shown in table 2-1.

Table 2-1. *Major Air Pollutants*

Main characteristics	Principal sources	Principal health effects
	Carbon monoxide (CO)	
Colorless, odorless gas with strong affinity for hemoglobin in blood; victim is usually aware of presence of CO only after early poisoning symptoms appear (such as nausea, headache, dizziness, difficulty in breathing)	Incomplete combustion of fuels and other carbonaceous materials, industrial processes, cigarette smoking, forest fires, decomposition of organic matter; natural processes produce ten times as much CO as automobile and industrial processes combined, but the problem is the high concentrations in urban environments	Absorbed by lungs; reduces oxygen-carrying capacity of blood; reduces tolerance for exercise, impairs mental function, affects fetal development, aggravates cardiovascular disease; several studies show that prolonged low-level exposure diminishes visual perception, manual dexterity, and ability to learn and perform intellectual tasks; other studies have produced no such adverse effects at low levels of exposure
	Hydrocarbons (HC)	
Organic compounds in gaseous or particulate form (such as methane, ethylene, acetylene); component in formation of photochemical smog	Incomplete combustion of fuels and other carbon-containing substances, such as those in motor vehicle exhausts; processing, distribution, and use of petroleum compounds such as gasoline and organic solvents; natural events such as forest fires, plant metabolism, and atmospheric reactions	Acute exposure causes eye, nose, and throat irritation; chronic exposure suspected of causing cancer; some groups of combustion hydrocarbons were especially implicated in induction of cancer in laboratory animals
	Lead (Pb)	
Heavy, soft, malleable, gray metallic chemical element; often occurs (as environmental contaminant) as lead oxide aerosol or dust	Ingestion by young children with pica (abnormal craving for nonfoods) who eat leaded paint and dirt; occupational exposure in industries such as smelting and battery making; airborne lead from nonferrous metal smelters; auto exhausts along highways; agricul-	Enters primarily through respiratory tract and wall of digestive system; more than 40 percent of lead inhaled is absorbed into bloodstream; accumulates in body organs; early signs of lead poisoning are impairment of mental function, behavior problems, and anemia; higher

(Table continues on the following page.)

Table 2-1 *(continued)*

Main characteristics	Principal sources	Principal health effects
	tural use of leaded arsenates; lead salts in some pottery glazes released when in contact with slightly acidic liquid or when heated; in moonshine whiskey, which is often made in apparatus with lead-welded copper tubing or in old automobile radiators	levels cause vomiting, cramps, serious impairment of kidneys and nervous system, and possible brain damage; study on rats and mice fed lead for life in concentrations comparable to levels in human tissues in the United States showed early mortality, shortened life span, increased susceptibility to infection, visible aging and loss of weight, hardening of the arteries and heart attacks; studies of the fetal development of mice show currently accepted safe blood levels of lead cause developmental deficiencies in certain individuals

Nitrogen oxides (NO_x)

Main characteristics	Principal sources	Principal health effects
Mixture of gases ranging from colorless to reddish-brown	Primarily from internal combustion engines; also high-temperature stationary combustion (power plants) and atmospheric reactions	Major role as component in creation of photochemical smog; also has distinct effects apart from those associated with smog; has been shown to be toxic to experimental animals; some studies indicate NO_2 produces animal diseases that have human counterparts (emphysema, other lung diseases); study of schoolchildren in high NO_2 areas (near TNT plant) found that children contracted significantly more respiratory disease than children in control area; has been shown to aggravate respiratory and cardiovascular illnesses and chronic nephritis

Table 2-1 *(continued)*

Main characteristics	*Principal sources*	*Principal health effects*
	Particulate matter	
Any solid or liquid particles dispersed in atmosphere, such as dust, pollen, ash, soot, metals, and various chemicals; particles often classified according to size, as settleable particles (larger than 50 microns), aerosols (smaller than 50 microns), and fine particulates (smaller than 3 microns)	Natural events such as forest fires, wind erosion, volcanic eruptions; stationary combustion, especially of solid fuels (as in coal-burning power plants); construction activities, industrial processes, and atmospheric chemical reactions	Direct toxic effects or aggravation of the effects of gaseous pollutants; aggravation of asthma or other respiratory or cardiorespiratory symptoms; increased cough and chest discomfort; increased mortality
	Photochemical oxidants (smog)	
Oxidizing type of pollutant found in many urban areas; results from chemical combination of reactive hydrocarbon vapors with nitrogen oxides in presence of sunlight; the resulting production of photochemical oxidants consists of a number of toxic compounds: ozone, peroxyacetyl nitrates (PAN), aldehydes, and other chemical compounds	Most hydrocarbons come from motor vehicle exhausts, and nitrogen oxides from motor vehicle exhausts and stationary combustion sources; photochemical smog is a problem not only in southern California but also in desert cities of the Southwest and in eastern cities that now may be receiving more sunlight because of reduction in smoke layer; meteorological conditions necessary for formation of oxidants are a stationary high accompanied by adequate sunshine with low wind speeds in early morning	Aggravation of respiratory and cardiovascular diseases, irritation to eyes and respiratory tract, impairment of cardiopulmonary function; some concern about possible mutagenic effects of ozone; one study of Los Angeles showed no association between "alert days" when oxidant levels were high and mortality increase; poorer athletic performance has been related to high oxidant levels; possibility of developing tolerance to oxidant pollution, as has been shown in experimental animals, may account for the relatively few changes associated with chronic exposure

(Table continues on the following page.)

Table 2-1 (*continued*)

Main characteristics	Principal sources	Principal health effects
	Sulfates	
Aerosol formed by sulfur oxides; in moist environment appears as sulfuric acid (H_2SO_4) mist or rain	Atmospheric reactions of SO_2; secondary chemical reactions in atmosphere from other sulfur compounds; recent indications that automobiles with catalytic converters designed to decrease hydrocarbon and carbon monoxide emissions may emit more sulfates than automobiles without converters	Aggravation of respiratory diseases, including asthma and chronic bronchitis; reduced lung function; irritation of eyes and respiratory tract; increased mortality
	Sulfur dioxide (SO_2)	
Colorless gas with pungent odor; oxidizes to form sulfur trioxide (SO_3), which forms sulfuric acid with water	Combustion of sulfur-containing fossil fuels, smelting of sulfur-bearing metal ores, industrial processes, and natural events such as volcanic eruptions	Classed as mild respiratory irritant; most SO_2 inhaled is absorbed in upper respiratory tract and never reaches lungs; penetrates when clings to particulate matter; aggravates respiratory diseases, including asthma, chronic bronchitis, and emphysema; can result in reduced lung function, irritation of eyes, and possibly increased mortality

Source: W. J. Baumol and W. E. Oates, *Economics, Environmental Policy, and the Quality of Life* (Englewood Cliffs, N.J.: Prentice-Hall, Inc., 1979); reprinted by permission of Prentice-Hall, Inc.

The chronic health effects of air pollution have by no means been limited to highly industrialized countries. For example, a city in a South American country reportedly has a high prevalence of lung cancer. Hydrocarbons produced by nearby oil refineries may be implicated.

Aside from the chronic effects of air pollution, acute impacts have been observed in localities which contain numerous industrial facilities emitting sulfur dioxide and which have been subject to thermal inversions (a meteorological condition which traps air particles in the lower atmosphere). In three well-documented incidents—the Meuse Valley in 1930, Donora, Pennsylvania, in 1948, and London in 1952—adverse weather conditions coupled with severe air pollution led to a significant increase in deaths from respiratory diseases in the course of several days.[4]

In addition to the widespread pollutants are other contaminants which may be hazardous or even toxic. The U.S. Environmental Protection Agency (EPA) has indentified forty-three such contaminants for further study.[5] By 1982, the EPA had listed seven substances as toxic air pollutants because of strong evidence that they are carcinogenic: asbestos, beryllium, mercury, vinyl chloride, benzene, inorganic arsenic, and radionuclides. Of these, emission standards have been set for only the first four. Table 2-2 summarizes the main characteristics and principal sources of these seven toxic air pollutants.

This list is likely to grow considerably in the future. Two other contaminants—acrylonitrile and coke oven emissions—are currently strong candidates for inclusion on the list, and other substances may follow shortly. Project planners and environmental authorities are advised to solicit current information on toxic contaminants during the planning phase of a new facility.

Regulatory Alternatives

The concentrations or quantities of specific air pollutants that may be discharged are specified in standards set to protect human health and the environment. Two types of standards are commonly used: ambient and emission. Ambient standards establish the concentration allowed in the surrounding air after proper mixing. These concentrations are designed to protect public health as well as to control secondary effects on vegetation and property. Emission limitations establish the levels of specific contaminants allowed at the point of discharge into the atmosphere; they usually assume use of the best practicable control technology and optimal operation and maintenance of a facility, but they do not indicate the pollution level allowed in the surrounding air.

Both emission and ambient standards should be established by each country or jurisdiction on the basis of its own needs and circumstances. To assist in project appraisal and supervision missions, the World Bank has established emission limitations for

Table 2-2. *Selected Toxic Air Pollutants*

Main characteristics	*Principal sources*
Arsenic(As)	
Volatile, highly toxic chemical element; cumulative protoplasmic poison; properties of both metal and nonmetal; occurs naturally in coal and oil; usually found as the sulfide, compounded with oxygen as arsenides, arsenates, and arsenites	Main use in the past was in pesticides and herbicides; now has limited agricultural use (with advent of organic chemical pesticides); some nonagricultural uses (weed killing along roadways and tennis courts); used in paint, glass, and ceramics industries and in wood preservatives; large quantities produced from smelting of lead, copper, zinc, gold ores, ginning of cotton, burning of coal
Asbestos	
Class of natural fibrous silicates; two important forms—chrysotile (most important as environmental contaminant) and amphiboles (amosite and corcidolite); widely used in the environment	Exposure from numerous sources including road building, construction, mining of asbestos, thermal insulation, asbestos plants, transportation of asbestos, cement, floor tiles, attrition of brake linings, fireproofing, demolition of old buildings in which asbestos was used as spray insulation, asbestos pipes, asbestos filters, effluent from mining operations and plants; occupationally exposed workers are themselves a source of contamination
Benzene	
A major industrial chemical derived mainly from petroleum; attacks the body's blood-forming system (especially the bone marrow) and causes blood disorders such as acute myelogenous leukemia	Major stationary sources are fugitive emissions (such as valve and pump leaks) from refineries and chemical plants, and emissions from the steel industry's coke by-product recovery plants; gasoline service stations also responsible for emissions of benzene to a lesser extent
Beryllium (Be)	
One of the most toxic nonradioactive elements known; light stiff metal with high melting point; increasing use in modern technology	Commonly used as component in alloys, particularly copper; major use in the past was in fluorescent lighting industry; discontinued in 1949 but brought to public attention berylliosis, occupational disease of beryllium workers; beryllium contamination of the environment largely confined to industrial plants that refine it or that use it in alloying or machining

Table 2-2 (*continued*)

Main characteristics	*Principal sources*

Mercury (Hg)

Heavy silver-white liquid metallic chemical element; toxic properties have long been known; certain mercury compounds, especially methyl mercury, extremely lethal	Occurs naturally from erosion and weathering; pollution results from mining, refining of mercury, combustion of fuels and refuse, and widespread use of mercury pesticides; used as fungicide to treat seed and as mildewcide in paints and textiles; in paper and pulp industry to prevent slime formation and improve storage properties; in chlorine-alkali industry as electrode; used in lamps, batteries, switches

Radioactive substances

Gaseous, liquid, or solid substances that give off ionizing radiation	Natural sources (rocks, soils, cosmic rays); nuclear weapons testing, nuclear power generation; uranium mining, refining, machining processes

Vinyl chloride (VC)

Monomer used in the production of polyvinyl chloride (PVC), the most commonly used clear plastic; affects flexibility and workability; not chemically bonded to matrix of PVC so can easily escape into air; low residuals of VC required in final PVC product	Routes of entry into environment are air (most important), water, and solid waste; occupational exposure in plants that manufacture or use VC (two major sources of VC emissions: polyvinyl chloride plants and ethylene dichloride vinyl chloride plants); potential sources of exposure to general population owing to use of (as opposed to manufacture of) VC in aerosol containers and in plastics used to wrap or package food and drinking water; used widely in industry, home, and medical science: in wall coverings, upholstery (accounts for "new car" smell), appliances, pesticide sprays, industrial oils, cosmetics, and perfumes

Source: W. J. Baumol and W. E. Oates, *Economics, Environmental Policy, and the Quality of Life* (Englewood Cliffs, N.J.: Prentice-Hall, Inc., 1979); reprinted by permission of Prentice-Hall, Inc.

several industries.[6] These may be useful to public agencies and private developers engaged in project planning. Ranges of ambient air quality levels for some major pollutants, from levels considered acceptable (uncontaminated) to those considered hazardous to humans, are shown in table 2-3.

A number of countries have established both ambient and emission standards for many contaminants. Table 2-4 presents the emission standards which various nations have set for stationary sources of the major pollutants.[7] Information on other pollutants is readily available in the literature.[8]

Although most nations apparently favor ambient standards and specific emission limits to control air pollution, in several instances regulatory authorities have instead used a system of emission fees. Japan, Norway, and the Netherlands have used this approach to reduce emissions of sulfur dioxide from power plants and other industrial facilities. Their emission fees or taxes depend both on the sulfur content of the fuel burned and on the final level of sulfur dioxide emitted into the atmosphere.[9] As a result of these programs, plants have increased their use of low sulfur fuels and have installed costly flue gas desulfurization equipment to remove sulfur dioxide from stack gases after combustion, but before the pollutant enters the atmosphere. Similar programs have been tried in the United States in isolated instances,[10] but several comprehensive studies have suggested that a system of emission taxes would be a viable way of further reducing air pollutants there.[11]

In establishing an appropriate regulatory framework, it is impor-

Table 2-3. *Uncontaminated and Hazardous Levels of Air Quality for Various Contaminants*

Contaminant	Uncontaminated	Threshold limit value[a] (ppm)
Carbon monoxide (CO)	0.03 ppm	35
Nitrogen oxide (NO_2)	4 ppb	3.0
Nitric oxiden (NO)	2 ppb	25
Sulfur dioxide (SO_2)	<0.002 ppm	2
Ozone (O_3)	0.01–0.05 ppm	0.1

Note: ppm signifies parts per million; ppb signifies parts per billion.

a. The time weight average concentration acceptable for a normal eight-hour work day and forty-hour work week.

Source: International Labour Organisation, *Encyclopaedia of Occupational Health and Safety*, 3d ed. 2 vols. (Geneva, 1983).

Table 2-4. *Typical Emission Standards for Stationary Sources of Various Pollutants*

Pollutant	Country	Standard	Unit	Remarks
Particulate matter	Australia	250	mg/cu.m	For all sources
	France	350	mg/cu.m	Coal burning, <20% ash coal
	France	500	mg/cu.m	Coal burning, >20% ash coal
	Japan	400	mg/cu.m	Sintering plants, most districts, under 40,000 cu.m/hr
	Japan	300	mg/cu.m	Sintering plants, most districts, over 40,000 cu.m/hr
	Japan	200	mg/cu.m	Sintering plants, special districts
	Mexico	1.0	kg/Mkcal	Coal burning, >40 Mkcal/hr
	Mexico	1.5	kg/Mkcal	Coal burning, <40 Mkcal/hr
	Mexico	45	g/Mkcal	Oil burning, >63 Mkcal/hr
	Mexico	80	g/Mkcal	Oil burning, <63 Mkcal/hr
	Germany, Fed. Rep. of	100	mg/cu.m	Refuse incineration <1.5 tons/hr
	Germany, Fed. Rep. of	100	mg/cu.m	Refuse incineration >20 tons/hr
	Germany, Fed. Rep. of	200	mg/cu.m	Refuse incineration <20 tons/day
	Germany, Fed. Rep. of	150	mg/cu.m	Refuse incineration >20 tons/day
Sulfur dioxide (SO_2)	Brazil	520	mg/cu.m	For ABC district, São Paulo state
	Great Britain	0.5	% of sulfur burned	New contact H_2SO_4 plants
	Sweden	20	kg/ton pulp	New sulfite pulp mills
	Sweden	20	kg/ton fuel	Oil-steam electric power plants over 300 MW
	United States	0.8	1b/MBtu	New liquid fuel power plants
	United States	1.2	1b/MBtu	New solid fuel power plants

(Table continues on the following page.)

Table 2-4 *(continued)*

Pollutant	Country	Standard	Unit	Remarks
Nitrogen oxides (NO_x)	Australia	350	mg/cu.m	Gas-fired power plants
	Australia	500	mg/cu.m	Any other processes
	Great Britain	1,800	mg/cu.m	Nitric acid production
	Japan	360	mg/cu.m	Metal heating furnaces 10,000 to 40,000 cu.m/hr gas
	Japan	360	mg/cu.m	Petroleum industry heating 10,000 to 40,000 cu.m/hr gas
	Japan	360	mg/cu.m	Nitric acid production 10,000 to 40,000 cu.m/hr gas
	Singapore	4,000	mg/cu.m	Nitric acid production
	Singapore	2,000	mg/cu.m	Any other processes
	United States	0.3	1b/MBtu	New liquid fuel power plants
	United States	0.2	1b/MBtu	New gas fuel power plants
	United States	0.7	1b/MBtu	New solid fuel power plants
Sulfates (as H_2SO_4)	Australia	1,000	mg/cu.m	Any trade, industry, or process
	Singapore	200	mg/cu.m	All processes except combustion and sulfuric acid production
	Germany, Fed. Rep. of	2	kg/ton acid	For SO_3 and H_2SO_4 production
Lead (Pb)	Australia	10	mg/cu.m	Any trade, industry, or process
	Japan	30	mg/cu.m	Refining copper, lead, or zinc; blast and sintering furnaces
	Japan	20	mg/cu.m	Glass production, using lead oxides; baking furnaces
	Japan	10	mg/cu.m	Pipe, sheet, wire, pigment, storage, battery production, etc.
	Singapore	200	mg/cu.m	All sources

Sources: World Bank, "Industrial Waste Control Guidelines" (Washington, D.C.: World Bank, Office of Environmental and Health Affairs, 1978 and 1979), processed; W. Martin and A. C. Stern, *The Collection, Tabulation, Codification and Analysis of the World's Air Quality Management Standards*, 2 vols., EPA-650/9-75-001-a (Washington, D.C.: Environmental Protection Agency, October 1974).

tant to understand that the impact on air quality of emissions from a particular project will depend on a variety of factors, including:

- Type of facility
- Size of the facility
- Raw materials used
- Local topography
- Local meteorological conditions
- How the surrounding property is used.

By varying one or more of the design or operating criteria or by siting in a more favorable meteorological location, it is possible to diminish the negative effects of a planned facility on air quality. During project planning, the potential air quality impact of a proposed facility (as well as projected level of emissions) should be identified and, to the extent possible, quantified. A three-phase process of analysis has been recommended by the U.S. EPA.[12] The first phase consists of a simple screening procedure to determine if there is a possibility of an air quality problem. If there is, then a detailed screening or basic modeling procedure should be conducted in the second phase. If this procedure indicates the likelihood of an adverse impact on air quality, then a refined analysis may be justified, with the use of more sophisticated air quality models to determine the precise level of impact under various scenarios.

Additional Considerations

A great deal of attention is currently being paid to the phenomenon known as acid rain. The incidence of acid rain appears to be growing in developed countries, and the global environmental consequences may be significant.

Acid rain is precipitation with elevated concentrations of sulfuric and nitric acid and a pH level below 5.6. Essentially, sulfur oxides and nitrogen oxides are discharged into the atmosphere (mostly from coal-fired electric utility plants) and converted into sulfates and nitrates. These compounds then react with moisture to form sulfuric and nitric acid, which often fall to earth many hundreds of miles from the initial source of the contaminants.

The impact of acid rain on aquatic systems can be severe. In many lakes in developed nations, fish populations have declined and even disappeared entirely. If the soil in a watershed does not contain limestone or other alkaline substances to neutralize the acidity, soils and vegetation may be damaged. Since the acid leaches toxic metals such as lead and mercury from the soil into surface streams and groundwater tables, acid rain may indirectly threaten human health by contaminating fish and water supplies.

Water Pollution

Sources of water pollution may be grouped into four broad categories:

- Municipal sewage
- Industrial wastewater
- Agricultural runoff
- Storm water and urban runoff.

Most research and technology development for the control of water pollution has focused on the first two categories; relatively little has been done, in either developed or developing nations, to control urban and agricultural runoff, particularly runoff carrying farm pesticides. As broadly scattered sources of pollution, these last two categories are more difficult to pinpoint and control. Still, the cumulative effect of all water pollution sources must be considered when evaluating the potential impact of a planned development project.

Principal Pollutants

Nine indicators are commonly used to measure the level of water pollution in a given water suppply:

- Dissolved oxygen
- Total dissolved solids
- Suspended solids
- Bacteria
- Nutrients
- Color and turbidity
- Oil and grease
- pH value
- Temperature.

Not only is excessive pollution of a water source a direct threat to individuals coming in contact with the polluted waterway, but there is also the danger that contaminants will work their way into the food chain and water supply and thus affect a large number of people. Water pollution may also upset the aquatic environment in a watercourse and damage important species of fish and other marine animals. The characteristics, primary sources, and principal effects of each major contaminant are summarized in table 2-5.

In addition to these broad indicators of water pollution, a growing number of potentially toxic chemicals have been found in the surface and groundwaters of developed nations. These chemicals must be taken into account in the project planning process.

The U.S. Clean Water Act identifies sixty-five substances or categories of substances which are classified as chemical pollutants. Tests have been conducted on most of these substances to determine the risks they pose to human health and the environment at varying levels of exposure. Although tests on the original sixty-five substances are not yet conclusive, and although additional potentially toxic chemicals have been identified since promulgation of the original list, there is strong evidence that many toxic chemicals have significant adverse effects on health and the environment. Twenty-one such substances, along with the suspected health and environmental impacts of each, are listed in table 2-6.

The acute health effects listed in the table have usually been demonstrated at levels of concentration somewhat higher than those typically found in polluted surface waterways. However, some of these chemicals have been found to be carcinogenic (cancer causing) or teratogenic (inducing birth defects) even at relatively low levels of exposure—particularly if the exposure is over a protracted period. Most of the adverse environmental impacts identified in the table have been observed at relatively low levels of concentration.

Industrial facilities are the largest source of potentially toxic contaminants in most watercourses, but the number and level of contaminants discharged varies considerably from industry to industry. Table 2-7 shows the usual industrial sources of twenty-one toxic chemicals in the United States, and it indicates the approximate percentage of facilities within a given industry which discharge each chemical. As the table shows, virtually all industries have the potential to discharge a large number of toxic chemicals.

Data are also available on the total quantities of toxics discharged by different industries. In the United States three industries—or-

Table 2-5. *Parameters of Major Water Pollution Indicators*

Indicator	Main characteristics	Principal sources	Principal health and environmental effects
Dissolved oxygen level	Dissolved oxygen is necessary in streams for fish and other aquatic life to survive. Soluble organics deplete the oxygen by the activity of aerobic bacteria. The quantity of soluble organics in a waste is measured either by biochemical oxygen demand, chemical oxygen demand, total organic compound, or total oxygen demand. These measurements calculate the quantity of oxygen which a given waste will take from a stream.	Soluble organics are contained in most industrial waste waters, but especially in waste liquors from pulp mills, canning plant wash effluents, meat packing wastes, textile scouring and dyeing effluents, milk product wastes, and fermentation wastes.	As the level of dissolved oxygen falls below five parts per million, adverse effects are observed on aquatic life. Many fish and marine species cannot survive significant reductions in dissolved oxygen.
Total dissolved solids (TDS)	TDS is a measure of the total inorganic salts and other inorganic substances that are dissolved in water.	Occurs in a wide variety of industrial wastes, but in particularly high quantities in the manufacture of fertilizers, organic and inorganic chemicals, and in wastes generated by leather-tanning processes	Accelerates corrosion in water systems and pipes, depresses crop yields when used for irrigation, and at high levels adversely affects fish and other aquatic life; may make water unfit for drinking
Suspended solids	Includes soil and other solid particles	Caused by soil erosion as well as by industrial processes such as the manufacture of aluminum, glass, cement, asbestos, fertilizers, chemicals, plastics, and pulp and paper; also caused by processing of meat and dairy products and petroleum refining	Turns waterways brown; adversely affects aquatic life; creates sludge blankets which can produce noxious gases; interferes with operation of water purification plants

Bacteria	Measurements are usually taken for one specific bacteria—fecal coliform—to indicate the presence of other disease-causing bacteria.	Household and municipal waste and animal waste; certain industries such as tanneries, pharmaceutical manufacturers, processors of food and livestock products	Creates strong potential for infection and disease
Nutrients (phosphorus and nitrogen)	Essential to aquatic life in small amounts	Produced in several industrial processes such as the manufacture of fertilizers	At high levels nutrients stimulate growth of algae and seaweed, tend to accelerate eutrophication, and increase oxygen depletion.
Color and turbidity	Produced by compounds such as lignins and tannin	Result from processes in the beverage, beet sugar processing, dairy, pulp and paper, and textile industries	Major aesthetic problem
Oil and grease	Oils and greases are generally biodegradable.	Generated by many industrial processes including those for palm oil, beverages, leather tanning, meat products, metal finishing, chemicals, plastics, pulp and paper, and steel	Unsightly and possibly flammable.
pH value	Measures acidity and alkalinity of a stream	Wastewater from virtually all industrial processes causes some change in the pH level.	Changes in the pH value may upset the ecological balance of the aquatic environment; excessive acidity may create air pollution problems from hydrogen sulfide.
Temperature	Increased temperature caused by discharge of industrial cooling water into streams	Steam electric power generation, petroleum refining, and the production of steel, cement, glass, and fertilizers	Decreases ability of water to assimilate waste; increases bacterial activity; may upset ecological balance of aquatic environment

Source: Research and Education Association, *Pollution Control Technology*, vol. 11 (New York, 1978).

Table 2-6. *Selected Effects of Twenty-One Toxic Chemicals on Health and the Environment*

| Chemical | Human health effects | | | Environmental effects |
	Carcin-ogen	Terato-gen	Other	
Aldrin/dieldrin	√		Tremors, convulsions, kidney damage	Toxic to aquatic organisms, causes reproductive failure in birds and fish, bioaccumulates in aquatic organisms
Arsenic	√	√	Vomiting, poisoning, liver and kidney damage	Toxic to legume crops
Benzene	√		Anemia, bone marrow damage	Toxic to some fish and aquatic invertebrates
Bis-(2-ethyl-hexyl) phthalate	√	√	Central nervous system damage	Eggshell thinning in birds, toxic to fish
Cadmium	√	√	Suspected causal factor in many human pathologies: tumors, renal dysfunction, hypertension, arteriosclerosis, Itai-itai disease (weakened bones)	Toxic to fish, bioaccumulates in aquatic organisms
Carbon tetrachloride	√		Kidney and liver damage, heart failure	Ozone-depleting effects
Chloroform	√		Kidney and liver damage	Ozone-depleting effects
Copper			Gastrointestinal irritant, liver damage	Toxic to fish
Cyanide			Acutely toxic	Kills fish, retards growth and development of fish
DDT	√	√	Tremors, convulsions, kidney damage	Reproductive failure of birds and fish, bioaccumulates in aquatic organisms, biomagnifies in food chain

Table 2-6 (*continued*)

| Chemical | Human health effects | | | Environmental effects |
	Carcinogen	Teratogen	Other	
Di-n-butyl phthalate			Central nervous system damage	Eggshell thinning in birds, toxic to fish
Dioxin	√	√	Acute skin rashes	Bioaccumulates
Lead	√	√	Convulsions, anemia, kidney and brain damage	Toxic to domestic plants and animals, biomagnifies in food chain
Mercury		√	Irritability, depression, kidney and liver damage, Minamata disease	Reproductive failure in fish, inhibits growth of and kills fish, methylmercury biomagnifies
Nickel	√		Gastrointestinal and central nervous system effects	Impairs reproduction of aquatic species
Polychlorinated biphenyls (PCBs)	√	√	Vomiting, abdominal pain, temporary blindness	Liver damage in mammals, kidney damage and eggshell thinning in birds, suspected reproductive failure in fish
Phenol				Reproductive effects in aquatic organisms, toxic to fish
Silver				Toxic to aquatic organisms
Tetrachloroethylene	√		Central nervous system effects	Ozone-depleting effects
Toluene	√			Toxic to aquatic organisms at high concentrations
Toxaphene	√	√		Decreased productivity of phytoplankton communities, birth defects in fish and birds

Note: Check marks indicate known effects of the substance.
Source: U.S. Council on Environmental Quality, *State of the Environment 1982* (Washington D.C., 1983), pp. 120–21.

Table 2-7. Discharge of Selected Toxic Chemicals to Surface Waters in the United States, by Industry, 1980

Industry	Aldrin/dieldrin	Arsenic	Benzene	Bis-phthalate[a]	Cadmium	Carbon tetrachloride	Chloroform	Copper	Cyanide	DDT	Di-n-butyl-phthalate	Dioxin	Lead	Mercury	Nickel	PCBs	Phenol	Silver	Tetrachloroethylene	Toluene	Toxaphene
Car washes, laundries	○	●	●	●	★	○	●	●	●	○	○	★	★	●	●	★	○	○	●	●	○
Electrical	★	●	○	●	●	○	●	●	●	★	○	★	●	●	●	★	●	●	○	●	○
Foundries	★	●	●	●	●	★	●	●	●	★	●	★	●	●	●	★	●	●	○	○	★
Iron and steel	★	●	●	●	●	○	●	●	●	★	●	★	●	○	●	★	●	●	○	●	★
Mechanical products	○	⋮	○	●	⋮	○	●	⋮	⋮	★	●	★	⋮	⋮	⋮	★	●	⋮	●	●	★
Nonferrous metals	★	●	●	●	●	○	●	●	●	★	○	★	●	●	●	○	●	●	●	●	★
Organics and plastics	○	●	●	●	●	○	●	●	○	★	●	★	●	○	○	●	●	○	●	●	★
Pesticides	○	○	●	●	○	●	●	●	○	★	●	★	●	●	●	○	●	○	○	●	○
Petroleum refining	○	○	●	●	○	○	●	●	●	○	○	★	●	★	●		○	○	○	●	★
Publicly owned waste water treatment works	★	⋮	○	●	⋮	★	●	⋮	⋮	○	●	★	⋮	⋮	⋮	○	●	⋮	★	○	
Pulp and paper	○	●	○	●	●	○	●	●	●	★	●	★	●	●	●	○	●	●	★	○	★
Timber products	★	●	●	○	●	★	○	●	★	★	○	★	●	○	●	★	●	○	★	●	★

Note: The percentage of firms within an industry found to be discharging a particular chemical:

● = more than 50 percent ★ = less than 1 percent
● = 11 to 50 percent ⋮ = unknown
○ = 1 to 10 percent
a. Bis-(2-ethylhexyl) phthalate.

ganics and plastics, metal finishing, and iron and steel—account for
more than 90 percent of all toxic discharges into waterways. Specifically, in 1981 the total quantity of toxic wastes generated from
several major U.S. industries was:[13]

	Millions of tons
Organics and plastics	780
Metal finishing	290
Iron and steel	125
Pulp and paper	22
Foundries	13
Petroleum refining	9

Regulatory Alternatives

To control water quality both "stream" and "effluent" standards
are used. A stream standard denotes the concentration of the pollutant in the receiving water, after it has been adequately mixed. An
effluent standard denotes the concentration of the pollutant just
before it is discharged into the receiving water.

The advantage of stream standards is that they establish a level of
quality at which the receiving water must be maintained regardless
of the quality or quantity of effluents discharged. These standards
are based on the volume of waste that a stream can assimilate, and
thus they protect the water for a variety of uses.

Effluent standards provide more control over individual discharges. Effluent limitations must be frequently reviewed and,
where necessary, upgraded in order to provide long-term protection for the receiving water. Effluent standards are usually based on
the treatment technology that is available, economic considerations,
and the proposed use of the water. Very different standards will be
appropriate for water used for recreation and that used for industrial
cooling. The effluent limitations help determine the degree of treatment required at individual installations in order to maintain stream
standards.

A useful and comprehensive compilation of information relating
to stream standards was developed by the U.S. Environmental
Protection Agency in 1972 and updated in 1976.[14] It presents recommended limitations for all water uses—public water supplies, recreation and wildlife, marine aquatic life and wildlife, industrial, and
agricultural. The information covers a wide range of physical conditions and contaminants and includes extensive background data
and references for recommended limitations.

Many countries have established stream standards for various uses of water. In Japan, for example, different standards have been established for a range of uses (for the standards applicable to rivers, see table 2-8). In Brazil, sources used for drinking water, irrigation, and primary contact recreation must meet the same standards (see table 2-9). Other nations have promulgated effluent standards for liquid domestic and industrial waste discharges that cover the contaminants of primary interest to them.[15]

In addition to setting standards, several nations (particularly in Western Europe) have used effluent charges to control water pollution. One noteworthy example of this technique has been in the Ruhr river basin in the Federal Republic of Germany. In that highly industrialized area, eight local government authorities have im-

Table 2-8. *Water Quality Standards for Rivers in Japan*

Purpose	pH	Biochemical oxygen demand	Suspended solids	Dissolved oxygen	Number of coliform bacteria groups
Water supply, class 1	6.5–8.5	1 ppm or less	25 ppm or less	7.5 ppm or more	50 MPN/100 ml or less
Water supply, class 2; fishery, class 1; bathing	6.5–8.5	2 ppm or less	25 ppm or less	7.5 ppm or more	1,000 MPN/ 100 ml or less
Water supply, class 3; fishery, class 2	6.5–8.5	3 ppm or less	25 ppm or less	5 ppm or more	5,000 MPN/ 100 ml or less
Fishery, class 3; industrial water, class 1	6.5–8.5	5 ppm or less	50 ppm or less	5 ppm or more	
Industrial water, class 2; agricultural water	6.0–8.5	8 ppm or less	100 ppm or less	2 ppm or more	
Industrial water, class 3	6.5–8.5	10 ppm or less	No floating matter such as garbage	2 ppm or more	

Note: Japan has separate standards for lake water and for coastal water. MPN, most probable number; ppm, parts per million.

Source: "Water Pollution Standards," *International Environmental Reporter* (1978), sec. 91, p. 1473.

Table 2-9. *Quality Standards for Raw Water for Domestic Purposes, Irrigation, and Contact Recreation in Brazil*

Constituent	Standard
Floating materials	Virtually none
Oil and grease	Virtually none
Substances imparting taste and odor	Virtually none
Fecal coliform	Not >1,000 cells/100 ml in 80% or more of at least 5 samples collected in any one month
Biochemical oxygen demand (5-day, 20°C)	<5 mg/l
Dissolved oxygen	>5 mg/l
Arsenic	Not >0.1 mg/l
Cadmium	Not >0.01 mg/l
Chromium	Not >0.05 mg/l
Copper	Not >1 mg/l
Lead	Not >0.1 mg/l
Phenols	Not >0.001 mg/l
Mercury	Not >0.002 mg/l
Nitrate	Not >10 mg/l as N
Zinc	Not >5 mg/l

Source: Legislaçao Basic-Portaria/GM/no. 0013, de 15 de Janeiro de 1976 (Brasilia: Ministerio do Interior, Secretario Especial do Meio Ambiento, 1976).

posed effluent fees on both the quantity and quality of waste discharges.[16] As a result, almost 40 percent of industrial acids used in the Ruhr Valley are now recovered, and the water quality is high enough to sustain fishing and other recreation in four of the five small rivers in the basin. Both France and the Netherlands have also placed charges on industrial polluters. These systems are not punitive, but rather tie the level of charges to the cost of programs to maintain water quality. The results have been promising, and they suggest that effluent charges may be an effective way to control water pollution.[17]

Additional Considerations

The protection of drinking water supplies presents a special problem in pollution control. In addition to standards for the sources of raw water, standards must be established for the treated water supplied to the consumer. Many pollutants, organic as well as inorganic, must be monitored in the supply and delivery system. The discussion in this subsection assumes that an adequate water system already exists in the locality. The problem of developing a system in communities where one does not yet exist is considered in chapter 8.

A number of organic compounds produced as a direct result of the water treatment process are potentially hazardous; the incidence of these compounds in drinking water must be closely monitored. Chlorine, which is used to treat wastewater and to purify drinking water, can react with other contaminants to form chlorinated organic compounds such as chlorinated phenols and trihalomethane compounds (for example, chloroform and bromoform). Chloroform is a known animal carcinogen and a suspected human carcinogen. In addition, the level of other organic chemicals (such as pesticides) in drinking water must be monitored and restricted.

Where nuclear materials are processed or used, such as in hospitals, laboratories, or nuclear power installations, the regulation of radionuclides in the water supply is particularly important. The U.S. standards for selected contaminants in drinking water are shown in table 2-10; table 2-11 provides the maximum permissible contaminant levels for radionuclides in U.S. water supplies.

Any planned industrial project with a potential impact on a drinking water system (that is, on the collection, treatment, storage, or distribution of water) must be analyzed with particular care. Planners must ensure that the project will not affect the integrity of the water system. Specifically, the project should not interfere with any of the following:

- Collection and storage of the water supply
- Effectiveness of water treatment procedures currently in use
- Proper functioning of the distribution system (no loss of water pressure, no cross-connections, and no back-siphonage)
- Ability to repair and expand the system as needed.

These concerns should be taken into account along with the possibility that an industrial source will add contaminants to surface or groundwaters which are used for drinking water.

Hazardous waste disposal sites represent another major source of groundwater pollution. The dangers posed by these sites are discussed in the following section.

Table 2-10. *Primary Standards for Drinking Water in the United States*

Constituent	Maximum levels
Arsenic	0.05 mg/l
Barium	1 mg/l
Cadmium	0.010 mg/l
Chromium	0.05 mg/l
Lead	0.05 mg/l
Mercury	0.002 mg/l
Nitrate (as elemental nitrogen)	10 mg/l
Selenium	0.01 mg/l
Silver	0.05 mg/l
Fluoride	2.4 mg/l (air temperature ≤ 12°C)
	1.4 mg/l (air temperature = 26.3–32.5°C)
Organic chemicals	
Endrin	0.0002 mg/l
Lindane	0.004 mg/l
Methoxychlor	0.1 mg/l
Toxaphene	0.005 mg/l
2,4-D	0.1 mg/l
2,4,5-TP	0.01 mg/l
Turbidity	5 units (average for 2 consecutive days)
Coliform bacteria	Membrane filter method: not >1 cell/100 ml as arithmetic mean of all samples in any one month
	Fermentation tube method: none present in >10% of portions examined in any one month, using 10 ml standard portions

Source: U.S. Environmental Protection Agency, "National Primary Drinking Water Regulations," *Federal Register*, vol. 47, no. 43 (March 4, 1982), pp. 9350–58.

Solid Waste Disposal

Unlike air and water pollutants, the contaminants which make up solid wastes cannot be easily listed or categorized. Solid wastes vary tremendously in composition and concentration, and during the past two decades their composition has changed considerably. Traditionally, solid waste consisted mostly of municipal refuse, and it was hazardous primarily for residents living near the local dump site. As a result of increased industrial development, however, more and more wastes are generated by industrial processes. These wastes are potentially far more hazardous than traditional solid wastes and

Table 2-11. *Maximum Radionuclide Levels
in Community Water Supplies in the United States*

Contaminant	Level
Combined radium-226 and radium-228	5 pCi/l[a]
Gross alpha particle activity (including radium-226 but excluding radon and uranium[b]	15 pCi/l
Annual dosage to the total body or any internal organ from average annual concentration of beta particle and photon emitters from man-made radionuclides in drinking water[c]	4 pCi/l

a. pCi, picocurie = quantity of radioactive material producing 2.22 nuclear transformations per minute.

b. Gross alpha particle activity = total radioactivity due to alpha particle emission as inferred from a dry sample.

c. Man-made beta particle and photon emitters = all radionuclides—except daughter products of thorium-232, uranium-235, and uranium-238—emitting beta particles and/or photons listed in U.S. Department of Commerce, *Maximum Permissible Body Burdens and Maximum Permissible Concentrations of Radionuclides in Air and in Water for Occupational Exposure*, NBS Handbook 69 (Washington, D.C., 1959).

Source: U.S. Environmental Protection Agency, "Drinking Water Regulations—Radionuclides," *Federal Register*, vol. 48, no. 194 (October 5, 1983), pp. 45502–52.

must be handled and disposed of with a great deal of caution. This section deals with solid industrial waste; other categories of urban refuse are discussed in chapter 8.

Principal Pollutants

It is difficult to define with precision what constitutes a hazardous waste. One broad definition often used is any waste that is ignitable, corrosive, reactive, or toxic. The danger is that these wastes may pollute groundwater used for drinking and soils used for grazing and farming. Toxic chemicals that thus enter the food chain represent a threat to human health.

Most industrial processes generate some hazardous wastes. Table 2-12 lists the approximate quantity of wastes generated by various U.S. industries in 1980. As the table shows, the chemical and primary metals industries were responsible for a substantial majority (about 70 percent) of all hazardous wastes generated.

In most industrialized nations the quantity of hazardous wastes generated is increasing, not only because of industrial growth, but also because of the installation of air and water pollution control equipment. Such control technologies as wastewater treatment

Table 2-12. *Hazardous Waste Generation, by Industry,*
United States, 1980

Industry	Quantity (wet weight in thousand metric tons)	Percent
Chemicals and allied products	25,509	61.9
Primary metal industries	4,061	9.8
Petroleum and coal products	2,119	5.1
Fabricated metal products	1,997	4.8
Nonmanufacturing industries	1,971	4.8
Paper and allied products	1,295	3.1
Transport equipment	1,240	3.0
Electrical and electronic equipment	1,093	2.7
Leather and tanning	474	1.1
Machinery, except electrical	322	0.8
Miscellaneous manufacturing industries	318	0.8
Rubber and miscellaneous plastic products	249	0.6
Textile mill products	203	0.5
Printing and publishing	154	0.4
Instruments and related products	90	0.2
Lumber and food products	87	0.2
Furniture and fixtures	36	0.09
Stone, clay, and glass products	17	0.04
Total	41,235	100.0

Source: U.S. Environmental Protection Agency.

plants and flue gas desulfurization equipment create large amounts
of sludge which must be disposed of.

Several risks associated with hazardous waste disposal sites may
be reduced if the sites are located far from areas where people work
or live. In that case, however, the wastes may have to be transported
many miles; such shipments can be costly and may create additional
risks of accidents and spillage. In any event, the options available for
hazardous waste disposal, and the risks associated with improper
disposal, must be taken into account in project planning.

Regulatory Alternatives

While regulatory activities with respect to air and water pollution
focus on establishing and maintaining ambient and effluent standards for individual pollutants, regulatory actions for control of

hazardous wastes have usually been directed at setting criteria for the handling of broad categories of wastes. An essential component of any hazardous waste regulatory program is the permit system. Any firm involved in the generation, storage, treatment, disposal, or other handling of hazardous waste materials must obtain a permit from the government agency charged with regulating solid wastes. Under the terms of its permit, the firm must keep certain records on the handling of any hazardous wastes, and it must submit to regulatory officials reports containing specified data.[18] In addition, many countries have established a manifest system, by which a written record is maintained of any and all movements of hazardous wastes. As such, it is possible to track these wastes from source to final disposal.

Hazardous wastes may either be disposed of by the generating agent on its own property or be sent to a commercial disposal facility, if one is accessible. Although the number of commercial disposal facilities in developed countries has grown substantially in the past decade, most wastes are still disposed of by the generator. In either event, landfill disposal of hazardous wastes is the most popular method. If not closely regulated, however, this technique may have adverse impacts on health and the environment. As previously noted, hazardous chemicals may leak from the site and contaminate groundwater or surface waters; various compounds can react together to produce toxic air pollutants. Contamination of the soil and possibly of food products grown thereon are other potential consequences of the improper disposal of hazardous wastes. It is also important to ensure that hazardous wastes are not deposited in or near any known or suspected important archaeological sites.

Regulatory requirements for the handling of hazardous wastes are varied and complex. In most developed countries these regulations are quite new, and difficulties with the regulatory process are still being worked out.[19] Still, the most satisfactory solution is to utilize in-plant processes that obviate waste production.

Additional Considerations

Even if land disposal is done properly, future disturbances of disposal sites could cause unwanted health or environmental impacts. Consequently, alternatives to land disposal may be desirable. Three alternatives are chemical or biological treatment, recycling, and incineration.

Although many chemical and biological processes for treating hazardous wastes are still in the development stage, others are already in widespread use. Essentially, chemical processes seek to change the structure of a substance to make it less toxic, while biological processes use bacteria to help decompose organic wastes into natural nontoxic substances.

Recycling is the process by which wastes from one plant or process are used as raw materials in another. In many developed countries, waste exchanges have been established to facilitate this type of recycling. According to one source, European exchanges are now transferring 30 to 40 percent of their listed wastes.[20] This practice merits thorough evaluation by planners in developing countries, particularly in areas where natural resources are scarce.

Finally, many hazardous wastes could be safely disposed of by incineration, provided proper air pollution control equipment is used on the incinerator and provided incinerator temperatures are continually maintained at sufficiently high levels (approximately 800° C to 1050° C, depending on the waste).

At this time, alternative solid waste disposal practices are, in general, more costly than the conventional practice of landfill. As the alternative techniques are perfected and put into more widespread use, however, they may represent a viable and least-cost option under certain circumstances.

Noise Pollution

Noise may be defined as any unwanted or excessive sound—in particular, sounds that produce undesired physiological or psychological effects on individuals. It is measured in units of decibels (dB). The decibel is equal to twenty times the logarithm of the ratio of sound pressure to a reference pressure of 0.0002 dyne per square centimeter, or

$$\text{Sound pressure level (dB)} = 20 \left(\log_{10} \frac{\text{Measured pressure}}{\text{Reference pressure}} \right).$$

Thus, a sound with ten times the pressure of another is considered to be 20 dB louder, and each succeeding tenfold increase adds another 20 dB to the sound level. The decibel level for various sounds is shown in table 2-13.

Table 2-13. *Relative Sound Pressure Levels*
for Various Sources of Noise

Apparent loudness	Examples	Relative sound pressure level dB	Ratio to 0 dB	Dynes per sq. cm
Deafening	Jet aircraft	140	10,000,000	2,000
	Threshold of feeling	130	3,162,000	
Very loud	Elevated train, thunder	120	1,000,000	200
	Subway train, riveting	110	316,200	
	Noisy industrial plant	100	100,000	20
	Loud street noise	90	31,620	
	Noisy office	80	10,000	2
Loud	Average street noise	70	3,162	
	Average office	60	1,000	0.2
Moderate	Moderate restaurant clatter	50	316	
	Private office	40	100	0.02
Faint	Rustling leaves	20	10	0.002
Very faint	Normal breathing	10	3	
	Threshold audibility	0	1	0.0002

Source: United States Gypsum, *Sound Control Construction Principles and Performance,*
2d ed. (Chicago, 1972).

The sound level meter is the basic instrument for measuring sound or noise. It electronically weights the amplitudes of the various frequencies in accordance with human hearing sensitivity and sums the resulting weighted spectrum into a single number. The A scale has been developed to approximate most closely the human perception of sound. The weighted sound level unit at the A setting is commonly designated as dBA, or as the A-weighted sound level.

Principal Pollutants

In the urban environment there are four principal sources of noise: aircraft, industrial operations, construction activities, and highway traffic.

Aircraft-related noises affect mainly the populations living near airports or in the flight paths of low-flying airplanes. Although many new types of jet-powered airplanes introduced since 1972 emit less noise than earlier models, noise continues to be one of the most serious environmental problems currently associated with airport operations. Mitigating measures consist of modification of flight paths and curtailment of airport activities during specified hours of the night.

Noises from industrial operations are usually confined to the plant structure. Machinery and equipment are the main sources, and the effects are felt mainly by individual workers. This kind of noise can be mitigated by control measures at the source (relocation, vibration control, dampening); by installation of acoustical shields, enclosures, or other barriers to interrupt the path of the sound; or by limitations on the duration of exposure. These measures also help reduce noise levels both in and outside the plant.

Although construction operations are not permanent, large projects can last for relatively long periods of time, so that measures to reduce noise levels are frequently required. Construction noises can originate from cranes and hoisting equipment, air compressors, concrete mixers, tractors and bulldozing equipment, and delivery vehicles. Mitigation procedures are similar to those mentioned for industrial operations.

The impact of vehicle noise on a population usually depends on traffic concentrations rather than on any individual vehicle. Although there are generally fewer trucks than other vehicles, trucks tend to make the most noise. Motorcycles are also significant. Vehicular noises originate from the exhaust systems, tires, engines, special equipment (such as the loading machinery on solid waste carriers and other heavy-duty trucks), and other features. The impacts of noise from traffic may be reduced by installation of special equipment on motor vehicles and by urban development plans which divert traffic away from residential areas.

The precise health and environmental effects of noise pollution are not fully known. Prolonged noise exposure may cause general personal stress, either singly or in combination with other stresses; sounds of sufficient intensity and duration can cause permanent damage to the auditory system. Exposure to moderate intensities in the environment does affect the cardiovascular system, but no definite permanent effects on the circulatory system have been demonstrated. Moderate noise levels have been known to cause vasoconstriction of the peripheral areas of the body and pupillary dilation, but there is no evidence that these changes are harmful over time.

Continuous noise levels above 90 dBA have detrimental effects on human performance, especially in so-called noise-sensitive functions, such as vigilance tasks, information gathering, and analytical processes. Noise levels below 90 dBA can be disruptive, particularly if they have predominantly high-frequency components and are intermittent, unexpected, and uncontrollable.

Regulatory Alternatives

Recommended allowable noise levels from individual sources may be mandated. Table 2-14 presents limits considered adequate for protecting the health and welfare of the general public in specific situations. These limitations, however, are only to prevent hearing impairment and do not take into account psychological effects of noise.

Alternatively, specific measures to mitigate particular sources of noise may be mandated by a local authority. For example, certain construction operations in urban areas (such as blasting) may be prohibited during specified hours.

Additional Considerations

An important secondary effect of noise on human health and welfare is noise-induced vibrations. Sound of sufficient intensity may cause buildings to vibrate (and become damaged) and windows to break. This is most likely in construction areas where explosives are used or where blasting operations are conducted. In such circumstances, it is important that precautions be taken to protect nearby structures.

Noise has the same general effects on animals as it does on humans. Noise of sufficient intensity can disrupt certain patterns of animal behavior: exploratory behavior can be curtailed, avoidance behavior can limit access to food and shelter, and breeding habits can be disrupted. Hearing loss and the masking of auditory signals can complicate an animal's abilities to recognize its young, detect and locate prey, and evade predators. Physiological effects of noise exposure—such as changes in blood pressure and chemistry, hormone balance, and reproductivity—have been demonstrated on laboratory animals and, to some extent, on farm animals.

Table 2-14. *Yearly Average Equivalent Sound Levels Required for Protection of Public Health in the United States*

Type of area	Measure[a]	Indoor			Outdoor		
		Activity inter-ference	Hearing loss consider-ation	To protect against both effects[b]	Activity inter-ference	Hearing loss consider-ation	To protect against both effects[b]
Residential area with outside space and farm residences	L_{dn}	45	—	45	55	—	55
	$L_{eq(24)}$	—	70	—	—	70	—
Residential area with no outside space	L_{dn}	45	—	45	—	—	—
	$L_{eq(24)}$	—	70	—	—	—	—
Commercial area	$L_{eq(24)}$	—[c]	70	—	—[c]	70	70[d]
Inside vehicles	$L_{eq(24)}$	—[c]	70	—[c]	—	—	—
Industrial area	$L_{eq(24)}$[e]	—[c]	70	70[d]	—[c]	70	70[d]
Hospitals	L_{dn}	45	—	45	55	—	55
	$L_{eq(24)}$	—	70	—	—	70	—
Educational area	$L_{eq(24)}$	45	—	45	55	—	55
	$L_{eq(24)}$[e]	—	70	—	—	70	—
Recreational area	$L_{eq(24)}$	—[c]	70	70[d]	—[c]	70	70[d]
Farmland and general unpop-ulated land	$L_{eq(24)}$	—	—	—	—[c]	70	70[d]

— Not applicable.

a. L_{dn} = day-night average A-weighted equivalent sound level, with a 10-decibel weighting applied to nighttime levels. $L_{eq(24)}$ = equivalent A-weighted sound level over 24 hours.

b. Based on lowest level.

c. Since different types of activities appear to be associated with different levels, identification of a maximum level for activity interference may be difficult except in those circumstances in which speedy communication is a critical activity.

d. Based only on hearing loss.

e. An $L_{eq(8)}$ of 75 dB may be identified in these situations as long as the exposure over the remaining 16 hours per day is low enough to result in a negligible contribution to the 24-hour average, that is, no greater than an L_{eq} of 60 dB.

Source: U.S. Environmental Protection Agency, *Information on Levels of Environmental Noise Requisite to Protect Public Health and Welfare with an Adequate Margin of Safety,* EPA-550-9-74-004 (Washington, D.C., 1974).

Conclusion

A wide variety of pollutants may be released into environmental media as a result of a development project. In some cases, even minute quantities may be harmful, while in others the dangers exist only at high concentrations. It is imperative that project planners know which pollutants may be released from the contemplated facility, the expected level of emissions, the assimilative capacity of the surrounding environment (discussed in chapter 6), and the possible health effects on nearby population centers. Regulatory options to control the quantity of pollution may take several forms, such as ambient or stream standards, emission or effluent standards, subsidies for pollution control equipment, or effluent charges. Although many developing countries seem to favor uniform regional or even national standards to control pollution, this may not always be appropriate. In many cases, individual standards tailored to a specific project circumstance may be preferable.

Notes

1. L. C. McCabe and G. D. Clayton, "Air Pollution by Hydrogen Sulfide in Poza Rica, Mexico," *Archives of Industrial Hygiene and Occupational Medicine*, vol. 6 (1952), p. 199.

2. H. Matsumoto, G. Koya, and T. Takeuchi, "Research Note," *Journal of Neuropathology and Neurology*, vol. 24 (1965), p. 563.

3. See National Academy of Sciences, *Biologic Effects of Atmospheric Pollutants: Fluorides* (Washington, D.C., 1971), p. 149; and H. L. Hardy, E. W. Rabe, and S. J. Lorch, "United States Beryllium Case Registry," *Journal of Occupational Medicine*, vol. 9 (1967), p. 271.

4. World Health Organization, *Health Hazards of the Human Environment* (Geneva, 1972), p. 25.

5. U.S. Council on Environmental Quality, *State of the Environment 1982* (Washington, D.C., 1983).

6. World Bank, Office of Environmental Affairs, "Environmental Guidelines" (Washington, D.C., 1982–84).

7. The most current information on the ambient standards and emission limitations of individual countries is in Bureau of National Affairs, Inc., *International Environmental Reporter* (Washington, D.C., 1983).

8. See W. Martin and A. C. Stern, *The Collection, Tabulation, Codification and Analysis of the World's Air Quality Management Standards*, 2 vols., EPA-650/9-75-001-a (Washington, D. C.: U.S. Environmental Protection Agency, October 1974); P. Jarrault, "Limita-

tion des émissions des pollutants et qualité de l'air-valeurs réglementaires dans les principaux pays industrialises—Specifications en vigeur in 1978," Pub. no. 63 (Paris: Centre de Documentation, Institut Français de l'Enérgie, July 1978).

9. See W. J. Baumol and W. E. Oates, *Economics, Environmental Policy and the Quality of Life* (Englewood Cliffs, N.J.: Prentice-Hall, Inc., 1979), p. 351.

10. See, for example, California Air Resources Board, "Report to the Governor on Acid Deposition Research and Monitoring Program" (Sacramento, Calif., 1983).

11. H. Bingham and K. Miedema with P. C. Cooley and J. C. Mathews, *Final Report, Allocative and Distributive Effects of Alternative Air Quality Attainment Policies* (Research Triangle Park, N.C.: Research Triangle Institute, October 1974); W. D. Watson, Jr., "Costs and Benefits of Fly Ash Control," *Journal of Economics and Business*, vol. 26 (Spring 1974), pp. 167–81; James M. Griffin, "An Econometric Evaluation of Sulfur Taxes," *Journal of Political Economy*, vol. 82 (July–August 1974), pp. 669–88.

12. U.S. Environmental Protection Agency, "Emissions and Diffusion Modeling Package—User's Manual," EPA-909-981-002 (Washington, D.C., 1981).

13. U.S. Council on Environmental Quality, *State of the Environment 1982*, p. 126.

14. See U.S. Environmental Protection Agency, "Water Quality Criteria—1972" (Washington, D.C., March 1973); and U.S. Environmental Protection Agency, "Quality Criteria for Water" (Washington, D.C., July 1976).

15. World Bank, Office of Environmental and Health Affairs, "Industrial Waste Control Guidelines" (Washington, D.C., 1978 and 1979); and World Bank, Office of Environmental Affairs, "Occupational Health and Safety Guidelines" (Washington, D.C., 1982–84).

16. A. V. Kneese and B. T. Bower, *Managing Water Quality: Economics, Technology and Institutions* (Baltimore, Md.: Johns Hopkins University Press, 1968), chap. 12.

17. See R. W. Johnson and G. M. Brown, Jr., *Cleaning up Europe's Waters: Economics, Management, and Policies* (New York: Praeger, 1976).

18. U.S. Council on Environmental Quality, *State of the Environment 1982*, p. 146.

19. See, for example, Bureau of National Affairs, Inc., *International Environmental Reporter*, August 10, 1983, p. 329.

20. U.S. Council on Environmental Quality, *State of the Environment 1982*, p. 171.

3

Health Considerations For Economic Development

The Arabian proverb, "He who has health has hope, and he who has hope has everything," underscores the importance of public health as a resource in the process of economic development. Certainly economic development can promote public well-being—by improving agricultural productivity and access to health services, and by providing safe drinking water and waste disposal, for example. But certain types of development projects may also have adverse effects on public health, both during and after construction.

The importance of health as a factor in World Bank–financed projects was articulated by former Bank President Robert McNamara in his address before the UN Conference on the Human Environment: "In those instances where a development project may threaten to create or intensify an existing disease problem, the Bank incorporates in the loan agreement appropriate arrangements for the requisite preventative health care measures."[1]

In addition to including measures for disease prevention, worker safety, and health care in development projects, the Bank has undertaken projects that directly improve the health care of people in developing countries.

This chapter focuses on the variety of direct and indirect threats which development projects may pose to the health of inhabitants and workers in the project area—by exacerbating conditions for the transmission of disease, introducing strains on sanitation facilities and the water supply, and placing additional burdens on existing housing and medical facilities. The chapter concludes with a guide to comprehensive planning for the control of the adverse health effects of development projects. (Risks to community health from the release of pollutants into the atmosphere by industry were discussed in chapter 2.)

Effects on Inhabitants of the Project Area

The construction of a major development project in an economically deprived area may have profound effects upon the health of the inhabitants. If there is an established community, however small, it is destined to undergo radical change. The existing level of sanitation, while primitive, may have been reasonably adequate to meet the needs of a small population. But with the arrival of many people from other areas and a rapid increase in population density, two problems are virtually certain to arise.

First, new arrivals may introduce new diseases or new strains of the causative organisms of locally endemic diseases, to which both residents and newcomers may be susceptible. The highly mobile workmen who tend to follow new construction projects constitute a serious source of disease. They arrive in large numbers, accompanied or soon followed by dependents. Camp accommodations may not be ready to receive all of them. Indeed, the first arrivals are needed to construct the early shelters and sanitary facilities, while they live under highly adverse field conditions.

Second, existing housing and sanitary facilities in the area quickly become overburdened owing to the arrival of nonproject people, including more job applicants than can be employed and many others who hope to profit from the work. This influx is likely to produce conditions that are particularly conducive to the spread of communicable disease.

In addition, economic development may promote an array of more subtle environmental and social changes that affect local inhabitants: dietary change, effects on surface and groundwater, changes in ecological balance and in agriculture, increased risk of road accidents, and threats to community health from certain industrial processes. Table 3-1 lists the categories of health-related impacts of typical watershed development and irrigation projects on inhabitants of the project area, describes the causes of such problems, and suggests appropriate control or remedial measures.

Transmission of Communicable Disease

As certain diseases spread rapidly among a susceptible group of individuals, the causative organism tends to become more virulent and the illnesses more severe. Of particular importance are gastrointestinal diseases spread by contaminated food and water, such as the common diarrheas, but also amoebic dysentery, typhoid, and cholera. Viral hepatitis is spread in the same manner and is a common hazard of the construction site and its fringe areas.

The respiratory diseases, such as influenza and pneumonia, are

Table 3-1. *Health-Related Impacts of Watershed Development and Irrigation Projects on Inhabitants*

Category	Subcategory	Cause	Control and remedial measures
Communicable diseases	Gastrointestinal diseases such as common diarrhea, amoebic dysentery, typhoid, and cholera	Contaminated food and water, untreated sewage, poor solid waste management	Provision of potable water, monitoring food distribution, sanitary disposal of sewage and solid waste
	Tuberculosis	Crowding, inadequate sanitation, food scarcity	Provision of adequate housing, control of number of occupants, case-finding and treatment
Housing and sanitary facilities	Unsanitary state of work camps	Inappropriate use and maintenance of shower and toilet facilities	Instruction in the appropriate use and maintenance of facilities plus supervision
Road accidents	Increase in mortality owing to motor vehicles	Inhabitants of project area unaccustomed to paved roads and high-speed transport	Driver training, adequate road markings, traffic control on access roads, adequate medical care for accident victims
Introduction of new disease vectors	Malaria mosquito vector	Introduction of vector in passenger compartment or hold of aircraft	Spraying of aircraft and vehicles from areas where vector-borne diseases are endemic
	Schistosomiasis aquatic snail vector	Vectors resistant to dessication and transported on the underside of vehicles or amphibious aircraft	
Public health care	Increased demands for medical care, for ensuring safe food and water supplies, and for enforcing sanitary regulations and controlling disease vectors	Increase in disease and injuries sharpens awareness among original inhabitants of the need for medical care of an international standard	Adequate planning for, and financing and staffing of, health care facilities

less of a problem, although tuberculosis, transmitted by close contact, is a threat where crowding, inadequate sanitation, and a scarcity of food occur. Other parasitic diseases are often introduced into project areas, especially in the tropics. These may spread rapidly, either because of the inadequate disposal of human excrement and garbage or because of the presence of insect carriers of disease. A special problem is an almost certain sharp increase in venereal disease, first among the migrant workmen and then the local population. (Specific diseases are discussed in detail below.)

When populations are relocated in new areas, the people may be exposed to diseases to which they have little immunity or for which no cure as yet exists. Certain insect vectors of disease are distributed according to rather sharp geographic patterns. For example, the black fly *(Simulium)* vector of onchocerciasis, or river blindness, breeds only in rapidly flowing streams. Wide areas traversed by such streams in sub-Saharan Africa have been depopulated in the past for fear of this insect. Sometimes the threat of river blindness has been forgotten or is overlooked, and vacant areas are resettled. The new settlers will thus be exposed to a disease of which they are unaware if they have been living along placid rivers where the fly does not thrive. A similar risk of sleeping sickness exists if people move into an area where the tsetse fly is or may become established, since it becomes infected with the parasite after biting sick persons and transmits the disease to others.

Newcomers to an area are often highly susceptible to locally endemic diseases. If displaced persons become exposed to leishmaniasis, which is transmitted by the bite of the sandfly *(Phlebotomus)*, the disease is likely to spread in epidemic proportions. This is a problem in countries such as Sudan, Ethiopia, and Somalia where both the parasite and the insect vector flourish.

Housing and Sanitary Facilities

Change from an accustomed environment as a result of a new development project may adversely affect both the people who move into the area and those who were original residents. The effects upon those moving into the construction area are the more obvious. In addition to the increased risk of communicable disease, marked psychological strains are readily observed.

Laborers who move to the construction site from the traditional life of a village may feel lost at first and confused when confronted with the strange life of the workers' housing with its new social patterns, its community showers, and its unfamiliar sanitary facilities. Unless the new migrants are carefully instructed in the use of such amenities and then closely monitored, difficulties arise. Foreign objects are discarded into toilets and drains, and sewer lines are soon clogged. These crises tend to discourage the further use of sanitary facilities, and the camp environment deteriorates rapidly to a septic state. Such stresses contribute to the psychological breakdown of some individuals and add to the aberrant behavior often observed on new projects. The problem is further aggravated by the almost certain overcrowding of whatever housing is provided.

Another group more seriously affected over the longer term are those local people who are displaced from their ancestral homes by the land requirements of the development project. These impacts on the human ecology are reviewed in Bank-supported projects, and a resettlement plan is a required component. In the case of a water resource project, such as a major dam or a large new lake, many thousands of homes or entire villages may be relocated. These migrations, involving the loss of ties to the land and the destruction of long-established traditions, may cause feelings of powerlessness and alienation which are not erased simply by building new towns for the displaced. The decline in health experienced by these groups cannot be attributed solely to their increased exposure to communicable diseases peculiar to the new village sites.[2] Change alone may have a harmful effect.

Involuntary resettlement as part of a development project is generally a politically sensitive measure. Therefore, socioeconomic studies of the population affected are started as soon as project design begins. It is becoming widely recognized that adequate resettlement can be more complicated than project engineering and more time consuming than project design and construction. When a large number of people is affected, the resettlement costs may approach the cost of construction.

The Bank now has a systematic and detailed policy designed to ensure successful resettlement.[3] This new policy is based on the precepts that the displaced people should be better off and certainly no worse off after relocation, and that the planning and financing of resettlement should be an integral part of the project. A resettlement plan must address such issues as the type of settlement, type of dwellings, compensation, and restoration of socioeconomic livelihood, and it must be tailored to specific areas.

Tribal Peoples

Another social problem occurs when projects cannot be sited away from areas inhabited by tribal people—vulnerable ethnic minorities. Such groups are not fully acculturated within the national society, do not know the national language, and have little or no political representation. Because they often subsist outside the national economy, they are extremely vulnerable to unwanted side effects of projects; their society may even be destroyed by the presence of a project unless special precautions are taken. The protection of tribal people's welfare, identity, and individual and collective rights should be treated as a moral imperative in project design. Furthermore, since tribal people have, over many centuries, accumulated a wealth of knowledge concerning practical uses of plant and animal species little known to scientists, their sudden physical or cultural demise causes the loss of much information of potential economic value.

Measures to guard the rights and interests of tribal people are essential, even though they are at times difficult to design and implement. Health services (for example, measles immunization), the protection of adequate land area, and representation in the decisions affecting them are especially important considerations in project design.[4]

Dietary Change

It is tempting to assume that the immediate economic benefits to workmen and to the community at the site of a development project will result in an improvement in the general nutritional status of the local population. This is not always the case. The introduction of Western-style convenience foods, such as prepared baby foods, may result in malnutrition in children unless milk is available as well.[5] Even the introduction of high-protein food mixtures, such as a corn-soya-milk preparation, is not an unmixed blessing, since its use may aggravate the nausea and diarrhea that accompany some cases of malnutrition. The distribution of unfortified dried skim milk, unless accompanied by the administration of vitamin A capsules, has been observed in northeast Brazil to aggravate the symptoms (such as eye defects) of vitamin A deficiency.[6]

The introduction of whole milk or milk products into the diet of populations in Africa and in Southeast Asia has been shown to cause distressing gastrointestinal symptoms, such as abdominal pain and diarrhea, in a significant number of persons. This condition, termed lactose intolerance, has an unusual racial distribution and tends to affect adults more than children. It is probably due to inherited enzyme deficiency.[7]

When rural peoples are removed from the path of rising water to new locations, they may substitute unfamiliar but toxic plants for food items to which they have been accustomed. This hazard has been noted among farmers who were displaced by the rising Zambesi River behind the Kariba dam.[8] If the staple diet is changed completely as a result of population movement, other difficulties may arise. In Thailand, for example, the staple diet of people displaced by a rising lake was changed to milled rice. A reduced growth rate was subsequently reported in children aged one to three and was attributed to relative malnutrition.[9]

Effects on Ground and Surface Waters

Industrial development projects, as well as large-scale watershed development and irrigation projects (see table 3-2), can degrade the quality of ground and surface waters and thus have broad negative repercussions on the health of the inhabitants of the project area. This is especially true when population growth is rapid.

The most obvious adverse effects on water quality in the project area result from the contamination of streams or lakes with sewage. Existing communities near the project site, and especially those downstream, risk having their traditional water source seriously affected by the discharge of project wastes. Besides the excrement from an enlarged human and animal population, other sources of contamination are encountered—the runoff from laundries, maintenance shops, laboratories, and health care facilities, for example. The risk of communicable disease such as viral hepatitis from contaminated water is a serious one. Sewage collection and treatment and a safe drinking water supply are essential, and these facilities should be scheduled for installation at the earliest stage of construction.

Debilitating and killing diseases, caused in part by lack of adequate water supply and poor or nonexistent means for disposing of human excrement, are a major impediment to development. The World Bank has estimated that disease in developing countries typically takes up about a tenth of the average person's potentially productive time. The control of diseases related to water and sanitation requires ample quantities of safe water, good hygiene, and sanitary disposal of excrement. The UN General Assembly declared the 1980s the International Drinking Water Supply and Sanitation Decade to draw worldwide attention to the serious nature and enormous magnitude of problems of water supply and waste disposal in the developing nations. At the same time, World Bank lending for water supply and waste disposal projects has assumed increasing importance in recent years.

Another hazard to water quality may result from chemicals held in settling ponds or lagoons for stabilization or evaporation; even trace amounts may leach out and contaminate the underlying water table. This is a particular risk of chemical plants operating on some types of terrain. A disturbance in the pH reaction of an underground water table may affect all those who draw water from wells or springs over a large area near the project. (These hazards are discussed in more detail in chapter 2.)

Changes in Ecological Balance

The introduction of a toxic hazard can disturb the ecological balance of a project area and adversely affect the nutritional state of the local population. This situation can occur if a water resource project introduces changes that affect aquatic life in a stream, a lake, or an inlet of the sea. Fish killed by reduced oxygen content in impounded water is an obvious problem.[10] A less dramatic but more serious consequence when deoxygenation persists is a long-term decline in fish spawning; people who depend on fish as a major source of protein then risk significant malnutrition. A similar threat may occur from thermal pollution caused by wastewater from power plant operations, a condition that also adversely affects aquatic balance and reduces fish populations.[11]

Changes in Agriculture

Irrigation projects may have an indirect effect on the health of people in the area if the poor drainage of surface water causes the water table to rise. The resultant waterlogging of agricultural land and the increase in the salinity of groundwater require changes in agricultural methods and in crops. This condition has been reported

Table 3-2. *Impacts of Watershed Development and Irrigation Projects on Water Quality*

	Impacts						
Category	*Surface water*	*Ground-water*	*Drinking water quality*	*Health*	*Fish and crustaceans*	*Comments*	*Appropriate control measures*
			Project infrastructure				
Introduction of un-treated sewage	Appreciable	...	Major	Major	Appreciable	Could cause epidemics of diseases such as cholera and infectious hepatitis	Well-designed and operated sewage collection and treatment system should be installed at project start-up
Untreated urban and other runoffs (such as from laundries, maintenance shops, laboratories, and health care facilities)	Appreciable	...	Appreciable	Appreciable	Appreciable	Could cause the introduction of appreciable amounts of toxic chemicals and heavy metals into the watershed	Implementation of an appropriate runoff management plan, incorporating collection, treatment, and disposal
Leaching of trace amounts of toxic chemicals and heavy metals from stabilization ponds and lagoons	...	Appreciable	Appreciable	Appreciable	Appreciable	...	Line ponds with well-maintained impermeable materials

		Impoundments				
Reduced oxygen content of the impounded water	Appreciable	. . .	Appreciable	. . .	Appreciable	Fish kills occur; long-term decline in fish spawning	. . .
Buildup of toxic materials (such as pesticides) in sediments that collect behind new impoundments	Appreciable	. . .	Appreciable	. . .	Appreciable	Dredging of sediments can worsen quality of impoundment water	Implementation of an appropriate erosion control management plan
Water diversion for irrigation							
Reduced volumes of water available for dilution	Major	Appreciable	Major	Possible	Major	Pollutants added below the diversion point will be more concentrated; productivity of coastal and estuarine systems is altered (especially fish production); availability of potable water is reduced, (saltwater-freshwater interface moves inland)	Economic, ecological, and health impacts of the reduced availability of water downstream from the diversion points should be taken into account at the earliest stage of project review

(Table continues on the following page.)

Table 3-2 (continued)

			Impacts			
Category	Surface water	Ground-water	Drinking water quality	Health	Fish and crustaceans	Comments	Appropriate control measures
Groundwater pumping							
Pumping rate greater than recharge rate	...	Major	...	...	...	Possible intrusion of saltwater and brine into freshwater aquifer	Control pumping rate so that it is less than recharge rate
Irrigation return flows							
Presence of dissolved salts	...	Major	Major	...	Major	Affects water hardness	Improve water management and agricultural practices; develop an appropriate tariff structure to minimize water consumption;

Buildup of biocides (herbicides and insecticides)	. . .	Major	Appreciable	Appreciable	Appreciable	. . .	introduce proper planning at the earliest stage of project review
Buildup of agricultural nutrients	Major	Major	Major	. . .	Major	Contributes to water-weed proliferation and eutrophication; excessive nitrates in water can cause methemoglobinemia in infants	

. . . Insignificant or unlikely effects.

Source: Robert E. Tillman, *Environmental Guidelines for Irrigation*, prepared for the U.S. Man and Biosphere Program and U.S. Agency for International Development (Washington, D.C., June 1981).

from the Indus Basin development in West Pakistan. The response of farmers in the irrigated districts of the Punjab has been to convert from wheat to rice cultivation.[12] If similar drainage problems occur in the tropics, farmers may become newly exposed to schistoso-miasis (bilharziasis, or snail fever), since the snail host tends to propagate in irrigation systems, and the parasite is often introduced by carrier individuals. Other parasites such as Guinea worms may also be introduced and spread under these circumstances unless the supply of drinking water is carefully monitored.

Increased Risk of Road Accidents

A sharp rise in the rate of serious injury from road accidents is so often related to development projects that it should be placed high on the list of risks to human health. Medical personnel on and near such projects regularly report that traffic injuries are among their most critical problems.[13] An alarming increase in mortality rates as a result of motor vehicle accidents has been documented as a regular concomitant of economic development.[14] It is often the neighbors of a development area, unaccustomed to paved roads and high-speed transport, who are struck down as they go about their own business on foot. Adequate provisions should be made to care for accident victims, and special consideration should be given to preventive measures, such as driver training, adequate road markings, fencing, and traffic controls on access roads.

Direct Effects on Project Workers

In addition to the general project-related effects on the health of local inhabitants, there may be adverse effects on the project work-ers themselves. Workers are subject to job-related accidents and are exposed to in-plant contaminants as well as to local disease.

Work Accidents

The risk of work accidents is of major concern to the project planner. Aside from the monetary cost—of medical care, disability payments, damage to facilities, and disruption of work schedules—there is the human cost and its impact on relations with workers and with the community. Construction work is among the most hazardous of occupations at best. If large numbers of the work force have had no prior construction or industrial experience, job safety can be a serious problem, especially during the early stages of the project. Introduction of safety measures, close supervision of safety procedures, and provision of facilities and staff for the care of injuries are a necessity.

After construction is completed, the operation of the project may demand an even higher level of safety awareness and competence on the part of workers. An adequately staffed safety unit, with provision for training and supervision of workers in safety on the job, is essential.

Exposure to Chemical and Physical Hazards

In addition to the risk of traumatic injury from on-the-job accidents, workers may be exposed to both chemical and physical hazards. In the operational stage of many development projects chemical hazards such as toxic liquids, gases, dusts, fumes, mists, and vapors are released that are potentially harmful to workers. Construction jobs may be accompanied by physical hazards: vibration, extremes of temperature and pressure, electromagnetic and ionizing radiation,[15] noise, and such special risks as, for example, caisson disease in the case of divers.

A detailed analysis of the anticipated hazards of each type of industrial, mining, or power project will indicate the steps that should be taken for their measurement and control. A useful source book to consult when compiling a list of health considerations on a given project is the *Encyclopedia of Occupational Health and Safety*.[16] Most industrial processes will require a more detailed treatment of health factors and reference to a larger library of sources on industrial methods and hygiene practices.[17] In addition, the World Bank Office of Environmental and Scientific Affairs has produced a detailed set of "Occupational Health Safety Guidelines."

Exposure to Local Diseases

The introduction of a work force and its followers into a project area, especially in a previously undeveloped region, may expose many nonimmune individuals to endemic diseases.

MALARIA. The classic example of the catastrophic effect of local disease is the havoc caused by malaria during construction of the Panama Canal. Malaria remains probably the most serious single threat to health throughout the tropics and subtropics. The *Anopheles* mosquito is the carrier insect of this disease.

A newcomer to an area in which malaria is highly endemic may be misled by the apparently robust health of most of the local people. The adults, however, are simply the relatively resistant survivors of a disease that regularly kills a large percentage of infants. The previously unexposed immigrant to virtually all of Africa, most of Southeast Asia, and much of Latin America is at grave risk of contracting malaria, some forms of which have a mortality rate of 10 percent in untreated cases. Military forces and construction crews throughout history have been inactivated by this disease. Experiences in Viet Nam and on construction projects in Africa continue to demonstrate that antimalarial drugs do not offer complete protection.[18] Malaria is almost always underestimated as to its very wide geographic distribution, the high risk of infection, and the severity of the disease in nonimmune subjects.[19]

In the 1950s efforts to control malaria were highly successful. Later programs were unable to sustain earlier gains, however, partly because of increased resistance to insecticides and drugs. In recent years malaria has exhibited a dramatic resurgence: between 1972 and 1980 the number of reported cases outside Africa more than doubled.

ONCHOCERCIASIS (RIVER BLINDNESS). Onchocerciasis is another important threat to the health of workers imported into many tropical areas where water resource projects are planned. Although not as frequent a cause of disability as malaria, it is often more feared because of its symptoms: first an intensely itching skin eruption and later the development of nodules seen or felt beneath the skin. Involvement of the eyes and eventual loss of vision is a dramatic and tragic complication that occurs chiefly among lifelong residents of a hyperendemic area.

Onchocerciasis is spread by the bite of several species of the black fly, in Africa especially *Simulium damnosum*, an aptly named blood-sucking pest that swarms in enormous numbers, inflicting painful and bleeding bites. Projects may be seriously interrupted by this biting scourge, and senior staff have threatened mass resignation when the rate of infection with onchocerciasis has risen among the workers. The black fly is virtually worldwide in distribution, but the species that are notable as vectors of onchocerciasis are encountered chiefly in East and West Africa and in Guatemala.

Where the disease is prevalent, infection rates of 99 percent in adult residents have been recorded. Under these circumstances, the number of infective flies in the *Simulium* population is high. Technically speaking, a single bite by an infective fly is sufficient to transmit the disease. Settlements in areas with rapidly flowing streams, as mentioned previously, have been abandoned all across sub-Saharan Africa because of the depredations of *Simulium* and the alarming disease it carries.

The large new dams of Africa have caused some new exposures to onchocerciasis. *Simulium* control may add appreciably to the overall cost of a dam in a fly-breeding area, notably the Kainji on the Niger. Some other development projects—coffee plantations in Guatemala and a timber project in Uganda—have also been afflicted by onchocerciasis.[20] During the actual construction of a dam in a black fly area, as the velocity of the river is temporarily increased by narrowing the channel or by diverting it around the main dam site, fly breeding may actually increase. After completion of the dam, breeding is usually arrested in the placid waters behind the barrier but may continue in the downstream runoff.

SCHISTOSOMIASIS (BILHARZIASIS, SNAIL FEVER). A third hazard to the workers on some development projects in the tropics and in some areas of the temperate zone is schistosomiasis. The disease is contracted by wading or bathing in water in which the parasite has been released by snails. The parasite penetrates the intact skin of humans and causes a chronic and progressive disease of either the urinary tract or the intestinal tract, depending upon the particular schistosome. The resulting disease is markedly debilitating and difficult to treat.

It is estimated that some 150 million people are victims of the three major forms of schistosomiasis. The distribution is shown on map 1.

The snail vectors propagate chiefly in shallow, sluggish water, such as in ponds, borrow pits, irrigation canals, and along the banks of lakes. The risk of infection is not so great during the actual damming of large rivers as it is when the lake behind the dam has filled, but workmen engaged in surveying, clearing, excavating,

Map 1. *World Distribution of Schistosomiasis*

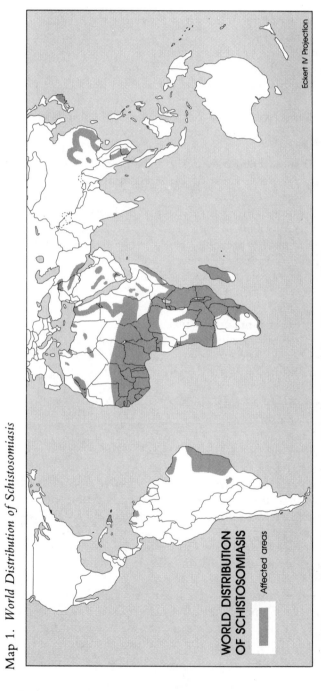

**WORLD DISTRIBUTION
OF SCHISTOSOMIASIS**

▓ Affected areas

Eckert IV Projection

Source: Based on World Health Organization, *World Health* December 1984). pp. 16–17.

70

and preparing a site may be exposed by wading or bathing in contaminated groundwater. A single exposure may be sufficient to contract the disease. Among people who have long been exposed, infection rates often exceed 90 percent of the population, and a sign such as blood in the urine occurs so commonly that it is locally regarded as a normal phenomenon. The risk that a new lake or the introduction of irrigation will increase the incidence of the disease in an endemic area is discussed more fully in the next section.

DENGUE (BREAKBONE FEVER). Dengue is a viral disease transmitted by the mosquito *Aedes aegypti*. It occurs in any warm, moist climate and is characterized by fever and excruciating pain in the joints and behind the eyeballs. A more serious form causes internal bleeding.

VIRAL ENCEPHALITIS. The most serious form of a disease caused by several viruses transmitted by mosquitoes, encephalitis is distributed worldwide. The relative risk of infection is determined by the presence of the disease locally in humans or animals and by the extent of mosquito infestation. Sandfly fever is a related disorder caused by a virus transmitted by the sandfly.

AFRICAN SLEEPING SICKNESS (GAMBIAN TRYPANOSOMIASIS). Caused by the bite of the tsetse fly transmitting the parasite, sleeping sickness is greatly feared throughout sub-Saharan Africa. A single tsetse inside a moving vehicle can panic the passengers and driver and is therefore a common cause of road accidents.

CHAGAS DISEASE (SOUTH AMERICAN TRYPANOSOMIASIS). A parasitic disease confined to Latin America, chiefly in Brazil and Peru, chagas is transmitted by the bite of the reduviid bug, found mainly in rural areas. The disease affects the internal organs, including the heart in some cases.

LEISHMANIASIS (ESPUNDIA, KALA-AZAR). A parasitic disease, leishmaniasis is transmitted by several species of sandfly of the genus *Phlebotomus*. A Latin American form, primarily affecting the skin, occurs in epidemic proportions when work parties, including some infected persons, enter a forest to cut lumber. A visceral form of the disease occurs especially in East Africa, India, and China.

BANCROFTIAN FILARIASIS (ELEPHANTIASIS). Caused by a microscopic worm transmitted by a mosquito, principally *Culex*, elephantiasis occurs throughout the tropics.

In addition to the above-listed diseases, which are transmitted mainly by insects, all development projects in the tropics carry a high risk of spreading a variety of intestinal parasites among newcomers. Meticulous attention to food sanitation is imperative. Viral hepatitis is also transmitted by contaminated food or water.

Completing the catalogue of risks to human health on development projects, especially construction jobs in the tropics, is exposure to venomous snakes, scorpions, large reptiles such as crocodiles, and dangerous fish.

Nutritional Status of Workers

A widespread problem of human health in poorer areas is malnutrition, most commonly a lack of sufficient protein in the diet. The result is diminished physical stamina and increased susceptibility to infection. On some development projects the health and productivity of workers have been improved by providing low-cost meals or supplementary food on the job. The best results have been attained when supplementary feeding is accompanied by instruction about the value of a balanced diet. This also provides an opportunity to emphasize food sanitation and to discourage the patronizing of itinerant food vendors, who often are a source of food-borne intestinal disease.

Introduction and Spread of Disease Vectors

A new development project may have a profound, if indirect, impact on human health by changing the ecology of an area. These changes can include the introduction of new disease vectors or the spread or intensified breeding of certain insects and aquatic species that provide a vehicle for the completion of the life cycle of some important parasites and viruses that afflict man. These vectors of disease, more common in the tropics than elsewhere, have been related most often to the construction of dams and other water resource developments (table 3-3). But there is a risk when any field

Table 3-3. *Some Human Parasites Related to an Aquatic Environment*

Parasite	Intermediate host	Method of infection	Diseases most commonly transmitted
Nematoda			
Onchocerca volvulus	Black fly (*Simulium*)	Fly bite	River blindness (onchocerciasis)
Wuchereira bancrofti	Several mosquitoes	Mosquito bite	Elephantiasis (filariasis)
Protozoa			
Plasmodium spp.	Anopheles mosquito	Mosquito bite	Malaria
Trypanosoma gambiense	Tsetse fly (*Glossina* sp.)	Tsetse bite	African sleeping sickness
Trematoda			
Schistosoma haematobium	Aquatic snail (*Bulinus*)	Bathing or wading in infested water	Urinary schistosomiasis (bilharziasis)
Schistosoma mansoni	Aquatic snails (*Biomphalaria; Australorbis*)	Infested water	Intestinal schistosomiasis
Schistosoma japonicum	Amphibious snails (*Oncomelania*)	Infested water	Visceral schistosomiasis
Viruses			
More than 30 mosquito-borne viruses associated with human infections	Several mosquitoes	Mosquito bite	Encephalitis; dengue

Sources: Adapted from C. C. Hughes and J. M. Hunter, "The Role of Technological Development in Promoting Diseases in Africa," in *The Careless Technology*, M. T. Farvar and J. P. Milton, eds. (New York: Natural History Press, 1972), pp. 69–101; and J. D. Thomas, "Some Preliminary Observations on the Ecology of a Small, Man-Made Lake in Tropical Africa," in *Ecology and Economic Development in Tropical Africa*, D. Brokensha, ed. (Berkeley, Calif.: University of California Press, 1965).

project brings people into an area where both the parasite and the vector thrive.

Introduction of New Disease Vectors

The movement of population induced by the establishment of a development project may introduce, or reintroduce, dangerous insects into an area previously free of them. The most conspicuous example is in sub-Saharan Africa where the tsetse fly has spread from heavy breeding areas to less affected areas along roadways.[21] Infective flies may travel great distances as "passengers" in conveyances, establishing new foci of sleeping sickness along the way. This accounts for the "sleeve" distribution of the disease in settlements along roads, tracks, and communicating streams of Africa. Where the fly finds new breeding grounds and human reservoirs of infection, outbreaks of the disease occur. This is most likely to happen on agricultural or livestock development projects, since cattle also attract the tsetse. However, the disease is transmitted only from one person to another by the bite of an infected fly.

New disease vectors, such as mosquitoes, may be introduced into a project area by aircraft, since insects may lurk in a passenger compartment or a baggage hold. It is also possible to bring in a snail vector of schistosomiasis on the underside of vehicles or on amphibious aircraft. Some aquatic snails, remarkably resistant to desiccation, have been transported for considerable distances in mud adhering to the bills and feet of wading birds, to the bodies of water buffaloes, and to the roots of transplanted shrubs and trees. A single snail is capable of producing many young and can quickly colonize a new habitat.[22]

New Infection or Reinfection of Existing Vectors

Vector-borne diseases of man become established in a population when three distinct conditions prevail: the vector is present; human or animal cases serve as a reservoir of the parasite; and previously uninfected individuals are exposed to the vector.

Control programs usually aim at all three factors: eradication of the vector; treatment of active cases in humans or destruction of an animal reservoir, such as rodents infected with the plague; and education, such as teaching the people to avoid water infected with parasites. Major emphasis is usually on vector control and treatment. The effectiveness of this dual approach has been well demonstrated, notably in the eradication of malaria from southern Italy, much of the Caribbean, most of Venezuela, and the southern United States.

Even when malaria has been eradicated, strict vigilance is required to avoid its reintroduction when surviving mosquitoes feed on humans who bring new infection from uncontrolled areas. This is a risk on development projects if labor is imported from malarial areas. In fact, the great mobility of the labor force is a significant obstacle to controlling malaria throughout Africa.[23]

Increased Propagation and Spread of Existing Vectors

A development project, especially a water resource plan, most seriously affects human health by changing the habitat of disease vectors, such as mosquitoes, black fly, and aquatic snails.

The mosquito population often increases in the early stages of clearing and constructing a project site, as breeding occurs wherever water collects—even puddles, vehicle ruts, and trash heaps containing discarded metal containers. Fortunately, it is relatively easy to reduce the number of mosquitoes by strictly controlling water accumulations and by spraying insecticides so that mosquito-borne diseases, such as malaria, can be held in check. Resistance to insecticides is increasing dramatically, however, and can negate control measures. Furthermore, unless the right pesticides are selected and used properly, they also constitute a public health problem.

Breeding of the black fly vector of onchocerciasis, *Simulium damnosum*, is usually arrested in the still waters of a lake rising behind a new dam, but very active breeding may occur around spillways or in the runoff stream below the dam where water velocity and turbulence provide a favorable habitat for the growth of larvae.[24] It is usually desirable to treat the stream with "safe" insecticides to discourage black fly breeding near dams in infected areas.[25]

The greatest risk is that water resource development will spread schistosomiasis in a previously endemic area or introduce it in any area that will support the growth of an aquatic snail vector of the disease. The snails that serve as intermediate hosts of schistosomiasis in Africa are of the genera *Biomphalaria* and *Bulinus*. In Asia, host snails are mainly of the *Oncomelania* genus, which is amphibious. The principal host snail in the Americas is *Australorbis*.[26]

The characteristics of snail habitats have been described as follows:

The snail intermediate hosts of schistosomiasis are adapted to a wide range of environmental conditions. They breed in many different sites, the essential conditions being the presence of water, relatively solid surfaces for egg deposition, and some source of food. These conditions are met by a large variety of habitats:

streams, irrigation canals, ponds, borrow pits, flooded areas, lakes, water-cress fields, and rice fields. Thus in general they inhabit shallow waters with organic content, moderate light penetration, little turbidity, a muddy substratum rich in organic matter, submergent or emergent aquatic vegetation, and abundant micro-flora. The snails may be found in isolated habitats quite independent of major drainage systems because snails or their eggs are sometimes carried passively to such habitats which seem favorable. Accordingly, to determine their habitats a systematic search for the snails must be conducted over a period of several seasons.[27]

Most likely to favor the increased propagation and spread of these snails are developments that impound water behind dams to serve hydroelectric plants, irrigation systems, or a fishing industry. The most conspicuous examples are those on the Nile that affect Egypt and Sudan. The spread of schistosomiasis there has been quite marked, with rates of infection rising to 75 percent or more in exposed populations.

In Ghana, as Lake Volta rose behind a large dam completed in 1964, an infective species of *Bulinus* snail was identified in the inundated area by 1966. The explosive growth of aquatic weeds favored massive reproduction of the snail. The parasite of schistosomiasis was present among people who had arrived from infested areas in the Volta delta, and it infected the local snail population. Outbreaks of the disease were soon observed in new townships along the lake. The rate of infection increased steadily, and within two years nearly all the children in these settlements were affected.[28] The snails also thrive in irrigation canals and ditches supplied with water pumped from underground, and along the shores of natural lakes, such as those of East Africa and the crater lakes of Cameroon.

Planning for Control of Adverse Health Effects

A major new project is likely to create heavy demands in the area for a variety of social services, including medical care for project personnel, their dependents, and the many additional people ordinarily attracted to a development site. In addition, public health measures such as monitoring the safety of water and food supplies, enforcing sanitary regulations, and controlling disease vectors must be considered.

All of these requirements are likely to overwhelm existing local resources, and governments may not be able to provide funds for additional facilities and staff to serve the expanded community. The following sequence of events may be expected:

- Arrival of project personnel and dependents
- Establishment of new communities
- Expectations of health services
- Arrival of nonproject people
- Increase in disease and injuries
- Increase in health awareness among original residents
- Demand for medical care of international standard.

More and more frequently, the project authority or developer is expected to furnish health services, either directly or by arrangement with contractors.[29] In fact, planning and financing of health care by the project authority is now required by many developing countries, a trend that is on the increase.

To prevent or control effectively the adverse effects of a development project on human health, there must be sound, comprehensive advance planning. Some factors that should be considered in preparing a comprehensive health management plan are listed in table 3-4. Specific authority and responsibility must be assigned among the official agencies and other organizations that have to deal with the project's impact on the community. Perhaps most important, adequate funding of control measures must be made available. For example, the World Bank frequently incorporates a health care management component in hydroelectric and irrigation projects which it funds, with special emphasis on the control of waterborne diseases.

A classic example of a complete assessment of the health risks anticipated on a major project, with a detailed plan for prevention and control, is contained in *The Volta River Project*, vol. 2, *Appendices to the Report of the Preparatory Commission*.[30] These observations and recommendations, prepared by the late Drs. Andrew Topping and George MacDonald of the London School of Hygiene and Tropical Medicine, constitute a model for the planner who is responsible for considering the human health factors of a development project. Their planning guide is presented below with a checklist of preventive measures to be considered in forestalling the adverse effects of large projects on health.

Table 3-4. *Considerations for a Comprehensive Health Management Plan*

Environment affected	Elements to be considered
Local community	Provision of adequate housing
	Control of number of occupants
	Provision of adequate sanitary facilities
	Education in use and maintenance of facilities
	Sanitary inspection and enforcement
	Early completion of safe water system
	Monitoring of water and food control
	Tuberculosis control
	Immunizations
	Instruction in general health issues with emphasis on prevention of waterborne diseases.
Work force	Worker safety training
	Prevention of communicable disease
	Education programs on the prevention of communicable diseases (including venereal diseases)
	Treatment of communicable diseases
	Immunizations
	Vector control at the work site through good housekeeping practices
	Supplementary feeding
Physical environment	Preliminary assessment of area ecology
	Effective sewage collection and treatment
	Industrial and all other effluent treatment
	Adequate drainage of project area
	Monitoring of air, water, fish, and vegetation
	Safe roadway design
	Driver education and license control
	Demonstration of efficient agricultural methods that minimize waste of water
General vector control	Organization of biological control services (entomologists, field control units, operations manuals)
	Preliminary survey of the project area for existing disease vectors
	Preliminary clinical survey of the population in the project area for vector-borne diseases
	Continuous biological surveillance of the project area for vector introduction
	Treatment of active and carrier cases of vector-borne diseases
	Spraying of aircraft and vehicles from areas where vector-borne diseases are endemic

Source: Donal T. O'Leary, "Health Aspects of Watershed Development and Irrigation Projects" (Washington, D.C.: World Bank, Office of Environmental Affairs, 1983).

Planning for Effects on the Local Community

Principal considerations for health planners are the anticipated effects of the project on housing and sanitary facilities in the local community and on the control of communicable diseases. Responsibility for planning usually lies with the central planning authority, the ministry of health, and the project authority. Implementing entities include local governments, the state and national agencies for housing and for health and sanitation, and the project authority and contractors.

Preventive measures include:

• Provision of adequate housing space
• Control of number of occupants
• Provision of adequate sanitary facilities
• Education in use of facilities
• Sanitary inspections and enforcement
• Early completion of safe water system
• Monitoring of water and food supplies
• Tuberculosis control
• Immunizations
• Instruction in nutrition.

Planning for Effects on the Physical Environment

Planning should take into account anticipated effects on the ecological balance of the project site and environs, including changes in the purity of groundwater and ambient air, changes in agriculture, and changes in the incidence of traffic accidents. Responsibility for planning usually lies with the central planning authority, the environmental protection agency, and the ministries of health, resources, and agriculture. Implementing entities usually include local governments; national and state water authorities, fisheries departments, and highway departments; and the project authorities and contractors.

Preventive measures include:

• Preliminary assessment of area ecology
• Provision of effective sewage collection and treatment

- Treatment or impoundment of effluents in impervious basins
- Engineering control of all effluents
- Prevention of the release of toxic effluents into air or water
- Adequate drainage of project area
- Monitoring of air, water, fish, and vegetation
- Vector control in the project area
- Safe design of roadways
- Driver education and license control
- Demonstration of safe agricultural methods.

Planning for Effects on the Work Force

The project work force may encounter on-the-job accidents, chemical and physical hazards, poor resistance to local diseases, or poor nutrition. Planning for the well-being of the work force is usually the responsibility of the central planning authority, the ministry of health, or the ministry of labor. Implementing agencies include the project authority, state and national agencies for health and sanitation and for industrial hygiene, and the contractors' medical units.

Preventive measures include:

- Assessment of industrial hygiene risks
- Engineering design to prevent job hazards
- Control of in-plant ventilation
- Medical examination of work recruits
- Strict medical selection and preparation of overseas staff and dependents
- Biologic monitoring of workers exposed to chemical hazards
- Provision of work safety training
- Treatment of communicable diseases
- Immunizations
- Vector control at the work site
- Supplementary feeding as indicated.

Planning for Effects throughout the Project Area

Health planning for the project area should anticipate the introduction of disease vectors, the infection of existing vectors, and the increased propagation of vectors as possible effects of the development project. The central planning authority, ministry of health, and ministry of agriculture usually formulate areawide plans, and they are implemented by the project authority and the state or national health and sanitation agency.

Preventive measures include:

- Organization of biological control services (entomologists, malacologists, field control units, operation manuals, and so on)
- Preliminary survey of the project area for existing vectors of disease
- Preliminary clinical survey of the population in the project area for vector-borne diseases
- Continuous biological surveillance of the project area for introduction of vectors
- Treatment of active and carrier cases of vector-borne diseases
- Spraying of aircraft and vehicles arriving from areas where vector-borne disease is endemic.

Specific preventive measures for the most important vector-borne diseases are given in table 3-5.

Planning for Health Care Services

The task of the health planner begins with the earliest conception of the development project. To determine the health needs of the project, a systematic assessment of the existing health situation in the project area is essential, with special emphasis on the acquisition of baseline data on communicable diseases and the potential for contamination. A standard method for conducting such a health survey has been outlined by the World Health Organization.[31]

Health services on the project site should be designed primarily to prevent and control communicable diseases and to provide medical care for injuries and illnesses that may arise out of project work. These requirements should be met without burdening whatever health services already exist in the area.

Project health services may be organized as follows:

> Therapeutic services
> > Comprehensive health care
> > Hospitalization
> > Ambulatory care

Table 3-5. *Preventive Measures for Selected Vector-Borne Diseases*

Disease	Preventive measures
Malaria	Identify, map, and number *all* human habitations in project area
	Periodically spray habitation walls with residual insecticide
	Eliminate or spray mosquito breeding areas
	Design irrigation systems and reservoirs for fluctuating water levels to discourage mosquito breeding
	Prepare banks of reservoir by removing vegetation
	Utilize predatory fish against mosquito larvae where feasible
	Avoid open dumps; incinerate or bury solid wastes
	Utilize antimalaria drugs as indicated
Onchocerciasis	Identify *Simulium* breeding foci
	Treat breeding streams with larvicide if feasible
	Spray aerially with insecticide where indicated
	Screen local residents and new arrivals for infection
	Treat active cases with caution
Schistosomiasis	Identify existing snail species before project work begins
	Design canals (with sharply sloping sides, high water velocity, and so on) to discourage snail breeding
	Utilize piping for irrigation where feasible
	Alternate irrigation and drying of fields where feasible
	Provide adequate drainage from irrigated areas
	Prepare reservoir sites before filling
	Control vegetation growth along accessible shorelines
	Control access to ponds and reservoirs where feasible
	Provide piped water to reduce visits to the lake
	Provide sanitary facilities in lakeside villages
	Maintain constant surveillance for evidence of snails
	Periodically introduce molluscicides into infested waters
	Screen local residents and new arrivals for infection
	Treat detected cases

Sources: Malaria: G. MacDonald, *The Epidemiology and Control of Malaria* (London: Oxford University Press, 1957). Onchocerciasis: B. B. Waddy, "Prospects for the Control of Onchocerciasis in Africa with Special Reference to the Volta River Basin," *Bulletin of the World Health Organization*, vol. 40 (1969), pp. 843–58. Schistosomiasis: J. P. Hughes, "Health Aspects of the Volta River Project in Ghana," in *Industry and Tropical Health*, vol. 5 (Cambridge, Mass.: Harvard University, School of Public Health, 1964); D. B. McMullen and others, "Bilharziasis Control in Relation to Water Resources Development in Africa and the Middle East," *Bulletin of the World Health Organization*, vol. 27 (1962), pp. 25–40; and M. J. Miller, ed., *Schistosomiasis: Proceedings of a Symposium on the Future of Control* (New Orleans, La.: Tulane University, 1972).

Preventive services
Occupational health and safety
Immunizations
Maternal and child health
Environmental services
Vector control
Sanitation
Safe water.

A modest ten-bed hospital of 500 square meters is shown in figure 3-1. This unit, which was planned for a development project in West Africa, is of modular design and was prefabricated so that it could be erected rapidly on the work site at the very beginning of the project. Complete medical care was available for the treatment of work injuries and acute illnesses during the critical early days of project construction. It may serve as the intensive medical care unit. One or more simple satellite units at the work site may be required for first-aid treatment of job injuries. Other satellite facilities for the care of ambulatory patients may be established nearer the housing areas. The cost of operation depends largely on the number of persons to be cared for, the availability of local rather than expatriate professional staff, the local availability of drugs and supplies, and the accessibility of referral centers.

The provision of community health services may become the responsibility of the project authority, at least temporarily, if government or private services are not established. It is highly desirable that what is done in this respect be consonant with the aims of national health planning in the country. There is a pronounced tendency to "spin off" the responsibility for nonindustrial health services from development projects to community organizations or to government as the project matures.[32]

Planning and Administrative Structure for Implementation

The responsibility for health factors on a development project is often shared by the project authority and the national ministry of health. Under these circumstances, the project authority may assign a portion of its task to the construction contractors under the terms of a master agreement. The authority may also operate a separate health unit, perhaps with personnel posted to it from the ministry of health, which is likely to serve as the main technical resource on

Figure 3-1. *Example of a Hospital Plan*

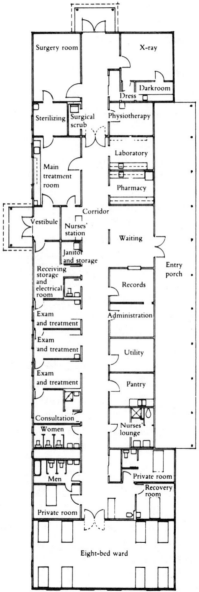

Source: American Hospital Association, "American-style Hospital for Ghana," *Hospitals*, vol. 43 (September 16, 1979), pp. 69–72.

health matters. Depending on project requirements, control teams may be organized for health survey work, for environmental sanitation, for vector control, and for other special measures deemed necessary. Provisions should also be made for the staffing and operation of hospitals, clinics, or dispensaries that may be established.

Various sanitary regulations are desirable for many development projects. These spell out specific responsibilities for each of the several entities that may be engaged in the project, such as government agencies, contractors, and the project authority.

Adequate funding of provisions to carry out health measures is an essential part of project planning, since even the most basic and indispensable health conservation activities cannot be carried out in the absence of fiscal provisions.

Conclusion

Improper attention to the overall effects of development projects on health will cause the health of project inhabitants and workers to deteriorate. Careful, comprehensive planning in advance to control such impacts and to provide for a health care delivery system in the developing area will contribute to the country's continued economic growth by assuring a healthy population and work force.

Notes

1. Robert S. McNamara, "Address to the United Nations Conference on the Human Environment," Stockholm, Sweden, June 8, 1972, in *The McNamara Years at the World Bank* (Baltimore, Md.: Johns Hopkins University Press, 1981).

2. J. R. Dyer, "Ivory Coast—Health Services on the Bandama Dam," in *Health Care for Remote Areas*, J. P. Hughes, ed. (Oakland, Calif.: Kaiser Foundation International, 1972), pp. 87–93.

3. World Bank, "Social Issues Associated with Involuntary Resettlement in Bank-Financed Projects," Operational Manual Statement 2.33 (Washington, D.C., February 1980).

4. Robert Goodland, *Tribal Peoples and Economic Development: Human Ecologic Considerations* (Washington, D.C.: World Bank, 1982).

5. F. T. Sai, "Opportunities and Responsibilities of Industry in the Field of Health in Developing Countries," *Industry and Tropical Health*, vol. 7 (Cambridge, Mass.: Harvard University, School of Public Health, 1970), pp. 11–17.

6. G. E. Bunce, "Aggravation of Vitamin A Deficiency following Distribution of Non-fortified Skim Milk, " in *The Careless Technology*, M. T. Farvar and J. P. Milton, eds. (New York: Natural History Press, 1972), pp. 53–60.

7. A. E. Davis and T. D. Bolin, "Lactose Intolerance in Southeast Asia," in *The Careless Technology*, pp. 61–68.

8. B. B. Waddy, "Medical Problems Arising from the Making of Lakes in the Tropics," in *Man-Made Lakes*, H. H. Lowe-McConnell, ed. (London: Academic Press, 1966), pp. 87–94.

9. B. G. Maegraith, "Symposium on the Health Problems of Industrial Progress in Developing Countries," *Journal of Tropical Medicine and Hygiene* (November 1970), p. 298.

10. P. Leentvaar, "The Brokopondo Research Project, Surinam," in *Man-Made Lakes*, pp. 33–42.

11. D. E. Abrahamson, "Ecological Hazards from Nuclear Power Plants," in *The Careless Technology*, pp. 795–811.

12. A. A. Michel, "The Impact of Modern Irrigation Technology in the Indus and Helmand Basins of Southwest Asia," in *The Careless Technology*, pp. 157–275.

13. See Dyer, "Ivory Coast—Health Services"; and C. Joubert, "Ghana—the VALCO Medical Service," in *Health Care for Remote Areas*, pp. 73–79.

14. A. Gabaldon, "Changing Problems of Preventive Medicine in the Tropics," *Industry and Tropical Health*, vol. 4 (Cambridge, Mass.: Harvard University School of Public Health, 1961), pp. 14–33.

15. Possible physical hazards from the spent wastes of nuclear power plants are not discussed in this volume because the World Bank has not assisted the financing of such installations.

16. International Labour Office, *Encyclopedia of Occupational Health and Safety* (Geneva, 1971); also published in a special edition (New York: McGraw-Hill, 1972).

17. See F. A. Patty, ed., *Industry Hygiene and Toxicology*, vol. 1, 2d ed. (New York: Interscience Publishers, 1958); and J. B. Olishifski and F. E. McElroy, eds., *Fundamentals of Industrial Hygiene* (Chicago: National Safety Council, 1971).

18. Dyer, "Ivory Coast—Health Services."

19. W. H. Wright and others, *Tropical Health: A Report on a Study of Needs and Resources*, National Academy of Sciences/National Research Council Publication no. 996 (Washington, D.C., 1962), pp. 69–77.

20. World Health Organization, *Expert Committee on Onchocerciasis: Second Report*, WHO Technical Report Series no. 335 (Geneva, 1966), pp. 26–27.

21. World Health Organization, *Expert Committee on Trypanosomiasis: First Report*, WHO Technical Report Series no. 247 (Geneva, 1962), pp. 25–26.

22. World Health Organization, *Snail Control in the Prevention of Bilharziasis* (Geneva, 1965), p. 21.

23. R. M. Prothero, "Population Movements and Problems of Malaria Eradication in Africa," *Bulletin of the World Health Organization*, vol. 24 (1961), pp. 405–25.

24. B. B. Waddy, "Onchocerciasis, with Particular Reference to Its Epidemiological and Economic Aspects," *Industry and Tropical Health*, vol. 5 (Cambridge, Mass.: Harvard University, School of Public Health, 1964), pp. 102–08.

25. J. P. Hughes, "Health Aspects of the Volta River Project in Ghana," *Industry and Tropical Health*, vol. 5, pp. 43–52.

26. World Health Organization, *Snail Control in the Prevention of Bilharziasis*, p. 21.

27. E. A. Malek, "Snail Ecology and Man-Made Habitats," in *Schistosomiasis*, M. J. Miller, ed. (New Orleans, La.: Tulane University, 1972), pp. 57–62.

28. I. Paperna, "Study of an Outbreak of Schistosomiasis in the Newly Formed Volta

Lake in Ghana," *Zeitschrift für Tropenmedizin und Parasit* (Stuttgart), vol. 21 (December 1970), pp. 411–25.

29. J. P. Hughes, "Economic Development and the Health Planner: Opportunity or Handicap?" in *Health Care for Remote Areas*, pp. 7–14.

30. *The Volta River Project*, vol. 2, *Appendices to the Report of the Preparatory Commission* (London: Her Majesty's Stationery Office, 1956), pp. 191–209, 325–50, 442–44, 457–59.

31. World Health Organization, *Local Health Service: Third Report of Expert Committee*, WHO Technical Report Series no. 194 (Geneva, 1960).

32. W. E. Wakeley, "Coordination of Medical Services in an Industrial Environment with those of Government and the Private Sector," *Industry and Tropical Health*, vol. 7, pp. 140–45.

4
Tropical Agricultural Development

Projects for agricultural development and production in the tropics claim the largest share of World Bank lending. These agriculture projects promote crop production and irrigation, livestock and fish production, and timber and fuelwood production. Food crops receive the most attention in agricultural projects because of the urgent need to provide more food for the world's increasing population.

Tropical agriculture refers to plant cultivation, animal husbandry, and forestry in climates characterized by equable temperatures and a uniform intensity of sunlight which often provides a year-round growing season. Tropical soils typically have a low nutrient content and are highly erosive.

Many countries' food needs exceed their agricultural production; as a result, close to 1 billion human beings suffer from hunger and malnutrition. The world community faces compelling problems of redistribution of food from areas of high production to areas suffering from low production and high consumption. The pressures to develop new agricultural projects, plus the loss of formerly productive land owing to poor farming and grazing practices, have focused attention on the need to implement methods of crop and livestock production that help protect and conserve existing agricultural resources.

Productive agriculture cannot be sustained unless the vital environmental resources of land, water, and natural biota are managed carefully to maintain their regenerative capacity. As energy costs rise, it will become increasingly difficult to offset environmental problems. Soil erosion and the depletion of nutrients, for example, have traditionally been combated by increasing energy-dependent inputs such as mechanized soil cultivation and fertilizers; in the future new methods will be needed.

In spite of increased inputs, the yields of grains per hectare globally have ceased to rise as fast as they once did. This is in part because of the degradation of arable land, the salinization and waterlogging of the soil, the loss of organic matter from the soil, and an increase in pest problems. During the 1970s and 1980s, the biological and physical resources of certain areas have been strained so much that food productivity per unit of land has declined just when there is a need for even higher productivity.

The most significant degradation of resources as a result of agricultural production projects is erosion and the resultant loss of productive soils. Tropical cropland, grazing lands, and forests are highly susceptible to erosion, which is extremely difficult and costly to rectify. Loss of the thin soils can be caused by certain planting and irrigating practices, overgrazing, clearcutting, and other aspects of development.

Even relatively minor environmental measures would help alleviate some adverse effects of agricultural development. This chapter emphasizes problems which should be considered in the design of agricultural projects. The environmental focus of this material is in no way intended to reduce the importance of economic, social, political, and agronomic factors in agricultural project design. Agricultural development that causes irreversible degradation of environmental resources, however, will, in the long run, result in both diminished production and pressures for more development.

These often costly effects can be significantly reduced through agricultural practices that minimize or mitigate adverse environmental impacts. Effective erosion control, conservation of water, efficient use of energy, careful management of forests, and protection of fisheries are required if tropical agricultural projects are to produce maximum yields and to sustain that productivity over time.

The chapter is organized to provide a description of three broad categories of agricultural projects assisted by the World Bank: crops, livestock and fish, and forestry. For each category, environmental problems are described and possible mitigating measures are suggested.

Tropical Crop Production

About 90 percent of all the plant food utilized by humans derives from only sixteen crops: rice, wheat, maize, sorghum, millet, rye, barley, cassava, sweet potato, potato, yam, coconut, banana, common bean, soybean, and peanut. The most important fiber crop is cotton.

Environmental tolerances of these crops determine to some extent where they are grown. Maize, for example, usually requires at least 65 centimeters of rainfall a year and a frost-free growing season of three to four months. Wheat can be grown in regions having only 40 centimeters of rainfall, and it can tolerate frost. Rice is particularly suited to the humid tropics and has become a staple food in those regions, but it can be grown in temperate areas and under both irrigated and rainfed conditions.

This section discusses the three main environmental issues related to tropical crop production—loss of soil because of erosion, use of biocides to control pests, and irrigation—and suggests measures to mitigate their adverse impacts.

Erosion

Acceleration of soil erosion is the principal environmental degradation of agricultural land.

Successful rainfed agriculture requires arable land (suitable for plowing and hence crop cultivation) with six favorable characteristics: 40–250 centimeters of rainfall annually, at least three to four months of favorable growing temperatures, suitable slopes, suitable soil texture, suitable organic matter, and sufficient nutrients for crop production. With proper management, arable land can be a renewable resource kept in use indefinitely.

In addition, it may be possible to bring some poor land into crop production. Best estimates are that world cropland resources might be expanded by about 15 percent (to 1.7 billion hectares) without great cost and effort. In addition, some arid lands could be irrigated to increase the potential by as much as 25 percent (to 2.1 billion hectares).[1] These endeavors would require such enormous inputs of energy and technology, however, that they might not be economically feasible.

Since the effects of soil erosion usually develop slowly and steadily, the annual loss incurred may be difficult to detect unless severe gully or sheet erosion has occurred. During the past 200 years, for example, at least a third of the topsoil on U. S. croplands has reportedly been lost. Various soil surveys have estimated that erosion has already ruined approximately 40 million hectares of arable land in the United States. Although this land can no longer produce crops, some of it is suitable for trees.

In India, soil erosion rates are three times more intense than erosion in the United States.[2] In Guatemala soil washed from maize fields on steep (20 percent) slopes can turn river water dark brown.

And in Haiti some cultivated slopes have had topsoil eroded away to the underlying bedrock, so that the land has been rendered totally unproductive. If deposited on flood plains or other usable sites, such alluvium can be valuable, but most is lost to bodies of water, where it may cause siltation.

Although in general wind-induced erosion is less severe than water-induced erosion, it is a serious problem in certain semiarid regions of the world. Some soils such as clays, those with low organic content, and those lacking a well-developed crumb structure are especially liable to erosion.

In addition to the outright loss of arable soils, erosion also significantly reduces the amount of nutrients available for crop production. The primary reasons for the reduced crop yields on eroded soil are low nutrient content, impaired soil structure, deficient organic matter, reduced moisture, and, in the long run, a system that is less buffered against environmental extremes.

Essential elements such as nitrogen, phosphorus, potassium, calcium, magnesium, and sulfur, as well as trace elements (for example, manganese, copper, and zinc) must be present in soil that is to be cultivated. If nutrient levels are too low to produce good crops, they can be raised by means of commercial fertilizer, livestock manure, organic compost, leaves collected from adjacent forests, waterweeds from nearby ponds, or other similar vegetation.

Soil erosion and exhaustion of nutrients are inherent with all annual row crops grown under intense cultivation. Row crops on slopes of 3 percent or more, tree crops on slopes over 15 percent, cultivation in high rainfall areas, churning and exposure of soil for the harvest of deep root crops and coarse grain crops in semiarid areas are examples of agricultural uses with a high erosion rate.

Ideally, crops and cropping systems should be selected which can be adapted to the environment. Where conditions are not suitable for a particular crop, however, various cropping, tillage, and land management techniques can be employed to reduce soil erosion and the loss of soil nutrients.

One traditional method of raising tropical food crops that has helped reduce their environmental impact is the culture of several crops in combination. The feasibility of this system, known as combination cropping, depends on the slope of the land, quality of the soil, available moisture, temperature, and potential pest problems.

Since multiple cropping may reduce the fallow period, soil nutrients must be continually restored. Numerous opportunities exist for preventing or reducing environmental losses in the growing of maize and other row crops, if appropriate systems of combination cropping are selected and the crops and the environment are carefully managed. Although many farmers have traditionally used such systems, some may need support and incentives to introduce the improved varieties, cultivation techniques, and fertilizers required for optimal yields. In addition, because the complex factors affecting crop production vary from location to location, proper testing, and in some cases research and development, should be employed.

On slopes of 2 to 12 percent, strips of carefully selected crops can be combined with row crops to help control soil erosion. For instance, if one cross-contour strip is planted with a row crop, the next downslope strip can be planted with a nonrow crop that will help capture soil washed from above. A workable crop sequence in a particular location might include maize, beans, mixed stylosanthes, or soya with grass hay. Rotating strip crops also prevents the buildup of insect and plant pathogens in the soil and helps control weeds because some weed species are poor competitors with particular crops. The weeds that are suppressed in maize production, for example, are different from those suppressed in alfalfa production.

In addition to these advantages of strip cropping, certain crops derive mutual benefits from growing together. Beans and maize, for example, have been combined for centuries. On the one hand, beans add nitrogen to the soil when nitrogen-fixing bacteria and favorable soil conditions are present, and they quickly cover the surface with vegetation and reduce the erosion associated with a row crop such as maize. Maize, on the other hand, can provide a support for climbing beans. Another advantage of mixing crops is that diverse host plants can be combined to reduce pest damage.

Combination cropping technology also helps maintain levels of organic matter and nitrogen in the soil. Some crops, such as maize and wheat, add large quantities of organic residue to the soil if erosion problems are under control. These crops must be supplied with adequate fertilizer, however, to sustain high yields and to compensate for the nutrients they draw from the ecosystem.

In addition to cropping systems, various tillage and land management techniques can be used to reduce or prevent soil erosion and water runoff. Although they cannot be implemented without an investment of energy, in general the return in crop yields is several times that of the energy investment.

Conservation tillage practices include contour planting accompanied by conventional tillage, crop rotation with conventional tillage, cover crops with conventional tillage, no-till culture, and combinations of these technologies. Simple contouring used with conventional tillage can reduce the average soil loss by 50 percent on moderate slopes. Planting a suitable cover crop such as grass along with legumes after harvest of the maize crop can reduce soil loss by more than 40 percent.[3] This combination of cover crops can provide about 8 metric tons a hectare of vegetation; grass is particularly effective in this mix because it provides a persistent mulch that does not decay as rapidly as that of the legume. Although cover crops offer no advantage over heavy residues of chopped stalks or straw in the prevention of soil erosion, they are more effective in reducing the leaching of nitrogen and in controlling weeds. Cover crops are essential if the crop residue is removed.

In no-till systems, seed is planted directly in uncultivated soil, which is covered by chopped stalks, small grain residues, or chemically killed cover crops.[4] Maize residues left on the land generally reduce soil erosion by about a third of that occurring when maize is grown by continuous conventional tillage on a 4 to 5 percent slope; combining no-till culture with a rotation of maize-maize-oats-hay reduces the rate of soil erosion to about a ninth of that occurring under conventional tillage. In certain instances, no-till planting in sod chemically killed with a properly applied herbicide may be even more effective since it can reduce soil loss to a twentieth of that in conventionally plowed sod.

Thus, while loss of arable soils to erosion is a worldwide problem of alarming proportions, encouragement of sound cropping systems and land management techniques should assist in preserving the soils necessary to sustain tropical crop production.

Pest Control: Use of Biocides

Pests reduce crop yields and consequently affect the world's potential food supply. About 35 percent of crops are lost worldwide because of pest activity.[5] These losses include destruction by insects, pathogens, weeds, mammals, and birds. Worldwide postharvest losses to pests range from about 10 to 37 percent.[6] The major pests of harvested foods are microorganisms, insects, and rodents.

This significant loss occurs despite all the methods now used to control pests. Developing countries can ill afford a loss of this magnitude in view of food shortages and ever increasing populations. Biocides help enormously to reduce food losses by controlling pests and disease. The term "biocide," meaning chemical killer of life, is used here deliberately as a reminder that the use of such substances can bring unwanted effects along with its benefits.[7] Because of their proven effectiveness, however, biocides will continue to be important in attempts to ensure adequate food supply for a growing world population while new control methods are sought.

About 2.3 billion kilograms of biocides are applied annually throughout the world. Pollution from the misuse and overuse of biocides is common in the developed countries in spite of their extensive knowledge of and ability to regulate these substances. The actual and potential impacts of biocides are far more severe and immediate in developing countries, however, because farmers do not know the proper methods of application and regulatory authority is often inadequate.

Some developing nations are repeating the mistakes initially made in the developed countries. Heavy and frequent applications of biocides initially produce boom yields, but these taper off over the years as pests and diseases develop resistance to biocides, as beneficial natural enemies of pests are reduced to low levels or annihilated, as previously unimportant organisms assume pest roles, and as the accumulation of biocides in the soil hinders crop growth and reduces yields.

Over the decades, biocides have provided important benefits to mankind by increasing crop production, but not without causing significant environmental damage and social problems. Serious accidents have occurred during the shipment and storage of pest control chemicals. Illnesses and deaths have resulted not only from the direct exposure of workers, but also from the consumption of food or liquids which have been contaminated by leaks or spills from improperly packaged biocides. Human poisonings, including deaths, can also be traced to the improper use of these chemicals. In Central America, for example, where large quantities of biocides are used on cotton, 3,000–4,000 human poisonings are reported annually, and the actual number may be much larger.[8] In the United States, there are an estimated 45,000 cases of pesticide poisoning annually, of which nearly 3,000 are severe enough to require hospitalization and about 200 result in death.

These data underscore the importance of taking precautions when handling biocides. Such precautions must be understandable and affordable, however, if they are to be heeded by farm workers worldwide, many of whom may be poor and illiterate. In a 1977 study of small farmers in a Latin American country, researchers followed the farmers from planting to harvest and noted the application of the biocides to crops and the care taken in handling. The studies disclosed widespread ignorance of safe handling and storage procedures. In addition, analysis of crop residues indicated potentially toxic amounts of two pesticides in 20 percent of the tomato and cabbage crops tested.[9]

Besides the direct impact on humans whenever biocides are used extensively, pest populations eventually develop some tolerance or resistance to the chemicals used. This tolerance creates the need for larger doses, more money spent on chemicals, a greater impact on the natural environment, and ultimately higher levels of resistance. One of the most alarming problems to arise from biocide resistance is the resurgence of malaria. Following the introduction of DDT in 1945 to control the malarial mosquito vectors, world malaria cases declined until 1960. In India, for example, malaria declined by about 100,000 cases a year, but by 1978 it had risen to 50 million cases a year owing to the increased resistance of the mosquitoes and a reduction in vector control operations.

In addition to humans, numerous other nontarget species are affected by the widespread use of biocides. Domestic animals are poisoned and livestock products such as meat and milk are contaminated.[10] Fish and shellfish in nearby waterways may be killed as the biocides move through the air and water of the crop ecosystem. Birds may die from eating sprayed crops, and groundwater supplies may become contaminated. Often less than 1 percent of the biocide hits the actual target pest population; this low level of control means that unnecessarily high levels of biocide are released into the environment and affect other nontarget organisms at random. Recent improvements in application methods such as ultra-low-volume sprays are expected to reduce these adverse effects.

Chemical weed control poses problems similar to those of chemical pest control, including contamination of waters, harm to fish life, herbicide resistance, change in weed species, contamination of crops, and harm to spray operators.

Herbicide controls of waterweeds can deplete the oxygen content of the water and reduce the fish population. Many herbicides, which now account for 50 percent by cost or weight of all biocides applied in the world, may persist in the soil and be detrimental to future crops. In addition, herbicides can increase the susceptibility of crops to insect and disease pests.

To mitigate the adverse impacts of biocides, new means of control are being considered. As the environmental and social costs of biocides are more widely recognized throughout the world, there are efforts to reduce the misuse of biocides and at the same time to improve pest control through integrated pest management (IPM) technology. This technology attempts to manipulate the crop environment to minimize chances of serious pest attack. Pest-resistant crop varieties are used if possible; times of planting may be changed to take into account the life cycles of pests; natural products or parasites may be encouraged or even introduced; mixed cropping may be used rather than monoculture. In addition, if biocides are used, the applications and dosages are based on a program to "treat only when necessary." Such a monitoring program helps reduce the quantity of biocides applied.

Because most pest problems are the result of a complex set of factors, no single approach is suitable for the control of all pests. A sound ecological approach combines environmental, biological, and chemical controls, modified to fit a particular crop ecosystem when sufficient knowledge becomes available. To be effective IPM requires a detailed understanding of the agronomy of the crop in question and the life cycles of the pests and their natural predators.

Biocide damage and other costs are so great and are increasing so quickly that IPM is being designed and implemented in a growing number of agroecosystems worldwide. One example of potentially significant IPM is an experiment to reduce biocide use for tsetse control in cattle projects by substituting the use of sterile males, fly traps, odor and sound schemes, and parasites.

When chemical controls are unavoidable, all precautions must be taken to ensure human safety and health as well as to avert environmental contamination. Water use downstream, proximity of homes to fields, storage and transport of biocides, and care in mixing and handling must be assessed.

Water Resource and Irrigation Projects

Because crop plants require substantial quantities of water for top yields, a lack of water limits crop production in certain areas of the world. One hectare of maize, for example, can transpire about 4.6

million liters of water during the growing season, and under arid conditions a maize crop may require about 12 million liters of irrigation water. Agricultural production in the United States uses about 83 percent of all water consumed, whereas industry and urban areas combined consume less than 17 percent.[11]

Industry and urban areas return most of the water they use to waterways, but agriculture consumes large amounts of the water it uses and returns much less to streams and lakes for reuse. That is, water contained in the crop, transpired by it, and evaporated from the field exceeds the return by drainage from the field. Nonetheless, the return flow still presents problems of runoff or leaching, discussed below.

World crop production can be increased by providing a reliable supply of water. Water can be delivered for irrigation by diverting it from streams and rivers, by developing impoundments or reservoirs, and by pumping it from groundwater supplies. Irrigation, which is being expanded in arid regions, serves two purposes in world crop production. First, it allows crops to be grown in regions previously unsuited for farming. Second, partial irrigation helps stabilize crop production in regions that have fluctuating rainfall.

Irrigation projects, however, are not without environmental impacts. The withdrawal of water from streams and rivers for irrigation may affect human communities downstream that use the water for drinking or to dilute and carry treated wastewater. If water diversion for irrigation is excessive during the dry season, the river's base flow will be significantly reduced. Wastes will not be adequately diluted and siltation and pollution may occur. Thus, human health could be threatened and the cost of purifying the water could increase.

Irrigation projects can degrade drinking water by increasing the leaching of biocides and fertilizers and by reducing the normal flow which previously diluted wastes. While adequate sewage treatment would mitigate the problem of insufficient dilution of waste streams, many rural areas do not have the facilities to do so. For example, of India's 3,119 towns, only 217 have any sewage treatment facilities.[12]

The combined effects of runoff from irrigated fields and reduced river flow can also raise the salinity of water and thereby reduce its quality for irrigation downstream. In some areas, reducing river flow creates breeding places for mosquitos, snails, and other organisms that are vectors of human diseases. At the same time, irrigation water moving through cropland may transport biocides back into streams inhabited by fish and other organisms sensitive to even relatively low levels of pollutants.

Effective controls must be instituted to prevent biocides and fertilizer from being carried into local waterways from irrigated croplands. Countries need to legislate and enforce adequate controls on the use of biocides and train people to take proper precautions. All biocide projects must be controlled to prevent pollution of domestic water supplies and damage to local fisheries.

Environmental costs associated with impoundments or water reservoirs, sometimes essential for an irrigation system, may include involuntary resettlement of human communities, flooding of upstream agricultural land, and destruction of forests and other terrestrial habitats by the rising water. Impoundments also provide a habitat for undesirable organisms such as snails, which are vectors of schistosomiasis. Furthermore, evaporation in the impoundment reduces the supply of water.

The growth of weeds on the surface of the water may contribute to water loss and may create an unsuitable environment for many types of fish and other desirable aquatic organisms that could serve as human food; such weeds can also block waterways and sluice gates. Weed control can become a major problem in impoundments, since chemical control may be only short-lived and mechanical control laborious. The detrimental effects of the weeds themselves must be carefully balanced against the negative effects of herbicides on water quality and the fish population.

Reservoirs and canals also provide ideal habitats for mosquitoes, snails, and other vectors of human diseases. Control of these vectors is usually expensive and is never completely effective. Thus, human disease is a social cost of some irrigation projects.

Groundwater may also be available for irrigation. More freshwater is stored underground than in rivers and lakes, but in some parts of the world it is now being pumped or mined at a rapid rate. Since agriculture consumes 80 to 90 percent of the water in arid regions, proper management of water resources is required to prevent an eventual shortage. The tradeoffs between agricultural and public needs must be carefully studied to protect the groundwater and to make the best use of this valuable natural resource.

The gradual buildup of salt (salinization) in soils caused by poor drainage, evaporation, and crop transpiration of irrigation water is a major environmental problem. From 33 to 80 percent of the world's irrigated land already has been affected to some degree by salinization, which seriously reduces the productivity of crops.[13] If the level of salt is high, the land may even have to be abandoned, as were millions of hectares in tropical regions in the past. Since crop productivity is reduced and inputs are not fully effective on these irrigated lands, energy resources used in fertilizers and irrigation pumps as well as human resources involved in crop production are wasted. In the end, food production declines.

Waterlogging, another serious environmental problem connected with irrigation, occurs when the water level in fields becomes so high that crop production is impossible. Plants drown or their yields are significantly reduced.

To make effective use of water and the nutrients present in human wastes, many communities are using sewage effluents and sludge treated in various ways as fertilizers and as sources of moisture. Raw sewage effluent that contains human disease organisms may contaminate food crops and threaten human health. Industrial effluent or sewage sludge containing heavy metals such as cadmium and lead creates another pollution hazard: the soil accumulates these metals, which are in turn absorbed and concentrated by the crop, and further concentrated—sometimes to harmful and potentially toxic levels—when people and livestock eat the crop. Regular analysis followed by appropriate treatment can prevent such problems.

In conclusion, adverse environmental and health impacts of irrigation can be reduced if projects are located on good soil with adequate drainage to prevent waterlogging, if there is ample water to flush out accumulating salts, and if expertise is available on how to use the water effectively to obtain high crop production. Since the implementation of irrigation projects increases the possibility of water-related diseases, these projects require health components to control such diseases, particularly schistosomiasis and malaria. (See the discussion in chapter 3.)

Livestock and Fish Production in Tropical Areas

Although not as important as plants are for food production in the developing countries, animals and fish are a valuable source of protein in human diets.

Livestock

Relatively few species of animals are used by mankind for the production of protein. About 90 percent of all animal products consumed come from dairy cattle, beef cattle, hogs, sheep, chickens, ducks, and turkeys. The type of livestock selected for production by societies in different parts of the world depends on the environmental resources available as well as on cultural preferences.

Meat production is the least efficient way to meet human protein needs. Raising grain-fed livestock wastes nutrients and energy when compared with direct human consumption of grain, and feedlot beef cattle are the most costly and least efficient of livestock at converting grain protein to animal protein. Small-scale milk and dairy production is valuable, however, especially if no special care is required. Similarly, livestock may be grown where cropping is not desirable, as on grassy sloping land and in drier areas. Small livestock, such as poultry and small mammals, may be regarded as environmentally beneficial and generally do not compete with crop production.

The main environmental problems of livestock production are the result of overgrazing or overstocking—that is, too many animals for the amount of feed available. Overgrazing damages vegetation and, by removing the plant protection of the soil, can accelerate erosion. Desertification, in arid regions, can be a serious result. Another problem associated with livestock production is deforestation to create cattle pasture.

Feedlots (where a large number of animals are maintained in a confined area) create large quantities of manure. Manure storage areas, if improperly managed, can contaminate nearby waterways.

New strategies are being developed to optimize livestock production within the limits of the range's carrying capacity, while preserving environmental integrity. Appropriate densities of cattle in combination with sheep or goats, for example, allow skilled pastoralists to make more effective use of the diverse vegetation maintained on the pasture or range.

Fish and Other Aquaculture Production

Although fish, shrimp, and other aquatic organisms in freshwater and marine environments provide a relatively small amount of the total protein consumed, they are a valuable source of protein in many tropical regions. Fish can be cultured in man-made ponds or in swamp habitats that may not be suitable for production of other livestock or crops. Some fish, such as certain types of carp, can be fed animal and household wastes and thus extend the resources available to a family or small community. Well-managed waste-water aquaculture systems may provide suitable environments for fish if no heavy metals or biocides are present.

Environmental dangers that threaten fisheries far outweigh the negative effects aquaculture projects may have on the environment. Deforestation, dams, irrigation schemes, biocides and heavy metals, flood control projects, drainage and land reclamation activities, harbor development, and the removal or alteration of coral reefs can wreak havoc on fish populations. In addition, industrial fishing fleets and overfishing have substantially reduced the numbers of certain species. Thus, all fishery projects must gather information on and monitor the population size and species composition in order to provide for a sustainable fish harvest.

Environmental problems associated with fish culture include: alteration of natural marsh habitats by the construction and maintenance of ponds, the cost of raising large quantities of grain if the fish are grain fed; pollution of waterways caused by the runoff of nutrient-laden water from ponds; the danger of releasing exotic fish species into the environment; the creation of habitats suitable for disease vectors such as mosquitoes and snails; and increased flooding of ponds if normal drainage has been improperly altered. Although some of these problems may be minimized by careful management, all aspects of aquaculture must be weighed to determine whether a given technique—for example, the introduction of fish that will eat mosquito larvae—is economically and ecologically feasible.

Timber and Fuelwood Production

Most people in the world use wood, dung, and crop residues as their primary fuels. Wood fuels in developing countries account for about 85 percent of the energy used for cooking and heating.

At current rates of world deforestation, the question is whether there will be sufficient firewood for people to cook their food, even if adequate amounts of food are produced in the future. Less than 29 percent of the world land area is covered with forests, and this resource is rapidly being depleted.[14] Because of greater demands for lumber, pulpwood, firewood, and food, the forest ecosystems of the world, especially those in the tropics, are at great risk. Deforestation at accelerating rates poses serious and widespread environmental threats, specifically the loss of tree species, wildlife habitats, and soils.

The two primary causes of worldwide deforestation are the clearing of land for agricultural production and the gathering of fuelwood. Although the forest area in developing countries is estimated to exceed 1,000 million hectares, it is being consumed for agricultural settlement at such a rate that it could disappear within sixty years if there is no extensive reforestation.[15] As the world population continues to grow rapidly, more land will be needed to produce more food. Since most of the more readily available land is forested, abandoned, or agriculturally depleted, existing forest lands are under great pressure, particularly where population growth is rapid.

Furthermore, because so many people use firewood for cooking, forests come under increasing pressure as the population escalates. On the average, one person burns about a metric ton of firewood a year.[16] Because of this fuel need, forests surrounding communities have been slowly removed. As nearby trees are used up for firewood, people travel farther to obtain wood, and the size of the deforested area expands.

The chief environmental impacts of deforestation are species loss, accelerated soil erosion, and increase in the rate of water runoff. Moreover, deforestation in arid regions may lead to desertification and laterized soils.

Land cleared of trees is exposed to erosion, which can be severe in deforested areas having slopes greater than 15 to 17 percent. If land is not disturbed any further and new growth becomes established, erosion may gradually subside. If, however, vegetation on the cutover land is continually removed by man or livestock, erosion will intensify and environmental problems can be severe.

When a forest is removed from a slope, the rate of water runoff is increased two- to tenfold or more, depending on the degree of clearing, slope, and rainfall. All too often this causes premature siltation of water impoundments and increased flooding of agricultural land in the lowlands. In Pakistan, for example, almost 2 million hectares of standing crops on the lowlands were destroyed by floodwater in 1973, and about 10,000 villages were wiped out. Since valuable soil is lost in floods, the quantity of the arable lands decreases. Alluvial silt deposited elsewhere is rarely usable enough to compensate for such losses.

Several means are available to reverse and reduce the impacts of deforestation. The World Bank is actively promoting rational forest management systems that encompass reforestation, watershed management, social forestry, "shelter-wood" and other selective harvesting systems, as well as agroforestry and village-based multiple-use woodlots.

In addition, agricultural projects can include components that explicitly conserve natural forest or reforest denuded lands and thus enhance agricultural production in a very cost-effective manner. A case in point is a World Bank–assisted irrigation project in Indonesia. To prevent deforestation of the watershed above the Dumoga Sulawesi irrigation works, the Dumoga National Park was established on 2,700 square kilometers. This cost less than 1 percent of total project costs, mainly to establish and demarcate park boundaries, develop a management plan, hire personnel, and provide necessary infrastructure and equipment. This relatively small investment protects the valuable irrigation investment by reducing sedimentation and maintenance costs, and by helping to ensure a steady, year-round flow of water necessary for optimal rice production. The park also preserves much of the rich flora and fauna that are unique to the island of Sulawesi.

In addition to the preservation of existing forests, reforestation is needed in many parts of the world. The increased removal of trees without replacement of them has already caused global concern.[17] Although the original species can be replanted in a forest, faster-growing trees are being planted as well because of the heavy demand for lumber, pulpwood, and firewood. Fast-growing plantations can ease the pressure to cut natural forests, while increasing the supply of fuel. Nonetheless, the planting of nearly uniform stands of fast-growing trees in place of primarily mixed forest raises the risk of serious outbreaks of disease and insects in these new monocultures and of species extinction. Effective reforestation measures include mixed-species tree plantations, compensatory preserves, and sustained yield programs.

Other problems of reforestation are related to human beings. The people still need firewood and may cut and burn newly planted seedlings before they mature. This has been a common experience in some parts of the tropical world. Since human depredations on young forests are difficult to control when people need fuel, it is necessary to plant special firewood lots. Recognizing these needs, the World Bank envisions a fivefold increase in its forestry lending program over the rate of the past decade.

Another method to reverse the trend would be agroforestry—combined agricultural and forest production—which is particularly valuable on steep slopes (10 to 30 percent) that must yield both food and forest products. Appropriate parts of the slope, for example, could be planted with rubber, nut, or fuelwood trees. If trees are suitably spaced, rows of grains and vegetables may be interplanted at least in the early years of the plantation. The trees in this case serve to hold the soil while a small section of land is used for crop production.

Another strategy would be to grow forage under trees to feed stabled animals or grazing livestock such as cattle or sheep. When trees are of sufficient size and the number of animals per hectare is carefully controlled, it is possible both to manage the forest and to produce livestock.

Conclusion

The rapidly growing world population is exerting great pressure on the arable land, water, and energy resources that are essential to a productive tropical agriculture. Increased use of fossil energy inputs, lack of arable land for crop production, and degradation and erosion of the soil are serious constraints on agricultural expansion throughout the world. Major efforts are needed to control erosion, to conserve water and forests, and to make efficient use of energy resources. Agricultural management and sound ecological practices can restore environmental quality for a sustained and productive agriculture.

Notes

1. See National Academy of Sciences, *More Water for Arid Lands* (Washington, D.C., 1974); and P. Buringh, H. D. J. van Heemst, and G. J. Staring, *Computation of the Maximum Food Production of the World* (Wageningen, Netherlands: Wageningen Agricultural University, Department of Tropical Soil Science, 1975).

2. Food and Agriculture Organization, *Soil Conservation and Management in Developing Countries*, FAO Soils Bulletin no. 33 (Rome, 1977).

3. D. Pimentel, ed., *Energy in Agriculture* (West Palm Beach, Fla.: CRC Press, 1981).

4. G. A. Watson and H. P. Allen, "Limited Tillage Around the World" (Washington, D.C.: World Bank, Operations Policy Staff and Agriculture and Rural Development Department, 1981; processed).

5. D. Pimentel, "World Food Crisis: Energy and Pests," *Bulletin of the Entomological Society of America*, vol. 22 (1976).

6. See M. C. Bourne, "Postharvest Food Losses—The Neglected Dimension in Increasing the World Food Supply" (Ithaca, N.Y.: Cornell University International Agriculture Program, 1977; processed).

7. See G. Hardin, *Exploring New Ethics for Survival* (New York: Penguin, 1977). Rachel Carson called attention to the undesirable effects of biocides earlier in *Silent Spring* (Greenwich, Conn.: Fawcett, 1964). Biocides include herbicides, insecticides, fungicides, miticides, rodenticides, acaricides, nematicides, and molluscicides.

8. International Institute for Tropical Agriculture, *Annual Report for 1977* (Ibadan, Nigeria, 1977).

9. U.S. Department of State, *Proceedings of the U.S. Strategy Conference on Pesticide Management* (Washington, D.C., 1979).

10. R. Goodland, *Environmental Management in Tropical Agriculture* (Boulder, Colo.: Westview, 1983).

11. Of all the water that reaches U.S. streams—1,260 billion gallons a day (1 gallon = 3.79 liters)—a third, or 420 billion gallons a day, is withdrawn, and of this only about 95 billion gallons a day are actually consumed.

12. Center for Science and Environment, *The State of India's Environment—1982: A Citizen's Report* (New Delhi, 1982).

13. See E. P. Eckholm, *Losing Ground* (New York: Norton, 1976); and U.S. Department of the Interior, "Desertification in the U.S.: Status and Issues," Working Review Draft (Washington, D.C., 1980).

14. Eckholm, *Losing Ground*.

15. See World Bank, *Forestry*, Sector Policy Paper (Washington, D.C., 1978).

16. K. Openshaw, "Wood Fuels the Developing World," *New Science*, vol. 61 (1974), pp. 271–72.

17. U.S. Council on Environmental Quality, *The Global 2000 Report* (Washington, D.C., 1980).

5
Industrial Development

In most developing countries, a substantial effort to industrialize is currently under way. Industrialization is often viewed as the quickest way to reduce poverty and to raise a country's standard of living. It should be recognized, however, that virtually every industrial facility is a source of pollutants, and these pollutants can adversely affect human health, the environment, and human ecology.

The most common problems associated with industrial facilities are air and water pollution, the creation of solid wastes, noise, modification of traditional land use, and problems associated with the settlement of workers and their families. Planners are often faced with a difficult choice between increased large-scale industrialization and preservation of some important aspect of the environment. These alternatives, while in conflict with one another, need not be mutually exclusive.

This chapter provides a framework for analyzing the environmental impacts of proposed industrial development projects. Since almost all of the potential impacts could be associated with many different kinds of industrial projects, this chapter does not focus on specific industries but instead provides a framework that project planners can use to identify, assess, and seek to mitigate the impacts of any industrial project. When applying the general principles to a specific industry, planners should turn to other sources for more detailed technical data on the impacts and control measures relevant to the particular type of facility under consideration.[1]

Assessments of industrial projects should have three main purposes: to identify potentially harmful effects of a particular project on the environment, health, and society; to ensure that appropriate mitigating measures are incorporated into the project; and to prevent unnecessary depletion of domestic natural resources. As discussed in chapters 2 and 3, the construction and operation of industrial facilities can significantly damage health and the environment. Typically, a small initial sum (relative to total project costs) spent on pollution control can satisfactorily reduce or even eliminate pollution damage. Failure to incorporate environmental controls into a project at the outset, however, generally results in vastly higher expenditures later on for curative health measures and programs to control air and water pollution and manage solid wastes. As a consequence of such experiences, many developed countries by law now require environmental impact assessments before a major industrial project can be sited and constructed.[2] One such law—the U.S. National Environmental Policy Act—requires the following information for an environmental impact assessment:

- Description of the proposed action or project, statement of purposes, and description of the environment affected
- Statement of the relationship to land use plans, policies, and controls for affected areas
- Discussion of the probable impact—positive and negative, secondary and indirect, as well as primary and direct—and international environmental implications
- Consideration of alternatives
- Mention of the probable adverse effects that cannot be avoided
- Statement of the relationship between local and short-term uses and long-term environmental considerations
- Statement of the irreversible and irretrievable commitment of resources
- Outline of the other considerations that offset adverse environmental effects of the proposed action or project and the relationship of such considerations to alternatives
- Comments from reviewers, other agencies, and concerned organizations and other relevant information.

The World Bank insists that potential environmental impacts be considered during the planning phase of a project and that steps be taken at the outset to mitigate anticipated adverse effects. These requirements have repeatedly helped developing nations avoid serious health and environmental problems and later costly clean-up programs. For example, in the Bank-assisted Pan African pulp and paper project on the Nzoia river in Kenya, project planners were required to design a system for intensive treatment of the plant's effluents and to monitor closely the river's water quality. As a result, the river, which already received municipal, industrial, and agricultural wastes, was kept from further degradation. A precarious ecological balance vital to a downstream fishing industry—an activity of great importance to the local communities—was thereby saved.[3]

A Bank-assisted pulp and paper plant in Turkey's scenic Antalya forest area was designed to maximize in-plant recycling and minimize treatment before final discharge. Bank planners also helped ensure that the facility was not sited near scenic beaches and areas of high tourist activity, even though engineering costs at these locations initially appeared to be lower than elsewhere.[4] In the long run, these types of decisions have been shown to be not only environmentally sound, but economically prudent as well.

This chapter considers the issues that must be addressed in the assessment and mitigation of environmental impacts of industrial development and suggests guidelines for both the project designers and the operating teams. Specific environmental concerns will depend on the nature of the industry or project, the scale of operations, local, regional, and national laws and regulations, and nearby community or industrial developments. In any event, it is essential that environmental specialists be a part of the industrial design team and that these issues be resolved before final plans are approved.

The assessment of potential environmental impacts of an industrial development project is discussed here under four broad topics: project design, site selection, project operations, and integration of all factors.

Project Design

The way in which a project is designed determines the level of environmental impacts associated with it. Three principal variables that influence the magnitude of impacts are the natural resources used as raw materials, the type of industrial processes used, and the pollution control features built into the project. For each one, there is a vast array of options to limit or reduce the adverse effects on the environment.

Natural Resources

All potential environmental consequences associated with the use of a given natural resource should be taken into account. Natural resources include all organic fuels (such as fossil fuels), organics not used for fuel, all inorganic ores used in fertilizers, ceramics, and cements, all metallic ores (whether complex or native metal), and all other primary and reusable materials.

The anticipated environmental impacts of a project should include those that may occur from the time the resource is extracted to the time it enters the project plant. For example, in a project to build a naphtha cracker (used to produce feedstock for polyethylene), the starting point is when a well is drilled or the crude oil arrives at the seaport. The assessment continues through the refining stage in which the naphtha fraction is separated by distillation and thence to building the cracker. Particular environmental problems to be considered here are those related to oil drilling (if new wells are required), storage, and transport, as well as those associated with refinery operations.

To minimize the potential for environmental damage, project planners should take into account the proximity of natural resources to the planned facility, the ease with which the resources can be transported, and the hazards involved in transporting them. In most cases, locally available resources will be preferable to those which must be transported great distances.

In certain instances it is appropriate to consider whether an alternative raw material may be preferable to the resource traditionally used in a particular industry. For example, bauxite ores are normally used in the aluminum industry, but these generate a large quantity of unusable solid wastes. Two alternative raw materials—nepheline-syenite and alunite ores—when pretreated with lime, can be used as well, and the residual solid waste can be used to make cement and other construction materials. If these ores are available, they may be environmentally preferable and a sound alternative to bauxite.[5]

Certain raw materials may be preferable to others on the grounds that they are inherently less polluting. For example, metallurgical coals used to make steel may have a low, medium, or high sulfur content. Those with a low sulfur content emit far less sulfur dioxide when burned and, if available, might be selected over the coals with a higher content, which require costly pollution control equipment known as scrubbers.

Industrial Processes

The processes used in a facility are among the most important determinants of the level of environmental impact. Traditional processes in many industries cause considerable environmental contamination. During the past decade, however, many new processes have been developed which are environmentally more sound, and not much more costly, than the traditional techniques. For example, the production of nitric acid has typically released large quantities of nitrogen oxides. A process developed in the Netherlands, however, uses high-pressure acid-resistant steel equipment to recover most of the oxides as nitric acid. The system also reduces energy demands by creating a series of heat-producing reactions.[6] Similarly, copper smelting has been a major source of sulfur dioxide in the atmosphere. A new furnace system developed in the U.S.S.R., however, recovers most of the sulfur dioxide as sulfuric acid, a usable by-product.[7]

In these cases and others, it may be less costly and more efficient to use a process which generates fewer pollutants at the outset than to design a more traditional facility and add costly pollution control equipment to it. Where alternative, less polluting processes are not feasible and a traditional system is designed, adequate pollution control equipment should be installed.

Pollution Control Equipment

A vast array of pollution control equipment can be used to reduce air emissions or water discharges from an industrial project. The equipment appropriate for a given project will depend on the level of control that is needed. This in turn is determined by such factors as baseline environmental conditions in the vicinity of the plant, the proximity of human communities, the sensitivity of ecosystems which might be affected by the project contaminants, the anticipated level of uncontrolled emissions, and of course the cost of various pollution control options.

The World Bank has established air and water effluent criteria for various types of industrial facilities.[8] These can be used as a starting point for assessing the pollution control measures and equipment that are appropriate for a given project. The general options for controlling air, water, and land contaminants are summarized in the following paragraphs.

The technology for air pollution control falls into three broad categories: adsorption, absorption, and chemical conversion. Adsorption is the process whereby gaseous contaminants are condensed on the surface of a product such as activated carbon, silica, fuller's earth, or other clays and then removed; in absorption, pollutants are absorbed by a liquid, dissolved, concentrated, and then removed; chemical conversion refers to the transformation of contaminants to harmless materials in a reactor, sometimes with the use of a catalyst. For many years, air pollutants have been emitted and dispersed through the use of tall stacks, but this method has become increasingly less attractive as new knowledge on the global dispersion of acid rain becomes available.

Table 5-1 summarizes some of the principal air pollution control options and includes comments on the efficiency and associated environmental impacts of each.

Water pollution from industrial processes may be controlled by any number of on-site treatments designed to handle specific contaminants, or the effluent can be discharged directly into municipal wastewater treatment systems if commingling of the waste streams does not endanger the biological oxidation process. Many on-site removal treatments have a high level of efficiency and a relatively modest cost. For example, a coalescing filter can remove 99 percent of the oil and grease from wastewater; a carbon adsorption process can remove 99 percent of dissolved organics. Both techniques can be implemented at a reasonable cost. An overview of principal wastewater treatment measures is shown in table 5-2.

Off-site treatment facilities also have several advantages. Since these systems are larger and are shared by several industrial facilities, and sometimes more than one municipality, the net construction and operating costs per plant are less than for several smaller systems. In addition, wastewaters emanating from one industrial source may be offset by wastes from another (as in the case of acids and aklalines), so that both sets of wastes are neutralized.

In solid waste disposal, the most important consideration is that the technologies be appropriate to the processes and the site. Project planners should emphasize utilization of all materials whenever possible, and disposal of solid wastes into the environment should be considered a last approach. Moreover, recyclable raw materials should be used if available. For example, in the production of phosphate fertilizer, the mineral fluorapatite, $CaF_2O_3Ca_3(PO_4)_3$, lends itself to good waste management. When it is acidified to produce the phosphate fertilizer, fluorapatite has two by-products: a fluoride gas and calcium sulfate. The gas can be collected in various ways and sold in that form, or it can be further processed into other marketable materials. Calcium sulfate is also readily marketable either as is or in other forms.

It is an axiom of solid waste management that everything goes

Table 5-1. *Selected Options for Control of Industrial Air Pollution*

Control option	Comments
	Dust particulates
Water sprays	Effective especially with wetting agents in fossil fuel and mineral mines
Cyclone separators	For particles larger than 5–20 microns in diameter, efficiencies of 80 percent achieved
Scrubbers (such as spray chambers, wet cyclones, mechanical scrubbers, Venturi scrubbers, packed towers)	Efficiencies of more than 90 percent achieved for particles smaller than 5 microns in diameter, with simultaneous high-pressure losses
Baghouse filters	Removal efficiencies of 99 percent achieved for particulates; popular in cement and steel plants
Electrostatic precipitators	Removal efficiencies of 99.9 percent reported
	Hydrogen sulfide *(processes with at least 98 percent removal efficiency)*
Stretford process	Absorption process; sodium metavanadate in the absorbing fluid; gas stream should be pretreated to remove COS and CO_2
Selexol process	Absorption process; removes sulfur compounds which cannot be processed in a Stretford unit
Claus process	Feed stream must also contain SO_2; produces elemental sulfur; maintenance and downtime potential problems
SCOT process	Catalytic converter; adversely affected by high CO_2 concentrations
Incineration	Converts hydrogen sulfide to SO_2
	Sulfur dioxide *(processes with 90 to 95 percent removal efficiency)*
Wellman-Lord	Produces concentrated SO_2 after a reaction with sodium sulfate; SO_2 then converted to elemental sulfur or sulfuric acid
Double-alkali process	Uses two regenerable alkaline scrubbing (absorption) solutions, sodium hydroxide and sodium sulfite
Lime/limestone scrubbing	Produces a nonregenerable sludge that includes gypsum
	Nitrogen oxides
Combustion control (low excess-air firing, staged combustion, recirculation of flue gas, water injection, reduced air preheat)	Controls oxygen content and temperature in the vicinity of the furnace flame

Table 5-1 *(continued)*

Control option	Comments
Hydrocarbons and carbon monoxide	
Proper unit design (including instrumentation operation and maintenance)	To avoid the incomplete combustion of fuel for boilers, furnaces, heaters, and diesel equipment
All pollutants	
Tall stacks	Care must be taken, in designing tall stacks, to take account of conditions of atmospheric inversion, which would limit dilution. Atmospheric scavenging, including precipitation washout, is a possible deleterious side effect: field and laboratory experiments have shown that sulfur and nitrogen oxides can be oxidized to sulfuric and nitric acid or acid salt in the atmosphere and eventually be absorbed from the plume of stack gases by drops of rain. Lake ecosystems hundreds of miles from a tall stack may be adversely affected by stack-emitted pollutants. Visibility can be affected by the sulfates formed.

Source: World Bank, Office of Environmental and Health Affairs, *Environmental Considerations for the Industrial Development Sector* (Washington, D.C., 1978).

somewhere; there is no ultimate disposal. Plans for disposal must be incorporated into the project design. Such plans may be as detailed as a mercury flowchart accounting for every gram, or they can be as basic as a quantification of the percentages of a given by-product which will be disposed of in various ways. In all events, the level of toxicity of the wastes must be identified so that appropriate disposal techniques may be planned. Project planners should recognize that if wastes are nondegradable or toxic, costs of disposal will be considerably higher than otherwise.

Solid waste disposal can take one of four forms: shredding, compaction, sanitary landfill, and incineration—all of which can be on-site or off-site, as described in table 5-3. Sanitary landfill, the most popular method, must be carefully designed to avoid the contamination of groundwater by leachate from the landfill. That problem can be reduced by leaving at least two feet (0.6 meters) of space between the groundwater and solid wastes and by filling the

Table 5-2. *Selected Options for Industrial Wastewater Treatment*

Contaminant	Technology	Removal efficiency (percent)	Relative reliability	Relative adaptability	Relative cost
Oil and grease	Dissolved air flotation	90	Very high	Very high	Medium
	Coalescing filter	99	High	High	Medium
	Clarification	80	Very high	Very high	High
Dissolved gases	Air stripping	80	High	High	Medium
	Steam stripping	95	Very high	High	Medium
	Flue gas stripping	95	High	Medium	Medium
	Biological oxidation	High	Medium	Medium	Low
Dissolved organics	Activated sludge	95 BOD/40 COD	High	Medium	Low
	Trickling filter	85 BOD	High	Medium	Low
	Aerated lagoon	80 BOD	Medium	Medium	Low
	Rotating contactor	90 BOD/20–50 COD	High	Medium	Low
	Anaerobic digestion	60–95 BOD	High	Medium	Low
	Wet air oxidation	64 BOD/74 COD	Medium	High	Very high
	Photolytic oxidation	99 BOD	Medium	Very high	Very high
	Carbon adsorption	99 BOD	Medium	High	Medium
	Chemical oxidation	90 BOD/90 COD	Very high	Very high	High
	Electrolytic oxidation	95 BOD/61 COD	Medium	Very high	High

Suspended solids	Clarification	50	High	High	Low
	Pressure filtration	95	High	High	Very high
	Multimedia filtration	95	Very high	High	High
Dissolved solids	Clarification	Low except for metals	High	Medium	Medium
	Distillation	99	Medium	Low	Very high
	Reverse osmosis	60–95	Medium	Medium	Medium
	Ion exchange	High	High	Low	High
	Electrodialysis	10–40	Medium	Medium	Very high
Sludges	Thickening	Product 6–8% solids	Very high	High	Medium
	Anaerobic digestion	Low	High	Medium	Medium
	Vacuum filtration	Product 20–35% solids	High	High	High
	Sludge-drying beds	Product 90% solids	Medium	Low	Medium
	Evaporation basins	Product 95% solids	Very high	Low	Low
	Filter press	Product 35% solids	Very high	High	High
	Aerobic digestion	Low	Low	Low	High

Note: BOD, biological oxygen demand; COD, chemical oxygen demand.

Source: Adapted from Hamilton Standard Division of United Technologies, "Oil Shale Report Wastewater Treatment and Control Technology," assessment prepared for the U.S. Congress, Office of Technology Assessment (Washington, D.C., July 1978), pp. 2-12 to 2-24.

Table 5-3. *Selected Options for Collection and Disposal of Industrial Solid Wastes*

Description	Comments
	Grinding (shredding)
Makes plant refuse more uniform, in size, shape, and consistency; requires increased power, little additional labor	Increases operating efficiency of incinerators; aids compaction, decomposition, rodent and odor control of waste destined for landfill; minimizes the amount of soil cover required.
	Compaction
Used particularly with municipal refuse; can reduce volume by 80 percent; can compact refuse to 1,500 pounds per cubic yard (592.7 kilograms per cubic meter)	Systems should be designed to prevent the springback of refuse; compaction done at the site of refuse generation will help maximize efficiency of delivery systems.
	Sanitary landfill
Disposes of refuse on land without creating nuisances or hazards to public health and safety; utilizes the principles of engineering to confine refuse to the smallest practical volume; covers it with a layer of earth at the conclusion of each day's operation or at more frequent intervals if necessary[a]	May be incorporated in a land reclamation program. Site selection, design, and operation should be based on a systematic integrated study and an evaluation of physical conditions, economics, and sociopolitical constraints. An *active* public information program is needed to explain what makes a sanitary landfill work well and what benefits can be expected.
Gases generated by biological degradation are allowed to disperse slowly, continuously, and completely into the atmosphere; in impermeable soils refuse gases are vented through gravel vents or gravel-filled trenches.	Aerobic decomposition of the landfill waste can produce CO_2 and NO_3; subsequent products of anaerobic breakdown include CH_4, organic acids, NH_3, and H_2S and other sulfides.

Table 5-3 (*continued*)

Description	Comments
Leachate controlled by a natural or artificial layer between the groundwater aquifer and the landfill; a minimum distance of two feet is advisable between the landfill bottom and the maximum groundwater level.	Leachate may contain heavy metals and toxic chemicals and may be acidic. The leachate collection systems should be designed to collect seepage and drainage from rainfall equivalent to a fifty-year flood.
Incineration	
Incinerators are designed to burn refuse completely (variable load daily) at relatively high tempertures (1500° F–1900°F); should be part of a system to recover resources (steam, fuel, electricity, materials). Primary chimney gases of incineration include CO_2, water vapor, nitrogen and sulfur oxides, and a solid residue of ceramics, glass, metals, and various other ashes.	Requires large capital and operating costs and sophisticated management and operating skills; appropriate air pollution control equipment includes settling chambers, mechanical cyclones, wet scrubbers, electrostatic precipitators, and baghouse filters.

a. Recommendation of American Society of Civil Engineers.

Sources: Research and Education Association, *Modern Pollution Control Technology*, vol. 2 (New York, 1978); World Bank, *Environmental Considerations for the Industrial Development Sector* (Washington, D.C., 1978).

space with inert material such as clay or a synthetic liner. Also, the surface of the fill should be graded to drain off precipitation. Finally, nearby surface streams should be diverted away from the landfill site. When fill consists of toxic wastes, even more stringent control measures—such as impermeable liners and continuous monitoring—must be taken.

Noise, unlike other pollution, can seldom be controlled by standard equipment. Instead, noise control involves a process-specific and circumstance-specific set of techniques. Possible measures are:

- Separation of humans from the noise source by use of sound barriers, other enclosures, or ear coverings
- Restrictions on the times when noise-producing processes are permitted
- Use of industrial equipment especially designed to limit output of noise.

For all types of pollution—air, water, solid waste, and noise—the widest range of possible control options should be investigated at the earliest stage of project planning. Detailed information is available on control options for various industrial facilities.[9]

The relative cost of each option is an important consideration. A methodology has been developed to estimate emission control costs for any given industrial process.[10] This methodology takes account of all the cost elements: capital costs (including design, land purchase, equipment and materials, site preparation, and construction), operating costs (labor, materials, energy, insurance, taxes, and disposal of any wastes produced by pollution control processes), and maintenance costs (repairs and any losses because of downtime).

The Organisation for Economic Co-operation and Development (OECD) has used this methodology to estimate pollution control costs for a wide variety of industrial processes. In the iron and steel industry, the OECD has determined that the cost of installing a minimum level of pollution control (defined as that acceptable in the United States in 1970) would be between 2 and 4 percent of the final selling price of the manufactured product. For the best practicable control technology, the cost would be between 8 and 12 percent of the selling price.[11] In many cases, pollution control costs represent an even smaller percentage of overall project expenditures. It is possible to design and construct wastewater treatment facilities for canneries, poultry processing plants, and tanneries which yield 85 percent biological oxygen demand (BOD) removal, at an incremental cost of about 1 percent of overall production costs. This amounts to less than $0.40 per 1,000 gallons of wastewater treated.[12]

In almost all situations, the cost of pollution control equipment will vary considerably depending on the method used and the level of control required. For example, the capital cost of solid waste disposal facilities ranges from about $400 to $4,000 a ton a day for sanitary landfill, but between $12 and $15 a ton for organic waste composting.[13] Similarly, air pollution can be controlled by using physical cleaning processes at a fraction of the cost of scrubbers.

This disparity in air pollution control costs is further discussed in chapter 6.

Site Selection

At the time project planners are considering which industrial processes and pollution control equipment to incorporate into a project, the assimilative capacity of several possible sites should be assessed. In the site selection process, two sets of environmental impacts must be considered: the direct effects of project pollutants discharged into air, water, and soil, and the indirect (or social) effects of changes in community living patterns occasioned by the new facility. At the outset, project planners should select several alternative sites for serious consideration.

Although the possible sites will be chosen principally on the basis of economic concerns, environmental factors should be taken into account even at this stage. In addition to offering easy access to necessary raw materials and suitable energy supply, the proposed sites should be

- Downwind of major population centers and not subject to thermal inversions
- Distant from fragile aquatic ecosystems
- Close to water capable of receiving effluent
- Of sufficient elevation to allow gravity flow of process wastewater
- On land not conducive to intensive agriculture
- Remote from areas with prime potential for tourism and recreation
- Accessible to labor and to support industries and services
- In an area designated for industry and where local people desire industrialization
- Close to good transport networks.

Furthermore, the sites should not interfere with endangered or rare wildlife, and conversion to industrial use should not displace people from their homes.

Once alternative sites have been chosen, the final selection should rest primarily on environmental and social factors. To predict the direct environmental impacts at each site, planners must first obtain baseline data on air, water, and land conditions and then calculate the probable emissions. A variety of techniques can be used to estimate the likely effect of project pollutants on the surrounding environment.

Meteorological and hydrologic conditions should play a large role in site selection and should be carefully studied at all sites before the final selection is made. A given level of emissions may be acceptable under the meteorological conditions at one site, but quite unacceptable at another site with very different climate and wind patterns. For example, although substantial quantities of sulfur dioxide are discharged into the atmosphere in and around New Delhi, India, the ambient levels of sulfur dioxide in the city are well below government-specified levels.[14]

Finally, project designers should consider any other projects or development activities currently planned or proposed in the vicinity, so that the cumulative impacts of all activities can be taken into account.

Existing land use patterns may help determine what constitutes acceptable levels of environmental impacts. For example, wastewater discharged into a stream used heavily for local recreation or for tourism may require more complete treatment than wastewater discharged into an unused waterway that passes through uninhabited areas. New projects in an industrial area that is already heavily polluted may require more stringent controls than those in a "cleaner" location.

The amount of capital financing a country or industry may be able to commit to pollution control equipment should also be an important factor in site selection. In a developing country with many competing demands for its modest financial resources, it may make more sense to locate a large industrial facility in an area where emissions will do less harm (either because of the site's remoteness or because of favorable meteorological conditions) than to locate it in a congested area and install capital-intensive flue gas desulfurization equipment. Of course, future growth patterns must be carefully projected so that a plant with minimal controls is not sited in a remote area that subsequently becomes highly industrialized.

Any assessment of the assimilative capacity of a site should not be restricted to the immediate environment of the project. The capacity of the surrounding community to absorb the industry must also be taken into account. This type of analysis requires a prediction of new settlement patterns likely to develop from the project and needs to consider a variety of factors:

- Existing levels of employment and supply of housing
- Labor requirements and availability of land to meet the requirements of an expanded labor force
- Water supply and sewage treatment capabilities for the community as well as for the proposed project
- Adequacy of community health services
- Adequacy of transport infrastructure
- Effect of projected community growth on local customs and living patterns.

Several of these factors are discussed further in chapter 7.

Project Operations

During the planning stages of an industrial development project, procedures should be established to monitor environmental and health impacts of the facility once it begins to operate. Staff should have or acquire expertise in environmental engineering pertinent to the proposed project. Environmental monitoring should cover the flow of material from input of raw materials to final product to ensure that tolerances are maintained according to design specifications. In-house research and development might be considered to ensure efficiency and conserve materials. Data compiled over time should be analyzed for deviations from baseline (starting) conditions and for possible overloads of the environmental systems affected. Environmental engineering expertise must be used when a process technology is to be changed or a project expanded. When feasible, simulation models should be developed and projected effects analyzed to determine the likely efficiency and environmental impact of the project.

Monitoring should include both chemical and biological analyses to identify deviations from baseline levels at the site. Staff working on these analyses could also be responsible for maintenance, be trained to handle safety and environmental problems, and, possibly, undertake research on the impacts of an expansion of the project.

In addition, the health and safety of project employees and of local and regional populations must be closely watched. In-house safety procedures should be clearly and concisely stated and made known to all employees. Suggested health and safety guidelines are available.[15] Job specifications are essential for safe and efficient operations; implicit and explicit hazards of the industrial processes and the raw materials used should be clearly defined for the protection of workers.

Exposure to toxic chemicals is particularly hazardous and must be carefully monitored. If toxic substances are either used or produced in the manufacturing process, project planners must incorporate extremely stringent health and safety standards into project operations. If the developers are unwilling or unable to design a facility to meet those standards, it may be appropriate to abandon the project. For example, the Mexican Ministry of National Planning and Industrial Development recently rejected a proposal to build a plant to produce asbestos products in Mexico.[16] If the use or production of toxic substances is unavoidable, however, plant operations must be checked regularly to ensure that worker exposure remains within acceptable limits.

Integration of All Factors

One way to integrate the issues considered in the first three sets of concerns is to conduct a cost-benefit analysis. After initial consideration of the various possibilities for process design, pollution control, site, and project operations, the leading alternatives should be compared and assessed. Such an assessment will augment traditional costing procedures, which focus almost exclusively on the economics and not on environmental issues.

A large body of literature exists on assigning costs. Economists distinguish between internal costs borne by the project, which may affect the financial rate of return, and external costs absorbed by society, which may affect the economic rate of return. Assignment of costs depends on circumstances, which vary from society to society. Planners, however, must consciously address the total costs of the project so that the design will be effective and the evaluation will be accurate.

Alternative modes of assessing costs require substantial theoretical treatment, because environmental cost estimation techniques are not as well developed as other economic guidelines. In general, information gathered in the first three areas should help to identify pertinent items of cost. For example, if sulfur dioxide levels exceed the threshold of human tolerance, some costs of air pollution can be quantified in terms of work days lost or the use of public health facilities. In addition, a qualitative judgment can be made of human suffering from respiratory illness. The costs of avoiding river pollution may be the cost of building a water treatment plant downstream to render water potable, the opportunity cost of using the ecological carrying capacity of the river for a more productive enterprise, or the opportunity cost of using that river for public recreation such as swimming or tourism.

Although costs of maintaining environmental quality are quantifiable, the benefits of doing so are not so easily calculated. It is much easier to determine the cost of equipment for reducing air and water pollution, for example, than to identify and evaluate many of the health, aesthetic, agricultural, recreational, and other benefits that result from cleaner air and water. The costs of pollution control are offset by such benefits as reductions in crop losses, less damage to structures sensitive to air pollution and lower cleaning costs for them, revival of fisheries and recreational industries, savings on medical services for diseases induced by air or water pollution, less working time lost, and increased productivity. Additional information on cost-benefit assessments is provided in chapter 1.

Conclusion

Every industrial development project is a potential source of pollution, but careful advance planning can minimize the level of pollution and its effect on the population and surrounding environment. In evaluating an industrial project, particular attention should be given to the interrelationship between choice of process and the potential for recycling, between plant location and direct environmental impacts, and between waste management and process design. If these and other issues are fully taken into account, it should be possible to design a project that is sensitive to human concerns and environmental needs.

Notes

1. See Research and Education Association, *Modern Pollution Control Technology*, vols. 1 and 2 (New York, 1978).

2. See, for example, U.S. Congress, *National Environmental Policy Act of 1969*, as amended, PL 71-900; and Australia, *Environment Protection Act*, no. 164 (1974).

3. Albert Wall, *Environment and Development* (Washington, D.C.: World Bank, 1979), p. 14.

4. Ibid.

5. World Bank, Office of Environmental Affairs, "Industrial Pollution Control" (Washington D.C., 1983), pp. 28–29.

6. Ibid., p. 27.

7. Ibid.

8. World Bank, Office of Environmental and Health Affairs, "Industrial Waste Control Guidelines" (Washington, D.C., 1978 and 1979).

9. Research and Education Association, *Pollution Control Technology*.

10. World Bank, "Industrial Pollution Control," pp. 13–14.

11. Organisation for Economic Co-operation and Development, *Emission Control Costs in the Iron and Steel Industry* (Paris, 1977).

12. World Bank, *Environmental Considerations for the Industrial Development Sector* (Washington, D.C., 1978), p. 72. (All costs are given in U.S. dollars and have been adjusted for inflation.)

13. Ibid., p. 79.

14. "India's Changing Landscape," *Economist* (March 5, 1983), p. 95.

15. World Bank, Office of Environmental Affairs, "Occupational Safety and Health Guidelines" (Washington, D.C., 1982–84).

16. H. J. Leonard, "Pollution Plagues Industrial Firms in Growing Nations" (Washington, D.C.: Conservation Foundation, 1982), p. 3.

6
Energy Projects

As developing nations become more industrialized, energy projects acquire greater significance. Projects to develop and use domestic energy resources (especially to generate electricity) can be environmentally damaging. In particular, certain fossil fuels used without proper controls can have serious environmental consequences. The use of renewable resources is often less damaging to the environment, although it, too, can have certain adverse effects. In deciding between a conventional project using fossil fuel and one using a renewable resource, the environmental impacts of each project should be taken into account along with economic considerations.

This chapter examines a full range of energy-related projects. The first section considers the development of fossil energy resources. When a project is to develop the supply of coal, oil, or natural gas, there is no choice as to the primary fuel, but choices often do exist with respect to the type of process used, the rate and location of development, and the method of transporting the fuel to market.

The second section of this chapter focuses on projects for the generation of electricity. Fossil fuel plants, large-scale hydroelectric projects, and smaller-scale projects which rely on renewable resources (such as sun, wind, water, and biomass) are considered. The environmental effects of each type of project and ways to mitigate those effects are discussed.

This chapter is more specific than chapter 5, which outlines a framework of analysis applicable to a large variety of industrial projects. Because of the smaller variety of energy projects, this chapter provides more details on the environmental impacts associated with each. The framework of analysis outlined in chapter 5, however, will be helpful in this context as well.

Development of Fossil Fuel Resources

Many World Bank–assisted projects involve the development of an energy resource. The following subsections focus first on oil and natural gas fields and then on coal mining. For each resource, the direct environmental impacts associated with exploration, production, and transport and ways to mitigate those impacts are considered. This is followed by a discussion of the indirect environmental impacts brought about by the socioeconomic changes associated with the development of each resource.

Oil and Natural Gas: Direct Impacts

The development of oil and gas may cause infrequent yet sometimes catastrophic impacts (such as blowouts and oil spills), as well as the more routine impacts associated with normal activities of resource development. Each kind of impact is discussed separately.

CATASTROPHIC IMPACTS. The potential for adverse environmental impacts begins during the exploratory phase. Both onshore and offshore, exploratory wells are usually drilled to reach a particular geologic formation that is believed to contain oil or gas. The most serious environmental effects of exploratory drilling, particularly offshore, are blowouts (uncontrolled release of oil or gas). Offshore blowouts may cause vast quantities of oil pollution and severely damage the marine environment, thereby harming important flora and fauna, dependent marine industries such as fishing, important food sources, tourism, and domestic recreational facilities.

Recent data on oil and gas operations in the United States indicate that, on the average, for every 10,000 wells drilled, a blowout occurs in 4.8 wells onshore and approximately 22 wells offshore. Of the offshore blowouts, 19 result from high-pressure gas wells and only 3 from wells producing oil and gas. Onshore, too, most blowouts occur in high-pressure gas wells.[1]

A particularly disastrous blowout occurred in June 1979 in an exploratory well in the Gulf of Mexico off the Yucatan peninsula. Initial attempts to control the well failed—even the blowout preventer, a device that shears through the drill pipe and closes it off, was ineffective. Only by drilling relief wells could the pressure on the runaway well be reduced sufficiently to cap it and stop the flow. Oil spilled into the Gulf of Mexico for more than four months.

There are comprehensive guidelines which should be followed to minimize the likelihood of a blowout.[2] Since blowouts cannot be totally avoided, a detailed contingency plan to contain a blowout and quickly clean up spilled oil should be drafted *before* any exploratory drilling. This plan should specify the equipment and dispersants to be used to clean up the oil.

Once it is determined that commercial quantities of oil and gas exist, development is planned. Wells are drilled to drain the reservoir as efficiently as possible. Equipment is installed to control the flow and dispose of brine, sand, and other impurities produced with oil and gas.

Development drilling uses the same techniques as exploratory drilling. Onshore, a single well may require a two-acre site for development.[3] A drilling rig is erected and dismantled when drilling is complete. Offshore, development drilling is usually done from fixed platforms rather than from mobile rigs. These platforms are individually designed and specifically built for each field to take account of various factors such as water depth, bottom conditions, weather, wave heights, and the possibility of earthquakes or hurricanes. The platform is constructed with drilling slots arranged in rows to form a rectangle. A movable drilling derrick is mounted on a grid somewhat resembling a checkerboard and is skidded from one drilling slot to the next. In this way the same platform may be used to drill twenty to thirty wells. After all wells are drilled, production equipment is installed on the platform in place of the drilling equipment.[4]

Development drilling is less hazardous than exploratory drilling because the characteristics of the geologic formations are known. The likelihood of blowouts is therefore smaller.

The large-scale oil spills that accompany blowouts are particularly serious when they occur offshore, since they are more difficult to clean up than those onshore. North Sea countries rely on dispersants, that is, chemicals that disperse, dissolve, emulsify, precipitate, or in some other way assist in removing spilled oil from the water. The United States favors mechanical cleanup with sorbents—inert, insoluble materials such as straw, paper fibers, and polyurethane foams. Mechanical devices are ineffective when waves are high or when a spill occurs in unprotected areas of open sea.

Most spills result from oil and gas transport systems. A recent study by the U.S. Environmental Protection Agency found that of 8,473 onshore and offshore oil spills, 52 percent were related to gathering and distribution systems, primarily pipelines.[5] Even though new pipelines are buried to reduce the chance of damage from anchors and other marine equipment, other factors such as human error can cause ruptures and leaks in a pipeline from over-pressurization. In older lines, failure from corrosion is frequent.

In the absence of pipelines, tankers usually transport oil to market. To minimize potential oil pollution from normal tanker deballasting operations, ballast treatment facilities may be needed. If tankers have segregated ballast facilities—that is, special tanks separate from cargo tanks and used only for ballast—then additional ballast treatment facilities may not be required.

Although tankers safely transport millions of tons of crude oil each year, they begin and end their voyages in crowded harbors and near the shore where the risk of accidents is high. Numerous small spills have occurred during loading and unloading operations. Many of these spills can be contained and removed by clean-up equipment. Some very large spills from tankers have occurred as a result of groundings, rammings, fires, and other accidents. These spills are usually very expensive to clean up and have received widespread publicity.

Although the number of spills and the amount of oil spilled vary widely from field to field, some estimates on the total volume are available. Table 6-1 shows that the amount spilled is about 1.4 times greater using tankers than using pipelines to transport oil from offshore fields.

The long-term costs of an oil spill—for example, the loss of marine resources and tourist income—are extremely difficult to estimate. Some figures have been reported for clean-up costs, however. The government of France spent F460 million (about

Table 6-1. *Oil Spilled over the Life of an Offshore Field*

Source of spill	Average number of spills	Total volume (metric tons)
Small find		
Platform	0.28	1,000
Pipeline	0.31	1,900
Tanker	0.41	2,700
Medium find		
Platform	1.3	4,600
Pipeline	1.4	8,700
Tanker	1.9	12,700
Large find		
Platform	4.7	16,600
Pipeline	5.2	32,100
Tanker	6.9	46,200

Source: U.S. Council on Environmental Quality, *OCS Oil and Gas—An Environmental Assessment*, vol. 1 (Washington, D.C., 1974), p. 76.

Table 6-2. *Large Oil Spills from Production Facilities*

Facility	Year	Estimated amount spilled (metric tons)	Estimated total clean-up cost[a] (million US$)
Union (Santa Barbara)	1969	2,500–107,000	10.6
Chevron (Gulf of Mexico)	1970	4,200	15.0
Shell (Gulf of Mexico)	1970	7,300–17,900	30.0
Amoco (Gulf of Mexico)	1971	60–70	15.4

a. The estimates include only the cost of cleaning up the spill, not the cost of the oil itself.

Sources: University of Oklahoma Technology Assessment Group, *Energy under the Oceans* (Norman, Okla.: University of Oklahoma Press, 1973), p. 90; and U.S. Council on Environmental Quality, *OCS Oil and Gas—An Environmental Assessment*, vol. 1, p. 69.

US$108 million) on cleaning up one of the largest spills ever caused by a tanker, after the wreck of the *Amoco Cadiz* off the coast of Brittany in March 1978. Estimates of the costs of cleaning up some oil spills that have occurred in U.S. waters are given in table 6-2.

The environmental impacts of an offshore oil spill depend on many factors:

- Type of oil spilled, in particular the concentration of low-boiling aromatic hydrocarbons
- Amount of oil
- Physiography of the spill area
- Weather conditions at the time
- Biota in the area
- Season of the year
- Previous exposure of the area to oil
- Exposure to other pollutants
- Method of treating the spill.

Most major spills cause severe, although not irreversible, damage to the marine environment and threaten health and environmental values.

ROUTINE IMPACTS. During both the construction and production phases of an energy project, environmental impacts must be contended with. The construction of a wide variety of facilities—platforms for offshore wells, pipelines, refineries, harbors, terminals, staging areas, and warehouses—can have considerable environmental impacts. Pipelines, for example, must often be constructed through wetlands, which are particularly sensitive areas since drainage patterns can be disturbed. Canals dug for pipelines can cause saline water to intrude into freshwater marshes and wetlands. Erosion can be accelerated and biologically productive land can be lost. Mangrove areas are particularly vulnerable.

Once an oil or gas field is producing, there are emissions into the air and water during routine operations. Oil and gas wells, storage tanks, compressor stations, gas separation plants, and other related equipment emit hydrocarbons, nitrogen oxides, carbon monoxide, sulfur dioxide, and particulates. Some of these emissions can be minimized by control equipment. Vapor recovery systems on loading stations and storage tanks or double-deck floating roof storage tanks, for example, can help minimize hydrocarbon emissions. Flaring rather than venting hydrocarbon gases during equipment upsets also helps reduce emissions.

The disposal of production wastewaters (brine) can also pollute water. Onshore, production wastewaters are often reinjected into the oil zones from which they were extracted.[6] This method has two advantages: it helps maintain pressure in the oil zone, thereby assisting in the ultimate recovery of the oil, and it eliminates a potential water pollution problem. When production waters are not reinjected into oil zones, they must be disposed of in lined evaporation ponds or in ponds having very slow percolation rates so as not to contaminate adjacent groundwater.

Offshore, production waters are commonly treated and released into the sea. It is estimated that during routine operations nine barrels of oil are released with the brine for every million barrels of oil produced.[7] The Gulf of Mexico has been subject to these chronic low-level discharges of oil from production operations since the 1950s. The ultimate effect on marine life is still unknown, but commercial fishing in the Gulf has not been affected.[8]

Since conventional methods of oil and gas production typically yield only 30 to 40 percent of the oil in a reservoir and about 75 percent of the gas in a formation,[9] special techniques are often used to increase the recovery of resources. These techniques, known as enhanced recovery, have the potential to create additional environmental impacts. One such technique is to inject a fluid into the reservoir to force the oil or gas out. In secondary recovery, water is used for this purpose; in tertiary recovery, other substances such as steam, carbon dioxide, chemicals, or a mixture of water and chemicals are injected.

Some environmental impacts of enhanced recovery are caused by drilling new wells to inject the fluids; tertiary recovery has additional effects from the production and use of chemicals and the production of steam. When chemicals are used, from 15 to 75 kilograms are required for each additional metric ton of oil produced.[10] These chemicals include surfactants, such as long-chain linear alkyl sulfonates—the same kind used in detergents. If the chemicals escape from the oil formation or are disposed of improperly and enter freshwater aquifers, they can cause foaming, bad tastes, and odors. In addition, because surfactants increase the solubility of crude oil fractions in water, escaping or improperly disposed of chemicals can carry with them traces of toxic crude oil fractions.

Oil and Natural Gas: Indirect Impacts

Large resource development projects generally create a need for housing, community facilities, and infrastructure. For example, Aberdeen and Peterhead, two cities on the coast of Scotland, were affected by the development of North Sea oil. During the peak development phase, the population of Aberdeen, a university and fishing city of 180,000, increased by more than 5,500. Peterhead, a small fishing town twenty miles farther north, increased from 14,000 to 16,000.[11] In another case, at the southern end of the Alaska pipeline, the population of Valdez swelled from 1,005 to over 7,000 during construction of the line and after completion leveled off to 4,205.[12] Labor shortages and population shifts are particularly acute problems in remote areas. Although immigration of construction workers and their families may be only transitory, the net result is usually an enlarged permanent population.

Socioeconomic impacts of oil and gas development depend on the relative amounts of oil and gas produced and whether the oil (if it is produced) is refined locally or exported. Estimates of typical employment and land requirements for facilities related to oil and gas development appear in table 6-3. Market conditions, the size of the oil and gas reserves, and other factors, such as the availability of land, influence the level of development.

Table 6-3. *Typical Requirements for Oil- and Gas-Related Facilities*

Facility	Size	Operating personnel (number)	Land requirement (hectares)
Gas processing plant	14 million cubic meters a day	55	10
Petroleum refinery	27,500 metric tons a day	555–850	500–600
Petrochemical complex (multiproduct)	454,000 metric tons a year	1,800–2,500	120
Offshore fabrication facility	—	1,500–2,500	400
Offshore oil and gas platforms			
Exploration	—	175	—
Production	24 wells	90	—
Onshore drilling rig	—	24	—
Major offshore oil area near the peak of its development stage	10 exploration rigs and 38 production platforms	5,170	—

Sources: Stanford Research Institute, *Impacts of Synthetic Liquid Fuel Development—Automotive Market*, vol. 2 (Springfield, Va.: National Technical Information Service, 1976), p. 67; U.S. Council on Environmental Quality, *Oil and Gas in Coastal Lands and Waters*, vol. 2 (Washington, D.C., 1977), p. 95; and U.S. Council on Environmental Quality, *OCS Oil and Gas—An Environmental Assessment*, vol. 4 (Washington, D.C., 1974), app. 1–4.

A recent study of the socioeconomic impacts of energy facilities in the United States estimates that in remote areas total population during the construction phase will increase by more than three times the number of construction workers. During the operating phase, the total population increases more than sixfold.[13]

A large peak in total population during construction makes planning for housing and community facilities very difficult. Often the costs of community facilities, infrastructure, and housing are not considered as part of the overall cost of an energy development project. Yet these costs are a part of the total impact of the development and must be taken into account.

Coal: Direct Impacts

Direct environmental impacts of coal mining include the potential for polluting ground and surface water; interrupting groundwater supply; disturbing the land with piles of solid wastes, fugitive dust, landslides, and surface subsidence; and creating noise and aesthetic problems. Specific water pollution problems include sedimentation, which occurs when organic and inorganic materials are carried and deposited by water, and acid mine drainage, which occurs when the iron sulfide minerals found in many coal deposits are exposed to oxygen and then dissolved in water. Since the direct impacts associated with underground mining and surface mining are different in many important respects, the two types are discussed separately.

UNDERGROUND MINING. Dust and methane gases released within the mine can be hazardous to miners' health. In addition, fire in an underground mine can cause serious problems, since the smoke contains such air pollutants as carbon monoxide and sulfur dioxide. Underground fires may burn for many years.

India's Jharia coalfield contains twenty-five active and dormant fires. These fires have consumed some 26 million metric tons of coal, and an additional 12.5 million metric tons cannot be mined because parts of the mines have been sealed in an attempt to extinguish the fires.[14]

Underground mining activity can cause both physical and chemical pollution of water. Physical pollution occurs when water from nearby underground aquifers enters the mine pit and becomes contaminated with acid, toxic materials, suspended solids, and other impurities. In this event, treatment is required before the water is released back to surrounding streams. Physical pollution may also occur when the erosion of surface piles causes siltation and deposition of sediments in valleys and streams.

Chemical pollution (or acid mine drainage) occurs when minerals, such as sulfides, are exposed to oxygen in the air; air makes the minerals more soluble, so that they dissolve on contact with water and form acids. Acid mine drainage from abandoned underground mines is a significant problem. With careful planning, however, a mine can be sealed, flooded, or backfilled when the mining work is completed to minimize the danger of acid drainage. When mines are located below drainage levels or when the overburden is alkaline, acid mine drainage is not a problem.

Two other principal environmental impacts of underground mining are subsidence and solid waste disposal. Subsidence is a lowering of the land surface; usually it is not uniform and occurs in isolated areas over a coal mine. When the mine is under populated or developed areas, subsidence can damage houses, buildings, and community facilities. The long-wall mining method (in which no pillars of coal are left to support the roof) usually causes more subsidence than the room-and-pillar method (in which coal pillars are left), but the subsidence is planned and controlled.[15] At the Blanzy coal mine in France, underground long-wall mining has caused subsidence of as much as 10 meters in some places. Reclamation of these areas as lakes is planned, but will be costly.[16]

Solid wastes are produced when the mine shaft is excavated, when coal is cleaned to remove unwanted materials, and when acid mine water is treated. Waste makes up approximately 25 percent of the material extracted from underground coal mines in the United States.[17] A significant amount of this waste is attributable to modern equipment, which removes approximately three times more roof and floor rock than was removed by hand methods. The waste material is disposed of on the surface in mounds ranging from a few hectares to wastepiles (also known as "tips") that are hundreds of meters high and more than 2 kilometers long. The wastes may be either acid or alkaline, but alkaline tips are easier to reclaim than acidic tips, which have to be neutralized by applying limestone or lime or by mixing with alkaline spoils. Often fertilizer must be applied before revegetation is successful.

Some of these wastepiles pose problems for public health and safety because of the possibility of fires, slides, or water impoundment. If the waste ignites, gaseous emissions can contain carbon monoxide, carbon dioxide, hydrogen sulfide, sulfur dioxide, and ammonia. In addition to damaging human health, these emissions can defoliate trees, cause crop damage, and discolor buildings for miles around.

The possibility of slides is another danger that indicates the need for proper disposal of coal waste. A major slide in 1966 at Aberfan, South Wales, caused 107,000 cubic meters of waste to flow from a 61-meter wastepile. In the United States in 1971 at Middle Fork, Buffalo Creek, West Virginia, another slide caused a flow of

497,000 cubic meters of water and 168,000 cubic meters of waste. At Aberfan 144 people were killed; in West Virginia 116 were killed and 4,000 were left homeless.[18]

Wastes are returned to the mine at many European sites. Although this option is technically feasible, its economic attractiveness varies from mine to mine and is a function of physical conditions, such as the existing transport system, the existence of injection boreholes on the surface, and the possibility that the leaching of wastes will contaminate groundwater.

Methane, which is present in underground mines, must be drained because of the danger of explosions. In England, the methane drained is usually used to power equipment in the mines, and in a few cases it is used in nearby industry. Methane may be recovered from the mine ventilation system and from holes drilled in the roof and floor.[19]

SURFACE MINING. The principal adverse impact from surface mining is the damage to surrounding ecosystems from direct mining activities as well as from disposal of the overburden (the material lying over the coal deposit). The possibility of soil erosion is of particular concern since this not only reduces the productive capacity of the land, but also may degrade the quality of nearby waterways.

The susceptibility of strip-mined land to erosion depends on the physical characteristics of the overburden, the steepness and length of the slope, climate, amount and rate of rainfall, and type and percentage of vegetative ground cover. Under almost any conditions, uncovered overburden and wastepiles are vulnerable to erosion and sedimentation.

Plans for controlling erosion and sedimentation should be developed before mining activities are started. Control of water flowing into, within, and from the surface of mining areas is essential. Sedimentation can be controlled by building catch basins and other structures, and it can be stabilized by applying chemicals or planting vegetation. Minimizing the area that is disturbed and the time of exposure also helps control sedimentation and erosion. Furthermore, careful design and location of coal haul roads can minimize the problem.

Regrading and revegetation after strip mining will help control erosion, siltation, and dust and will reduce or eliminate acid mine drainage. An important aspect of reclamation is segregation of overburden material so that toxic, acid, or salt-producing strata are buried and topsoils and growth-supporting materials are placed on top.

A technique that has potential for both the reclamation of land and the disposal of solid wastes from a power plant is to mix the surface mining spoils with fly ash. The Turoszow mine in Poland, adjacent to a 2,000-megawatt power plant, mixes fly ash from the plant with overburden (10 percent ash and 90 percent overburden). The alkaline ash helps to neutralize the spoils. It also makes it possible to establish a vegetative cover,[20] thereby reducing the possibility that the wastepiles will slip.

Backfilling and grading should be kept current with the mining operation, and revegetation should follow grading as soon as possible. Although trees may be planted in combination with grasses, trees alone may require up to ten years of growth before they can effectively control erosion. Grasses and legumes should be planted on all areas. The choice of species will depend on local conditions. Although initially certain species that promote rapid stabilization may be planted, ultimately the dominant vegetative cover should consist of native, self-sustaining species.[21]

In arid areas management of the revegetated area may be necessary for several years until a self-sustaining cover can be established. Fertilizer and irrigation will probably be essential in establishing a vegetative cover. In addition, special regrading techniques can be used to create small basins and traps to catch and hold rainwater.

Surface mining can also interfere with local water supplies, as happened at the Adamow mine, a large open-pit lignite mine near Konin, Poland. The normal water table in the vicinity of the mine is six meters below the surface. When the mining company tried to lower it to 60 meters, many local wells dried up. As a result, the coal company is now responsible for supplying water to local farms that lost their own supply.[22]

Although not a major concern, wind-blown particulates from surface mining may pollute the air. Emissions can be minimized by applying calcium chloride and sodium chloride to coal haul roads or by wetting down these roads with water.

Other environmental effects of surface mining are the annoyances of vibration and noise. Some mines, for example, use explosives to remove 30 to 50 percent of their overburden. Blasting is also used at many mines to break coal seams.[23] This activity can cause unpleasant vibrations for residents near the mine and frighten birds or animals from nearby habitats. Awareness of prevailing wind direction, blasting only during daylight hours, and careful consideration of charge size can minimize this type of noise pollution and surface damage.

Another unpleasant side effect is the unaesthetic appearance of a strip mine. The scar on the land can be almost entirely mitigated over time, however, by the reclamation techniques already discussed.

Coal: Indirect Impacts

The indirect environmental impacts that occur during the development phase of a coal mine are related primarily to the construction of roads, mine entries, and buildings, which creates local air pollution and changes patterns of surface water runoff. If the mine is in a remote area, housing and community facilities must be provided for construction workers and later for miners and their families.

The severity of the socioeconomic impacts of mine development and production depends on whether coal deposits are in a remote area or near a large city. A complicating factor occurs when towns and villages lie over deposits that can be mined only by surface methods, since villages are then destroyed and residents have to be resettled. West of the populous area of Düsseldorf and Cologne in the Federal Republic of Germany, for example, the lignite or brown coal mining operations of Rheinische Braunkohlenwerke AG have caused the relocation of some fifty villages and hamlets as well as farms, railroads, and highways.

For the most part, the indirect impacts discussed in the section on oil and gas projects apply equally to coal projects.

Production of Electricity

This section focuses on projects designed to produce electricity, rather than to develop an energy resource. Three types of projects are considered: conventional fossil-fuel generating plants, large-scale hydroelectric facilities, and smaller projects using alternative sources of energy: sun, wind, water, and biomass. (Nuclear power plants are not considered because the World Bank has not been involved in financing such installations.) For each type of energy

Table 6-4. *Typical Characteristics of 1,000-MW Fossil-Fuel Power Plants, with 75 Percent Load Factor*

Options	System efficiency (percent)	Annual air emissions (thousands of tons)			Annual solid waste (thousands of tons)	Increased electricity costs (percent)
		SO$_x$	NO$_x$	Particulates		
Conventional coal-fired boiler; no controls; average coal[a]	40	120	22	48	300	Baseline
Conventional coal-fired boiler; particulate precipitators and tall stacks; average coal	40	120	22	3	345	0.5
Conventional boiler; physically cleaned coal; particulate precipitators	36	60	22	2	345	6
Conventional boiler; chemical coal cleaning; particulate precipitators	34	12	22	1	50	40
Coal-fired boiler, FGD (throwaway)	37	12	22	1	1,000	10
Coal-fired boiler, FGD (regenerable)	35	12	22	1	350	13
Atmospheric fluidized bed (throwaway)	39	12	10	0.5	1,000	10
Pressurized fluidized bed (regenerable)	38	12	5	0.5	350	13
Oil-fired boiler; average residual oil;[b] no controls	40	74	21	2	0	Baseline
Oil-fired boiler; desulfurized residual oil; no controls	37	15	21	0	0	13

a. Average coal assumes 6,650 kilocalories per kilogram, 2.6 percent sulfur, 12.5 percent ash.
b. Based on 2.5 percent residual oil.

Sources: "Energy Alternatives: A Comparative Analysis," Science and Public Policy Program, University of Oklahoma, May 1975; W. H. Ponder, R. D. Stern, and G. G. McGlamery, "SO$_2$ Control Technologies—Commercial Availabilities and Economics," Third International Conference on Coal Gasification and Liquefaction, Pittsburgh, Pa., August 1976.

facility, potential adverse environmental impacts and possible control measures are discussed.

Fossil-Fuel Generating Facilities

Associated with both coal-fired and oil-fired plants are air pollution, water pollution, and solid wastes. The principal measures to mitigate these impacts are described here. Some of the control technologies are relatively simple and inexpensive and may therefore be well suited for use in developing countries. Other technologies, while possibly more effective, are so costly to build and to operate that they may be appropriate only for use in heavily polluted areas in the developing world. Also discussed is how pollution control technologies applied to one environmental media may in fact generate pollutants in another media—a consideration which may be relevant for many types of development projects.

A coal-fired generating facility without controls is a major source of air pollution. Although the level of pollution will depend on the coal's heating value, sulfur content, and ash content, an average coal burned in a 1,000-megawatt (MW) plant will emit each year about 120,000 tons of sulfur dioxide, 22,000 tons of nitrogen oxides, and 48,000 tons of particulates.[24] Installation of air pollution control equipment can vastly reduce these emissions, and in most cases with relatively little reduction in operating efficiency.

Table 6-4 shows the level of air emissions for an uncontrolled 1,000-MW generating plant (burning an "average" coal) and emission reductions with various types of control technologies. Emissions of sulfur dioxide (SO_2) from a high-sulfur coal can be reduced by a physical process which removes pyritic sulfur from the coal before combustion. The reduction of sulfur emissions will depend on how much of the sulfur in the coal is in the pyritic form. This is a very simple and inexpensive procedure (about $15 per kilowatt, compared with a total power plant cost of about $1,000 per kilowatt). Over 90 percent of the SO_2 can be removed by throwaway or regenerable flue gas desulfurization (FGD). Regenerable FGD is very expensive (between $200 and $250 per kilowatt) and complicated to operate, but it is efficient, leaves no solid waste, and generates marketable grades of sulfur or sulfuric acid. Throwaway FGD is less expensive and less complex to operate. For example, a wet limestone scrubber used with a high-sulfur coal has a capital cost of approximately $165 per kilowatt.[25] But this process creates a considerable quantity of sludge, which poses a disposal problem.

Emissions of particulate matter can be reduced by about 70 to 85 percent (depending on the coal being burned) by using multitube cyclones, an inexpensive ($10 per kilowatt) technology that is simple to operate. Over 99 percent removal of particulate matter is possible by using either baghouses or electrostatic precipitators (ESP), but these technologies are much more costly: to achieve 99 percent removal with either technique would involve a capital cost of between $40 and $60 per kilowatt.[26]

Two new boiler technologies still in the experimental stage are atmospheric fluidized beds and pressurized fluidized beds. These technologies can substantially reduce emissions from burning coal, but they are still being evaluated for commercial feasibility.

Oil-fired generating stations generally create less air pollution than coal-fired units. As table 6-4 shows, even an uncontrolled oil facility emits about 60 percent of the SO_2 emissions of an uncontrolled coal plant and less than 5 percent of the particulates. Use of low-sulfur oil or desulfurized oil reduces these emission levels even further.

Water pollution from fossil fuel facilities is a less critical, but still important, concern. Several pollutants (such as chromates, chloride, sulfates, and phosphorus) are discharged into the water used for cooling in fossil fuel plants. In addition, this water becomes hot, and if it is discharged directly into rivers or streams can adversely affect the receiving aquatic environment. The heated water can lower the level of dissolved oxygen, asphyxiate fish, kill eggs and larvae, scald certain marine species, and render spawning grounds unsuitable.

The four principal methods of cooling a fossil fuel plant are once-through cooling, cooling ponds, wet cooling towers, and dry cooling towers. The cheapest, most popular, and simplest method for a conventional fossil fuel facility is once-through cooling. With this method, an average 1,000-MW plant (coal or oil) will require about 1.1 billion cubic meters of water a year.[27] Almost none of this water is consumed by the facility; the water is discharged back into a stream, thus increasing the stream's temperature considerably.

Cooling ponds use less than 3 percent of the water needed by the once-through method, but require a large land area adjoining the generating plant (about 420 hectares for a 1,000-MW facility). Wet cooling towers also require a relatively small quantity of water and have the additional advantage of needing only a small parcel of land. They may be considered unsightly, however, and they usually emit

Table 6-5. *Comparison of Power Plant Cooling Systems*
(based on 1000-MW plant with 38 percent efficiency)

Cooling system	Water requirements (10^6 cu. m/yr)		Land requirement (hectares)	Plant efficiency	Increased electricity costs (percent)
	Intake	Consumed			
Once-through	1,140	small	0	38	Baseline
Cooling ponds	34	21	420	38	6.0
Wet cooling towers	22	13.6	Varies	37.5	2.5
Dry cooling towers	0.25	0	Varies	35	17.0

Source: "Energy Alternatives: A Comparative Analysis," Science and Public Policy Program, University of Oklahoma, May 1975.

heat and water vapor, thereby increasing local humidity and possibly fogging the neighboring area. Dry cooling towers require almost no water or additional land and do not emit water vapor. Nonetheless, they are even larger and more unsightly than wet cooling towers, they cause a considerable loss in power plant efficiency, and they increase the cost of electricity by 15 to 20 percent. The characteristics of these four methods of power plant cooling are shown in table 6-5.

Although bottom ash must be disposed of, solid waste is less of a problem with a fossil fuel plant unless the plant has installed FGD to control SO_2 emissions. A 1,000-MW plant with a throwaway FGD system can be expected to generate about 1 million tons of sludge annually. This sludge, which consists of fly ash, calcium sulfite and calcium sulfate, while not toxic, still presents a serious disposal problem.

In sum, the environmental impacts associated with conventional fossil fuel plants can be considerable—not only from mining, developing, and transporting the fuel, but also from producing electricity. In the following sections, various alternatives to fossil fuel plants are considered.

Large-Scale Hydroelectric Projects

Using rivers to generate electricity is a well-established energy technology. The size of hydroelectric projects may vary considerably from less than 1 MW of power to more than 1,000 MW; potentially, hydro projects can produce vast quantities of energy.

At present the world's largest hydroelectric project, at Itaipu on the border of Brazil and Paraguay, has a capacity of 12,600 MW. In the past, many hydro projects have been large. During the 1970s, however, as smaller and more localized energy sources became technically feasible and more attractive politically, small-scale hydro projects gained in popularity. This subsection focuses only on the conventional large-scale hydro projects (15 MW or more); small hydroelectric projects are discussed later with other projects to tap alternative forms of energy.

Large-scale hydro projects do not damage the environment as much as conventional fossil fuel projects: they have none of the impacts associated with resource exploration and mining and virtually no air pollution problems, and they do not deplete a natural resource. Nonetheless, they do have a broad range of negative impacts. To a large extent, the larger a project, the greater the potential adverse impacts. But when appropriate river resources are available and environmental impacts can be minimized, large-scale hydro projects may still offer an attractive, low-cost source of electricity in developing nations. In fact, 50 percent of the world's hydro potential is in developing countries, yet less than 10 percent of that potential power has been developed.[28]

The adverse impacts of large-scale hydro projects fall in three categories: social (human ecology), environmental, and health. Social impacts are particularly important. Creation of a reservoir may require flooding a large area occupied by many people. Since many hydro projects are in rural areas, the local inhabitants often have close ties to the land; their families may have lived in the area for decades. Many are tribal peoples who have developed survival skills that can be used only in specific areas. Resettlement of these peoples is a major concern. (For a discussion of the issues of resettlement and tribal peoples, as well as the related problem of worker migration into the project area, see chapter 3.)

Other social impacts of hydroelectric projects may stem from the quick and dramatic alteration of land use patterns. For example, if a large amount of productive farmland is flooded to create a reservoir; many employment opportunities for local farm workers will suddenly be wiped out. Changes in the flow regime of a river may severely damage a downstream commercial fishing operation. Finally, alterations in the local ecology could adversely affect wildlife in the region, which in turn could hurt any families or local industries that are dependent on the area's wildlife. Each of these potential social impacts must be taken into account when planning a large-scale hydroelectric project.

The environmental impacts of hydro projects are on both the aquatic environment and the surrounding land. After construction of the reservoir directly behind a dam large quantities of trees and vegetation are often flooded. When that vegetation decomposes, the reservoir water undergoes profound changes (oxygen reduction, eutrophication, and production of hydrogen sulfide), and these in turn change the biotic environment of the river downstream. The water quality deteriorates, ecosystems are altered, and some species of fish may not survive the changes.

These problems can be mitigated, however. For example, if the impoundment area is partially or fully cleared before flooding, there is less decomposition and fewer changes in the aquatic environment. Also, if the project is designed so that the reservoir is relatively shallow and the spillway can be opened at frequent intervals to keep fresh water flowing through, the effects of decomposition are reduced.

A related environmental problem is sedimentation, which occurs particularly in reservoirs built in heavily farmed areas where slopes are steep. Earthen particles collect in the reservoir as the result of erosion of surrounding lands. Sedimentation can have a disastrous effect on fish populations and on dam machinery; it also reduces the storage capacity of the reservoir and shortens the reservoir's life. Since erosion may occur a considerable distance upstream from the reservoir, a watershed management program for the entire catchment should be implemented. Planting trees along the perimeter of the reservoir and on nearby high ground can reduce erosion and hence mitigate siltation in the reservoir.[29]

Another problem caused by hydroelectric projects is that migrating fish may be unable to swim upstream over dams. In some cases, fish ladders are effective, but in others they are not. For certain species, the ladders must be placed at a very small incline if the fish are to make the climb. At such an angle, however, the ladder may need be so long that the fish tire before reaching the reservoir. Fish hatcheries have been successfully operated in many hydro reservoirs to overcome the problem of migration. They work particularly well for lotic fish in tropical and subtropical waters. These species do not migrate from the sea into freshwater streams, but only up and down the same river or river system.[30] In any event, the potential effect of a dam and reservoir on all aquatic populations (and the ways to minimize those effects) must be carefully assessed before a hydro project is begun.

Other potential environmental impacts of a large-scale hydroelectric project involve ecological effects on surrounding communities. Most important is the risk of flooding downstream as a result of dam failure or sudden high releases. Such problems can be minimized, however, if the project is carefully designed to take into account local weather patterns, soil conditions, topography, vegetation, and the seasonal flow rate of neighboring waterways.[31] Optimal operation of the spillway can further reduce the risk.

Reservoir-induced seismicity is another problem that should be taken into account. For the most part, it has been confined to sites where natural stresses in the underlying rock mass have already developed to a state very close to rupture. A comprehensive seismic investigation in the early stages of site selection should identify such areas. The extent of the problem will determine whether project size and operations have to be modified.

In addition to environmental effects, certain health problems may be associated with hydroelectric projects. Still water reservoirs in remote areas are often ideal breeding places for insect vectors of human diseases such as malaria. Other vectors, such as the fly vector of onchoceriasis, breed in the turbulent reservoir overflow. These insects thrive on fast-growing floating water weeds which are often abundant in reservoirs. Construction workers and residents in the area may easily become infected. As the workers and local inhabitants leave the dam site and move to other parts of the country, they can spread the disease over an extended area.

To prevent or reduce this problem, several steps may be taken:

- Elimination of water weeds by using biological or chemical controls
- Elimination of the disease vectors and their hosts (fish and amphibians that feed on insects and host snails have been successfully used for this purpose in many tropical areas)
- Control of access to the reservoir
- Strict medical supervision of all construction workers at a dam site
- Prevention of water contamination by untreated sewage, hazardous waste products, fertilizer, and pesticide runoff.

Possible adverse health effects of projects of this type and ways to mitigate them are discussed more fully in chapter 3.

The Aswan High Dam, completed in 1971 on Egypt's Nile river, presented many of the social, environmental, and health problems associated with large-scale hydroelectric facilities. Some of these problems were mitigated successfully; others were managed less effectively.[32] For example, the dam required resettlement of approximately 100,000 Egyptian and Sudanese Nubians. Although the education and health services available to many of these people were significantly upgraded after resettlement, their economic self-sufficiency decreased and their dependence on the government increased. An ecological effect of the project was the substantial reduction in the quantity of nutrient-laden silt downstream from the reservoir. Since local sardines feed in this silt, the fishing industry at the mouth of the Nile has had a severe setback. This adverse impact was countered, however, by a government program that created several inland fisheries upstream at the reservoir. The loss of silt downstream also created a serious erosion problem, which has not yet been remedied and which continues to worsen each year.

Alternative Energy Projects

This section considers projects which utilize renewable sources of energy (such as the sun, wind, and water) to generate heat or electricity. Typically, these projects are on a smaller scale than conventional energy projects. They do not deplete existing resources and have few adverse environmental impacts. Nonetheless, most of these projects have some negative effects that should be considered. In certain circumstances, alternative energy may be the most attractive option for purely economic reasons; for example, a small, isolated rural community might be served by a fossil-fuel generating station only at great expense. A joint U.S. National Academy of Sciences–National Science Research Council study of Tanzania suggested that small-scale renewable technologies were able to compete with the use of diesel power or a grid extension to provide electricity for a remote Tanzanian village of about 300 people.[33] In other cases, even when an alternative energy project is not the least expensive option, it may still be more attractive than a fossil fuel plant once the environmental benefits and the conservation of resources are fully considered.

Alternative energy projects rely on resources which often are abundant in developing nations. The energy resources examined in this section are wind, sun, small-scale hydroelectric power, and

biomass. For each type of project, there is a brief review of the
technology and a description of the environmental impacts associated with it.

WIND POWER. The ability to harness the wind has existed for
centuries; windmills have been used to pump water in rural areas as
well as to turn grinding wheels for various grains. Until cheap oil
became available, Denmark regularly used wind-generated electricity. In recent years, interest in using this technology to produce
electricity has mounted as a new generation of wind turbines has
been developed.

The first and most obvious consideration in the use of wind
power is the availability of a strong, reliable wind resource. Persistent winds are often found in deserts and mountainous regions.
Before a decision to begin development of a wind farm, the resource
must be observed and measured over time to make sure that winds
are of sufficient strength and persistence. Although the initial capital
outlay for equipment is high, fuel costs are nil, which makes wind
energy a desirable means of providing electricity. The technology
may be particularly attractive in remote locations where the cost of
extending transmission lines from existing power plants could be
high.

A typical system to convert wind energy into electricity consists
of a support tower, a rotor, a power transmission system or gear-
box, and an energy converter such as an electrical generator. Transmission lines will be required to deliver electricity from generator to
consumer. In an area with heavy winds, a series of turbines would
usually be arrayed on a wind farm to capture the maximum amount
of wind.

The use of wind for the generation of electricity avoids pollution
of air and water and the social impacts associated with conventional
fossil-fuel-fired power plants. Nevertheless, wind energy conversion systems are not without negative impacts. One possibility is
that they will interfere with other land uses. In the case of a wind
farm, windmills may have to be dispersed over a large area to allow
enough space between towers for maximum access to the wind;
access roads and transmission lines will criss-cross the landscape
between units. Although agriculture or animal grazing are land uses
not incompatible with windmills, as a practical matter the windmills may interfere with viable agricultural operations.

Windmills also have a visual impact, although there is a high degree of subjectivity as to how windmills are perceived. In remote areas of natural beauty, wind farms may be considered unsightly and unaesthetic. If so, tourism values may suffer.

Once a site is selected, the area needs to be prepared for the windmill towers. Construction machinery will create dust and noise, and without proper grading and control measures there is a danger of soil erosion and the siltation of nearby surface waters. Mountainous areas are more susceptible to these impacts than is flat terrain, because the landform must be more drastically altered to accommodate the towers.

After construction, the operating phase of a wind farm may affect the microclimate, animal life, public safety, and noise levels.[34] The absorption and deflection of wind currents by the turbine blades could directly modify the temperature, air pressure, and moisture of the microclimate. These changes will occur above ground and in most cases will not be considerable. If a wind farm is sited near the route of migratory birds, there is some possibility that the birds will collide with the blades. The major concern, however, is that wind farms will interfere with the human population—that people will be disturbed by the noise of the turbines or endangered by a thrown blade if a machine fails. Noise impacts can be minimized by careful siting decisions, and the blade safety issue can be taken care of by a buffer zone around the towers.

SOLAR POWER. Solar energy systems can be designed to heat water or space directly for residential, industrial, or agricultural uses, or to convert solar energy into electricity. Water heating and space heating by flat plate collectors are the solar technologies most advanced technically and most feasible economically at this time.[35] In these systems a working medium such as water is pumped through a collector panel (usually consisting of a metallic absorber plate), where it is heated to a desirable temperature. The heated water is then pumped through a heat exchanger to heat a secondary working medium, or it is pumped directly to the end use. In many localities, solar heaters are already the least expensive option available for water heating.

Photovoltaic cells can be used to convert solar energy into electricity. Such systems have been demonstrated to be economically feasible only in a few remote locations where a small amount of electricity is required. Technical improvements in design are still being made, and in the near future these systems may become cost-effective for such activities as irrigating small farms and pumping village water supplies.[36]

The environmental impacts associated with solar energy systems are minimal. Land requirements for solar energy systems are huge and may compete with other uses. Air and water quality is affected only in the manufacture of materials (aluminum, steel, copper, glass, fiberglass, polyurethane, and cement) for the components of the systems. But these impacts are considerably less than the air and water pollution that would be generated by a fossil fuel plant producing the same amount of energy.

One other potential adverse environmental effect is associated with the operation and maintenance of solar systems for water or space heating. Some systems use a nonpotable heat transfer or storage medium containing toxic additives. If the system breaks down or a crack develops in the storage tank, additives might leak onto the ground and contaminate nearby groundwater or surface waters. Proper design of the system and regular monitoring of operations can minimize this risk.

SMALL HYDRO. Small-scale water-driven generators or low-head hydroelectric systems may be an attractive way to generate electric power in developing countries. A primary advantage of low-head hydro projects is that they do not require major impoundments of water as do large-scale hydroelectric projects. Small hydro projects usually have capacities between 5 and 50 kilowatts and provide electricity to a few users or to individual villages. Implementation of this technology is now most advanced in the People's Republic of China, which currently has an enormous number of small-scale hydropower projects in operation. Because power is lost over the lines transmitting the electricity to users, however, it must be generated close to demand if the technology is to be commercially viable.[37]

In general, small-scale hydro systems are environmentally benign. They may have modest environmental impacts, however, because a dam, no matter how small, interrupts the stream flow by diverting it above the reservoir and by channeling water through a penstock below the reservoir. Even small dams may impede the upstream migration of spawning fish, and even a small reduction of instream flows will alter the aquatic ecology downstream. For a single small hydro project, these impacts are minimal, but a large number of small dams on the same river could have significant cumulative effects. These can usually be mitigated by installing fish ladders and by maintaining sufficient instream flows.

BIOMASS. Biomass is essentially any plant material, ranging from algae to wood. The main sources of biomass are timber logging residues, crop residues, agricultural residues accumulated at processing plants, and municipal trash wastes.

The energy content of biomass is relatively uniform: about one-half to two-thirds the heating value of coal. It can be converted to liquid fuels (ethanol and methanol) and gaseous fuels (biogas) and can be burned directly to generate heat and electricity.[38] A large-scale and highly successful program of ethanol production has been under way in Brazil since the late 1970s.[39]

The advantages of biomass fuel are that it contains virtually no sulfur and thus produces no SO_2 when burned; it generates little ash; and it is continually renewable (if properly managed).

There are, however, also several drawbacks. Because of its relatively low heating value and the cost of transporting large quantities of biomass, it must often be used at or near its source to be economic. More important, however, is that certain types of fuel, such as ethanol, are produced by the fermentation of food crops such as sugarcane, cassava, corn, and sweet sorghum. Sugarcane is the most efficient in terms of net energy yield. The large-scale use of such crops to produce fuel could seriously deplete the food supply in local communities. Even crop residues could be more valuable to local farmers as a soil conditioner than the fuel which could be produced from these residues. Still, in certain circumstances (particularly remote rural areas), biomass may be the most appropriate, least-cost option for generating electricity.

All methods of converting biomass to energy have environmental impacts. Combustion or conversion of biomass can produce emissions of particulates, carbon monoxide, nitrogen oxides, and organics. The mix and quantity of pollutants generated will depend on the technology and raw biomass material used. At present, the scale of operations and level of emissions is relatively small, and since biomass combustion and conversion usually occur in relatively remote areas, the associated health impacts should be minimal in most cases. A variety of technologies are available to reduce air emissions from biomass operations, and these should be investigated if the scale of operations increases.

Virtually all biomass conversion processes produce effluents which may pollute nearby surface waters and groundwater. Again, the type and quantity of effluents vary considerably according to the process used, but in many cases they can be profitably recycled. Either an on-site or an off-site water treatment program should be incorporated into the overall process (see chapter 5).[40]

A final environmental impact associated with biomass combustion and conversion is that the removal of large quantities of biomass from a given locality will produce changes in soil and aquatic biota. For example, depleting the vegetation from a stream may deprive certain aquatic species of nutrients necessary for survival; taking large quantities of vegetative ground cover from the soil may increase erosion. Consequently, project planners must have a complete understanding of the local ecology before initiating a biomass project, and they should make sure the project design anticipates adverse impacts and minimizes them.

Conclusion

Energy projects vary widely in their impact on the environment. Conventional fossil fuel projects have potentially the greatest adverse impacts, both during development of the natural resource and in the use of the resource to generate electricity. Low-cost technologies are available which substantially reduce the level of pollution from most processes, although in some instances the cost of removing 90 percent or more of a particular pollutant will be quite high. Large-scale hydroelectric projects generate less pollution, but they may damage nearby ecosystems and their biota and may also force the human populations to resettle elsewhere. Energy projects which rely on renewable resources generate much less pollution and help to conserve natural resources. Consequently, they should be given high priority and careful consideration by project planners. Even these projects are not completely without adverse impacts, however, which should be anticipated and minimized to the extent feasible.

Notes

1. U.S. Department of Energy, *Draft Environmental Impact Statement on Petroleum Production at Maximum Efficient Rate, Naval Petroleum Reserve No. 1 (Elk Hills), Kern County, California* (Washington, D.C., June 1978), pp. 1–42; University of Oklahoma

Technology Assessment Group, *Energy under the Oceans* (Norman, Okla.: University of Oklahoma Press, 1973), p. 285.

2. American Petroleum Institute, *Recommended Practice for Blowout Prevention Systems*, RP53 (Washington, D.C., 1978).

3. U.S. Department of Energy, *Draft Environmental Impact Statement on Petroleum Production*, vol. 1, p. 32.

4. U.S. Council on Environmental Quality, *OCS Oil and Gas—An Environmental Assessment*, vol. 1 (Washington, D.C., April 1974), p. 60.

5. U.S. Council on Environmental Quality, *OCS Oil and Gas*, vol. 1, p. 169.

6. U.S. Department of Energy, *Draft Environmental Impact Statement on Petroleum Production*, vol. 1, p. 76.

7. University of Oklahoma, *Energy under the Oceans*, p. 292.

8. U.S. Council on Environmental Quality, *OCS Oil and Gas*, vol. 2, app. K, pp. 34–43.

9. U.S. Council on Environmental Quality, *Energy and the Environment: Electric Power* (Washington, D.C., 1973), pp. 47, 52.

10. Ibid.

11. University of Oklahoma Technology Assessment Group, *North Sea Oil and Gas* (Norman, Okla.: University of Oklahoma Press, 1973), p. 106.

12. U.S. Council on Environmental Quality, *Oil and Gas in Coastal Lands and Waters* (Washington, D.C., 1977), pp. 60–79.

13. Murphy/Williams Urban Planning and Housing Consultants, *Socioeconomic Impact Assessment: A Methodology Applied to Synthetic Fuels* (Washington, D.C.: U.S. Department of Energy, April 1978).

14. A. K. Ghose, "Coal Mining and the Environment—An Overview from a Developing Nation," Transactions of the Ninth World Energy Conference (Washington, D.C.: McGregor & Werner, Inc., 1975), vol. 4, pp. 414–23.

15. University of Oklahoma Technology Assessment Group, *Energy Alternatives: A Comparative Analysis* (Washington, D.C.: U.S. Environmental Protection Agency, 1975), pp. 1–53.

16. R. D. Hill, "France and Poland," trip report (Washington, D.C.: U.S. Environmental Protection Agency, September 1978).

17. National Academy of Sciences, *Underground Disposal of Coal Mine Wastes* (Washington, D.C., 1975), p. 9.

18. Ibid., p. 23.

19. R. D. Hill, "Poland and England," trip report (Washington, D.C.: U.S. Council on Environmental Quality, October 1974).

20. Ibid.

21. U.S. Environmental Protection Agency, *Environmental Protection in Surface Mining of Coal* (Washington, D.C., 1974), pp. 149, 192.

22. Hill, "France and Poland."

23. U.S. Environmental Protection Agency, *Environmental Protection in Surface Mining of Coal*, pp. 82, 99.

24. W. W. Ponder, R. D. Stern, and G. G. McGlamery, "SO$_2$ Control Technologies—Commercial Availabilities and Economics," Third International Conference on Coal Gasification and Liquefaction, Pittsburgh, Penn., August 1976.

25. Stearns-Roger Engineering Corp., "Economic Evaluation of FGD Systems," prepared for Electric Power Research Institute, Research Project 1610-1 (Denver, Colo., 1983), p. 1-3.

26. Stearns-Roger Engineering Corp., "Economics of Fabric Filters and Electrostatic

Precipitators," prepared for Electric Power Research Institute, Research Project 1129-9 (Denver, Colo., 1983), p. 5-1.

27. Organisation for Economic Co-operation and Development, *The Siting of Major Energy Facilities* (Paris, 1979), p. 68.

28. World Bank, *Renewable Energy Resources in the Developing Countries* (Washington, D.C., 1980), p. 46.

29. F. M. G. Budweg, "Environmental Engineering for Dams and Reservoirs in Brazil," *Water Power and Dam Construction* (October 1980), p. 21.

30. Ibid., p. 20.

31. R. S. Panday, *Man-made Lakes and Human Health* (Paramaribo, Suriname: University of Suriname, 1977), pp. 10–20.

32. H. M. Fahim, *Dams, People, and Development: The Aswan High Dam Case* (Elmsford, N.Y.: Pergamon, 1981).

33. W. Holdgate, M. Kassas, and G. White, *The World Environment, 1972–1982* (Dublin, Ireland: Tycooly International Publishing, 1982), p. 452.

34. California Energy Commission, *Final Environmental Impact Report for the Solar Program and Wind Program* (Sacramento, Calif., 1980).

35. Ibid.

36. World Bank, *Renewable Energy Resources in the Developing Countries*, pp. 13–14.

37. Idaho Water Resources Institute, *Low-Head Hydro* (Moscow, Idaho, 1978).

38. N. Cheremisinoff and others, *Biomass Applications, Technology, and Production* (New York: Marcel Dekker, Inc., 1980).

39. Holdgate, Kassas, and White, *The World Environment, 1972–1982*, p. 485.

40. N. Cheremisinoff and others, *Biomass Applications, Technology, and Production*, 1980.

7
Urban and Regional Development

Many cities in developing countries suffer from overcrowding and pollution far worse than that in the industrialized, developed part of the world. Metropolitan authorities in developing countries must cope with environmental problems commonly associated with large human settlements—solid waste disposal, sewage treatment, and industrial pollution, as well as the sociocultural impacts of overcrowding and congestion. If facilities for a safe water supply, sewage treatment and disposal, and collection and disposal of solid waste exist at all in such cities, the systems are often inadequate. In part, this is because developing countries lack the necessary financial resources to provide essential urban services. In addition, many cities grew up so quickly that there was little forethought or time to develop a rational urban plan to accommodate the vast influx of rural poor drawn to the city.

This chapter presents a planning framework for assessing the environmental impacts associated with urban and regional development. The first section reviews environmental issues arising in the overall development process and discusses specific approaches to planning and managing urban and regional development. It also demonstrates how environmental considerations can support the development objectives of economic efficiency and social equity. In particular, this section highlights some major environmental concerns in urban development, such as the provision of necessary infrastructure and management for water supply, sanitation, and solid waste disposal. The second section discusses the possible environmental effects of transport networks such as highways, airports, and ports.

The chapter concludes with a description of a system for establishing and using environmental planning and impact analysis to assist in the formulation of environmental policies and strategies, as well as in the design and appraisal of development activities in the urban context. One role for the World Bank, as discussed in chapter 1 of this book, is to increase awareness of the critical environmental issues in urban and regional development, and to help countries develop approaches and processes that will address and resolve those issues.

Planning and Managing Urban
and Regional Development

Poverty, unemployment, and inadequate housing, infrastructure, and services are common urban problems. What most distinguishes those of developing countries is their scale and intensity. The severity of these problems is due primarily to the rapidity of overall population growth and to the acute shortage of resources to cope with demand.[1] Both factors are manifestations of a general transition taking place in the developing countries that is altering the relationship between the agricultural and the industrial and commercial sectors and is bringing rapid changes in cultural, social, and political conditions.[2] The most promising opportunity for improvement lies in the efficient and equitable use of severely limited resources to provide adequate urban development.

How can these overriding objectives be achieved? Cities cannot be planned and built like large pieces of architecture. They grow and change in response to a dynamic interplay of private and public interests that the government can at most attempt to harness and direct toward a more livable environment. Models on which to plan and manage urban development change as experience is gained. Emphasis has shifted in recent years from static-physical to dynamic-financial concepts, and environmental considerations have too often been largely abandoned in the process. To determine how and in what form environmental issues can be productively reintroduced, current trends in urban development need to be examined.[3]

Since the late 1960s the action planning concept has gradually replaced the static master plan for land use. The maxim has become short-range, dynamic, implementation-oriented public action through projects selected after a review of economic and social costs. The maxim also emphasizes benefits that are internal to the project and its sector and that may or may not relate to a broader development strategy. Primary emphasis is placed on public finance and on the ability of sectoral agencies to rapidly produce projects that can catch up with the backlog in urban services and at the same time address the health and environmental conditions of the urban poor.

This general approach to urban development has been strongly influenced by international development agencies, whose economists and planners have pressed for realistic action and immediate results. It has undoubtedly led to an acceleration of program and project implementation in many cities of the world's developing countries. An overemphasis on the need to get things done, however, has created certain weaknesses. The appraisal of physical development projects on economic grounds has not led to their integration with socioeconomic programs. Intersectoral linkages, environmental impacts, and institutional coordination have frequently been neglected, as have long-range and areawide strategies that can tie projects together into an efficient pattern of development.

Environmental Considerations

Environmental considerations should serve alongside the objectives of economic efficiency and social equity in urban development. The following examples illustrate the important role environmental parameters can play.

In upgrading sewage disposal for a low-income fishing community in Central America, it was decided not to discharge sewage into available natural drainage channels but to conduct the effluent through an expensive ocean outfall offshore, where currents guaranteed sufficient dispersal. This solution protected the habitat of shrimp, which constituted most of the local catch. The cost of the additional conduits and pumping stations was shown to be much lower than the economic and social costs of the loss of the seafood resource and the costs of relocation, job creation, and retraining that the community otherwise would have incurred. Environmental considerations contributed in this case to the economic efficiency of urban development.

In another case, however, a large, exclusive hotel in West Africa attempted to save construction and maintenance costs for treatment facilities by discharging untreated wastewater into a nearby lagoon. The lagoon was a valuable resource, providing protein-rich, inexpensive food, as well as employment. The sewage discharge gradually poisoned the seafood harvest on which a local village depended and finally eradicated all life in the lagoon, in addition to presenting a human health hazard. The village is now abandoned; most of its inhabitants have joined the masses of the jobless urban poor. In addition to demonstrating economic inefficiency (the fishermen put the lagoon to a far more productive use than the hotel), this case demonstrates how the neglect of environmental factors can lead to social inequity in development in that a low-income community had to pay a high price for a small saving to the hotel.

Environmental analysis can also identify the impacts that an action in one area of a city will have on another, distant section. In Lagos and Manila, some swamp and coastal lands were recently filled to form construction sites. Only an areawide perspective could have shown that in both cases, the fill would block the waters of an extensive river system that seeps to the sea through wetlands. As a result of the landfill, large urbanized areas in both cities are now periodically flooded.

Both intersectoral and spatial linkages have been emphasized in recent work by the governments of Indonesia and the Philippines. Their strategies for the urban services and spatial expansion of metropolitan Jakarta and Manila, respectively, include an analysis of environmental costs. In Jakarta, because of the lack of piped water, many people use private wells. Unconstrained contraction of groundwater, however, has caused salt water from the ocean to intrude into the aquifer in the northern part of the city, and the shallow wells have become saline. Extensive development in the southern part of the city, combined with more distant deforestation and dumping of solid and liquid wastes into the rivers and canals that drain the city, has led to increased runoff and heavy flooding in the north. Most of the city's poor live in the northern area and are debilitated by disease from the polluted floodwaters. To buy drinking water from vendor-drawn handcarts they must pay as much as 15 or 20 percent of their income, or twenty times the unit cost of piped water.

An analysis of the linkages among water supply, waste disposal, and the location of development in Jakarta, and of their effects on the environmental conditions of the poor, suggests that certain investments and policies could help improve conditions for the low-income group. For example, the environmental analysis indicated that expansion to the east and west would be the least-cost development solution, would have the lowest impact on the natural environment, and would be favorable to new low-income settlements. Unit costs of development would be roughly half those for the northern zone. As a result of this work, sectoral programs are now being reoriented to encourage new development in these directions.

Consideration of environmental issues should also identify long-term costs and adverse impacts that are likely to occur some years in the future. The following examples illustrate how such problems might be avoided by environmental analysis in advance of a project.

A new, high-capacity international airport was recently built in an African city on land well outside the existing urbanized area. Within the next twenty years, however, it is expected that the population of the city will triple and an additional 80 square kilometers of land will become urbanized. If the city expands in an environmentally sound pattern, the airport will be in the center of the future urban area, and its noise impact zone will cover large tracts of developed land. This possible problem could have been avoided had the airport been built in a different segment of the surrounding area, where major residential growth is not projected and where the flight paths would be tangential to the future perimeter of the city.

The second example concerns a site for a new town that a Middle Eastern country needed to serve a large new port and oil refinery. The proposed location was close to the port and future source of employment. But further investigation of soil conditions and analysis of air movements at that site suggested that the costs of development were likely to be high and that industrial pollution would seriously affect health. A wider search turned up a site without these problems some distance from the port. Further analysis revealed that subsidized transportation for workers could minimize the problem of distance, and this cost would be more than offset by much lower overall development costs and a healthier setting.

Common Urban Environmental Problems

Environmental issues should be approached practically and realistically in the planning, management, and coordination of urban projects. The most common environmental problems of cities in developing countries are similar to those in developed countries, except that they are usually more severe. Rapid growth and a lack of resources make it difficult for developing countries to deal with the pressures that high population densities exert on the environment.

Human and solid wastes that are not removed from populous areas pose the most serious problems to human health.[4] Domestic wastes may pollute aquifers that feed shallow wells on which many low-income families depend. Untreated wastes pollute watercourses, destroy freshwater or marine life that may be an economic resource, and may render the water dangerous to use. Urban and agricultural populations downstream may also be affected. The costs of piped sewage and treatment systems are high, however, and may not be affordable in many situations.[5] Directing development to areas that can absorb these impacts and restraining development on sensitive land and water systems help reduce these costs. Nonetheless, managing and directing development in the urban areas of developing countries are two current challenges.

Industrial wastes pose problems similar to those of domestic waste. They are usually not strictly controlled in developing countries, and industry is often closely mixed with residential areas. Thus, although the volume of waste produced is much less than in developed countries, the exposure level is higher and dangers to human health are greater. Although some large industries might be relocated in industrial parks, the massive segregation of industrial and residential land use is neither practical nor economically desirable. A more productive approach may be to control wastes better, to guide new development, and to encourage the recycling of wastes by locating waste-consuming industries near waste producers.

Unfortunately, however, in developing countries wastes are often viewed as merely a nuisance. Even those societies in which resources are scarce have not yet recognized the potential for recycling wastes. Moreover, the health and economic costs of the failure to provide for adequate collection, management, and disposal of urban solid wastes are rarely considered. Where a water supply program has been funded, however, a solid waste program may be necessary to realize the anticipated health benefits of the improved water system. To protect the purity of an urban drinking water supply, processes and facilities for collection, treatment, storage, and distribution of the water must be uncontaminated by waste. This is a monumental problem in developing countries.

Evaluation of a water system must critically consider at least the following points that could pose a threat to health:[6]

- Quality of source
- Output of source
- Protection of source
- Adequacy and reliability of treatment
- Distribution systems (quality, pressure, continuity)

- Quality control (records, sampling, tests)
- Control of cross-connections and back-siphonage
- Chlorine residual in the distribution systems
- Construction and repair procedures (including disinfection before services are initiated or resumed)
- Maintenance procedures
- Standards of operation.

As in cities in the developed nations, the generators of solid waste are households and commercial and industrial operations, but in developing nations they often use the city streets as a dumping ground. In addition to general refuse (household garbage and rubbish, residential ashes, commercial and institutional refuse, construction and demolition debris, dead animals, catch-basin and drain-cleaning wastes, building wastes, abandoned vehicles, and sanitation residues), streets in developing country cities can contain human excrement where sanitation facilities are inadequate and manure where animal populations roam the streets.

Thus, in the management of urban wastes, the most urgent job for developing countries is to get the refuse off the streets. It has been estimated that in cities of developing countries, 30 to 50 percent of solid wastes generated are often uncollected.[7] Such refuse accumulates, washes into the water supply, and clogs drains. The refuse itself and the stagnant water it creates serve as breeding grounds for vectors of disease. The poorer neighborhoods, of course, suffer the most.

Municipalities in developing countries, with the assistance of international funding institutions, must implement effective solid waste management programs. The essential elements of such a program include storage of solid waste at the source, periodic removal to a local collection point, collection by manual or mechanical means, transfer and hauling of the waste to the ultimate disposal site, and finally disposal.[8]

While open dumping remains the most prevalent form of solid waste disposal in developing countries, sanitary landfills would be the most cost-effective method for most cities. Nonetheless, the recovery of resources from the organic portion of urban solid waste is technologically feasible. With favorable climatic conditions for the biological decomposition of moist organic wastes, composting, biogas conversion, or methane recovery from landfills may be appropriate. The United Nations Development Programme and the World Bank are undertaking a joint global research project to develop state-of-the-art appropriate technology for resource recovery in developing countries; it is expected to yield findings of practical importance.

Inappropriate urban land development is another cause of environmental degradation that may impose heavy costs in the future. When steep slopes are stripped of vegetation and no ground cover is planted or contouring done before buildings are constructed, the soil will erode rapidly, especially in tropical climates. Both the microclimate and soil are then reduced to a poor state for residential settlement, but even more serious results of erosion are polluted rivers, clogged irrigation and drainage systems, and frequent floods in other communities downstream. Uncontrolled stripping of vegetation reduces the soil's capacity to retain moisture and causes rapid runoff that exacerbates flooding.

Similar problems of flooding occur when marshland or swamps, which act as natural sponges, are filled for industrial and other urban use. These wetlands are also productive biological areas and form a critical link with marine life. Since fishing remains an economic activity of many low-income people in developing countries, the livelihood of these communities is often threatened by this type of coastal development.

To prevent these damaging patterns of development, attention must be given both to proposed projects and to land use allocations. Much could be achieved by establishing and enforcing controls that would encourage developers to maintain existing vegetation and land forms, minimize erosion, increase planting, and maintain natural watercourses. Municipal governments should acquire information on the land types, water flow, and air currents of the urban region so that urban development can be directed into areas that are capable of absorbing the impacts.

Development of Transport Networks

To encourage economic growth and to provide the means for shipping raw materials, manufactured goods, and agricultural inputs and products, developing nations need adequate transport networks. Ports and airports are required near major urban and industrial centers. Highways must also be constructed to connect the ports and airports with cities as well as with rural areas. In addition, a country which imports or exports liquid petroleum products or bulk cargoes may need to develop new port facilities or expand and modernize existing ports.

This section discusses the environmental impacts of the construction of highways, airports, and ports and suggests measures to prevent or mitigate those impacts. The development of new modes of transport in otherwise rural areas, unaccustomed to quick access to more populated areas, could have major environmental, social, and economic effects.

Adverse environmental impacts could occur both during and after construction of a transport system. During construction, there is extensive disturbance of the natural environment and major socioeconomic impacts when a large construction force moves into the area. After construction, impacts are related primarily to the operation of the facility, and secondarily to the new settlements which spring up along roads and around major transport centers. Often the population growth and development of new areas associated with highway construction will create significant impacts.

Highway Construction

Construction of highway projects can adversely affect water quality, air quality, noise level, wildlife habitats and migration routes, and patterns of growth. In rural areas in developing nations, there is the possibility that existing settlements or tribal peoples will be affected as well. In addition to the direct impacts on the physical environment, unplanned settlements can frequently be expected along the route of new highways that traverse rural or undeveloped areas.[9]

WATER QUALITY. Major road development requires substantial cuts and fills, soil compaction, and removal of vegetation. When tropical soils are exposed during the construction phase, there can be substantial erosion, with increased turbidity and silting of nearby streams and reservoirs. As a result, fish and other aquatic life may be harmed or killed, downstream drinking water degraded, nearby agricultural lands damaged, natural water systems altered, and operating costs of affected reservoirs increased.

Road construction can alter the natural drainage system of a watershed if it is necessary to build stream crossings or diversions, relocate a river bed, fill in estuarine areas, marshes, and swamps, or drain such areas. Rechanneling a watercourse can increase runoff and velocity and cause downstream flooding. Because of the key role of estuarine areas in the local ecosystem, the disturbance of natural flows and the alteration of marshes and swamps can cause fish, shellfish, and wildlife to disappear. Such activities can also affect local agricultural practices if salt water intrudes, groundwater recharge areas are decreased, or native forests are destroyed.

In addition to increased siltation during the construction phase, water quality can be impaired in the long term by biological and chemical components of storm water that runs off road surfaces. Where storm water would previously have infiltrated the ground or run off at natural levels, impervious roadways can create runoff of such volume and velocity that it causes downstream erosion or even flooding, depending on the magnitude of the surfaced area. In addition, oil and fuels deposited on the roadway surfaces are washed into local waters along with animal and human wastes, pesticides, and other pollutants. The result could be degradation of fisheries, drinking water supplies, and irrigation water.

The potential impacts of highway construction on water quality can be mitigated by appropriate design, engineering, and construction techniques and practices. Minimizing cuts and fills, restricting the removal of vegetation, and phasing construction can contribute to erosion control. Adequate drainage systems designed for local storm patterns with catchment basins, protection of natural drainage patterns, revegetation, and other measures to curb erosion and runoff would reduce sedimentation and contribute to an effective program.

Minimizing construction in groundwater recharge areas and adopting appropriate road designs could prevent pollutants from reaching local water systems used by people, fish and wildlife, and agriculture. Finally, estuaries, marshes, and swamps should be neither filled nor drained, given their importance to the local food chain.

AIR QUALITY. Air pollutants include dust and particulate matter stirred up during construction and the emissions generated by increased vehicular traffic once the roads are completed. Depending on meteorological conditions and the existing level of air pollution, the impacts could be significant. Mitigating measures would include emission controls on vehicles if warranted by the quality of the ambient air. Areas with pristine air may be most obviously affected if dust and haze suddenly become noticeable.

NOISE. The impact of noise would be most conspicuous when a new road is being constructed in a rural area. In addition to its effect on the human ear, noise may also affect wildlife.

SETTLEMENTS OR TRIBAL POPULATIONS. Highway routes through rural areas in developing countries are likely to disrupt settlements and force the inhabitants to relocate. The final route selected should result in the least amount of involuntary resettlement possible. If resettlement is unavoidable, an adequate resettlement plan should be part of the project. In addition, a proposed transport corridor may cut through an area used by tribal peoples for hunting, cultivation, or seasonal migration. The effects of the project on such people should be assessed, and potential adverse impacts should be mitigated. The Bank's policies with regard to resettlement and tribal peoples are discussed more fully in chapter 3.

WILDLIFE. The construction of new highways may divide wildlife ranges, alter migratory patterns, and in other ways cause the degradation or destruction of highly productive wildlife, fish, or shellfish and their habitats. Since some forms of wildlife are frequently a source of food and livelihood for rural people, these adverse effects of roads may be more extensive in rural than in urban areas. Careful site selection and corridor planning based on knowledge of local wildlife and migratory patterns can reduce the negative consequences.

GROWTH. The inducement of growth is always a significant secondary impact of construction of highways. By providing easier access to remote rural areas, new roads offer the opportunity for new living situations. Large tracts of land which were previously difficult to reach are opened to unplanned, spontaneous settlement. As people gather in these newly settled areas, there is a greater chance that diseases and their vectors will be spread to surrounding and distant areas and introduced to previously unexposed communities.

Airport Construction

The principal problem associated with airports, and one which has caused considerable controversy between neighbors and airport operators in developed nations, is noise. Airport projects also affect water and air quality and have secondary socioeconomic impacts. As opposed to the development of highways, which opens up previously remote rural areas, airports are likely to be located in more industrialized, urban areas.

NOISE. Design decisions on runway orientation, flight paths, and scheduling of aircraft arrivals and departures can mitigate the impacts of noise. When the site is being selected, consideration should be given to the unique land use of the area surrounding the airport. The needs and desires of the broad community served by the airport, the nature of freight to be handled, and present and future uses of the adjacent land must be assessed. Careful attention must be given to zoning and, where possible, land in the immediate vicinity of the airport should be restricted to activities that are compatible with airport operations. Proper siting and land use measures are also needed to minimize undesirable consequences of congestion arising from airport development.

AIR POLLUTION. The impacts of airport operations on air quality should be analyzed, particularly their cumulative effect on air already severely polluted in urban areas. The total amount of pollutants emitted as well as the effect on ambient air quality should be considered. In addition to emissions from aircraft and fueling operations, there will be emissions from the many surface vehicles attracted by the airport. Siting the airport away from (or at least far downwind from) major urban population centers is probably the most effective mitigating measure.

WATER QUALITY. The impacts on water quality will be similar to those discussed above with regard to highway construction, but will probably be greater because of the large land area required for airports and the concentrated nature of the development. Extensive grading for airport buildings and runways may cause erosion unless control measures are in effect as discussed above. Moreover, the large areas of impervious pavement will increase runoff unless measures are taken to channel storm water harmlessly. Residues such as oil, asbestos, rubber, jet fuels, and heavy metals can be washed from the surface of landing fields and runways by heavy rainfall and pollute fisheries, drinking water supplies, and irrigation water.

SOCIOECONOMIC IMPACTS. In addition to the possible displacement of communities for airport construction or expansion, the location of an airport can cause population and industry to shift and thus increase demands for governmental services. Unless proper planning manages such growth through zoning and other land use controls, the concentration of industry and population around a new airport can place on the environment the heavy stress typical of urban degradation in many developing nations.

Port Development

Port activities occur in the coastal zone—that relatively thin strip of land and water which hosts one of the most productive and complex biological systems on earth. By their nature, port operations (such as ship traffic and loading, unloading, and storage of cargo) interact extensively with the physical, chemical, biological, and social environment. In addition to the potential adverse impacts on air, water, and land, ports attract a number of other activities which themselves can also affect the environment.[10]

The environmental impacts derive primarily from two sources. First, the development of the port itself permanently alters the environment, not only through the development and maintenance of harbors and channels but also through the construction of berthing facilities and terminals for handling and storing cargo. Second, the operations of the port introduce pollution from cargo spills (especially oil), waste discharges, and vessel traffic. Although preventive measures should be built into the design and operation of port facilities to reduce or mitigate these impacts, there always remains the possibility of damage from oil spills as the result of an accident. Thus, each port must have containment and clean-up equipment on hand and effective contingency plans (discussed further in chapter 6).

DEVELOPMENT AND MAINTENANCE OF HARBORS AND CHANNELS. The chief adverse effects of harbor and channel development stem from dredging activities to open and maintain channels and from the disposal of the resultant spoils. Dredging disturbs the bottom sediment and affects water quality by increasing turbidity, changing salinity, and increasing heavy metal concentrations. If the increase in turbidity is more or less permanent as a result of continual dredging for maintenance, the penetration of sunlight might be reduced enough to decrease photosynthesis in marine plants. This could interfere with the feeding of shellfish and adversely affect commercially important species. In addition, the intrusion of salt water could debase the quality of freshwater aquifers.

When bottom sediment is removed by dredging and the suspended dredge spoils are deposited elsewhere, the marine habitat can be changed so significantly that not only are resident species forced to leave but also their attempts to recolonize are impeded. Dredge spoils that are deposited on wetlands could conflict with the preservation of such areas, which should be considered off limits as disposal sites.

BERTHING FACILITIES AND MARINE TERMINALS. The construction of onshore terminals creates a land use problem because cargo handling, processing, storage, and transfer facilities require a large amount of space. New ports enjoy the luxury of having plenty of room both for immediate requirements and for expansion, whereas existing ports may have to deal with intense competition for limited space. But the luxury of space has the disadvantage that paving over large land areas could significantly alter runoff unless proper measures are incorporated into the design, as discussed in the preceding sections.

Depending on the nature of the processing facilities in the port area, air and water emissions may also be a source of concern. Proper site selection, design, and planning can alleviate many of the problems caused by new ports by regulating the nature of the bulk processing facilities or by requiring that mitigating measures be incorporated into the design of such facilities. In addition, port construction will eliminate the previous use of the coastal area and will further affect the environs as truck and rail traffic moves goods in and out of the port.

VESSEL TRAFFIC OPERATIONS. The physical movement of ships within the harbor areas, as well as discharges and accidental spills, may adversely affect the environment. Irregular currents or turbulence caused by deep draft ships within tight channels could, if strong enough, erode the shore or stir up sediment. Measures requiring treatment of discharges from ships can mitigate pollution of the harbor. Nonetheless, accidental spills of fuel and hazardous cargoes during transfer operations or as a result of collisions or groundings may harm shore areas, marine life, and migratory birds. The severity of such a spill depends on a variety of factors such as the nature of the coastal environment, prevailing winds and tides, the content and quantity of the material spilled, and the sensitivity of bird or marine life in the area. Oil spills can also pollute beaches and adversely affect a tourism industry. Oil spill emergency contingency plans and response capability are a must.

Utilizing Urban Environmental Information

Although action will be required at the national level to initiate broad policies and approaches for dealing with environmental problems, the technical work of identifying the problems and solutions will have to be done at the city and regional levels of government. The problems and solutions will vary in each case, but it is possible to define a set of objectives and a methodology that can be used in different settings to analyze the relationships between the natural environment and development.

Information gathering and mapping of the data are the first steps in addressing serious environmental issues. Environmental information can normally be collected and applied without changing existing local planning capacities. One approach outlined below provides a consistent and common framework for public and private planners and decisionmakers, makes public and private decisions more predictable, assists in setting priorities for special studies, and avoids wasteful and confusing duplication in data collection.

Types of Environmental Analysis

Before an information system can be developed, it is necessary to review briefly the objectives of the environmental analysis:

- *Identification of urban development patterns.* The natural environment provides important guidance for efficient urban growth patterns and public infrastructure investments.
- *Selection of locations for development projects.* In most cases, compatibility between a development scheme and its environmental

setting is a compromise. In these cases, the natural environment will dictate design and engineering measures to overcome potential conflicts.

- *Evaluation of compatibility between a development scheme and its location.* The environmental analysis can be used to identify projects that will alleviate problems resulting from conflicts between existing developments and the environment. It is also used for the environmental assessment of projects.

To meet these objectives the analysis must consider three basic interrelated aspects: the geographic location of the project, the design characteristics of the development, and the compatibility between the development and alternative locations. The third aspect deserves special attention because it will determine the location and design of the project. The information required to determine environmental compatibility can be divided into four categories, which are treated separately during the information collection stage:

- *Description of the environmental setting.* Definition of the nature and location of physical constraints to development in the project area should include sensitive resources to be preserved and hazards to be avoided.
- *Description of development implications.* An analysis of the environmental impacts is required in order to define the factors associated with project construction and operation which may conflict with environmental constraints.
- *Identification of conflicts between urban development and the environment.* This task describes the type and magnitude of conflicts and the social and economic impacts that may arise from certain urban development actions.
- *Formulation of policies, regulations, standards, and design recommendations.* These formulations establish permissible levels of impact on the environment, together with mechanisms for mitigating negative impacts in the design, construction, and treatment of wastes in each major development sector.

In an environmental review the available information is compiled and organized in such a way that it is readily understood. An environmental data base can be formed gradually without extensive additional surveys and research by using experience from the past and information produced from ongoing and future projects. It can be compiled without the aid of computers, by means of transparent map overlays and files of short descriptions; furthermore, information can be added incrementally. The data base can help planners, developers, and decisionmakers to link previously isolated facts and issues without preparing a major study for every project; to evaluate environmental compatibility between a given development scheme and a given location; and to identify and describe a spatial development pattern at the local or regional level that minimizes costs as well as conflicts between urban development and its environmental setting.

The environmental review can be modest in the beginning and can be expanded or modified according to need and the availability of data. The use of such a tool at the outset can heighten environmental awareness, permit the establishment of priorities for information collection, create a better perspective for urban and regional policy formulation, and assist in environmentally responsive project design and evaluation. Ultimately, it will improve the efficiency and equity of urban development. The potential benefits of avoiding future development costs appear to be great and seem to outweigh the small costs necessary to establish such an information and review system. Further details on such an information system are found in the next section.

Collecting, Analyzing, and Applying Environmental Information: A Systematic Approach

Comprehensive environmental planning and management requires project-by-project analysis as well as a comprehensive information base and coordination of policies across sectors, space, and time. Not only will this approach help establish consistent policies to guide development, but also the reuse of information common to all projects will economize on data collection and analysis.

The basic function of the environmental planning and management tool described here is to translate relevant facts and policies into practical project-level recommendations.[11] Three groups of tasks are performed: information collection, contribution to policy formation, and guidance in the development of plans and projects. These activities are continuous, and the information flow among them is cyclical (figure 7-1).

Figure 7-1. *Environmental Planning and Management: Functions, Activities, and Information Flows*

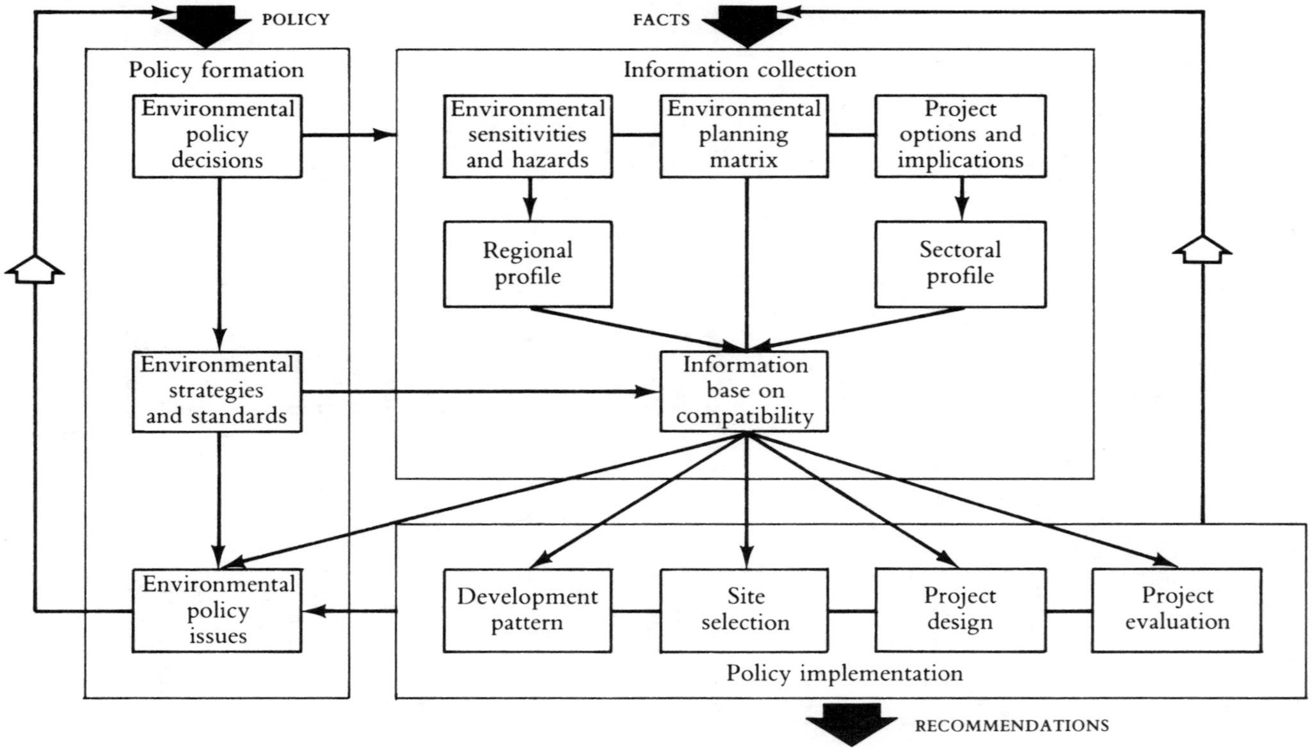

COMPILING AN INFORMATION BASE. It is important to distinguish between two major categories of environmental information: location-specific information (regional profiles) and project-specific information (sectoral profiles). A regional profile consists of a description of the environmental settings in a specific region and of their compatibility with a potential project. A sectoral profile consists of the description of development options for a specific type of project and of their potential impact on the environment.

Regional and sectoral profiles can be combined in different ways to form an operational information base to determine environmental compatibility. Both can also be used individually. Development agencies can thus maintain separate sectoral profiles for frequently executed types of project and regional profiles for areas in which many projects are located.

The regional profile describes the location, type, and significance of environmental constraints in a study area; potential conflicts with urban development; and policies, standards, regulations, and existing legislative and administrative provisions for dealing with these conflicts. The central part of data preparation for the regional profile is the mapping of environmental features that represent a constraint to development.

Each constraint is documented separately (see figure 7-2), and different degrees of constraint are indicated by alphanumeric and color codes on maps. Although constraints derive from and often coincide with identifiable features, most features need to be translated into constraints before they are intelligible to planners and decisionmakers. Soil classifications used by geologists, for example, need to be translated into levels of bearing capacity to identify foundation constraints; into levels of fertility to identify constraints on agricultural productivity; and into levels of percolation capacity to identify runoff coefficients and the suitability of the land for septic tanks with drainage fields. Although expertise may be required to define the more complex types of constraints, rule-of-thumb approximation is generally adequate for initial decisions on location and scale of development and is preferable to neglecting a constraint entirely.

In a matrix like the one shown in figure 7-3, each environmental constraint is related to a standard set of implications of the project (such as grading or emission of pollutants) in a way that identifies potential conflicts (the dots in the conflict matrix). The develop-

Figure 7-2. *Example of an Environmental Constraint Map*

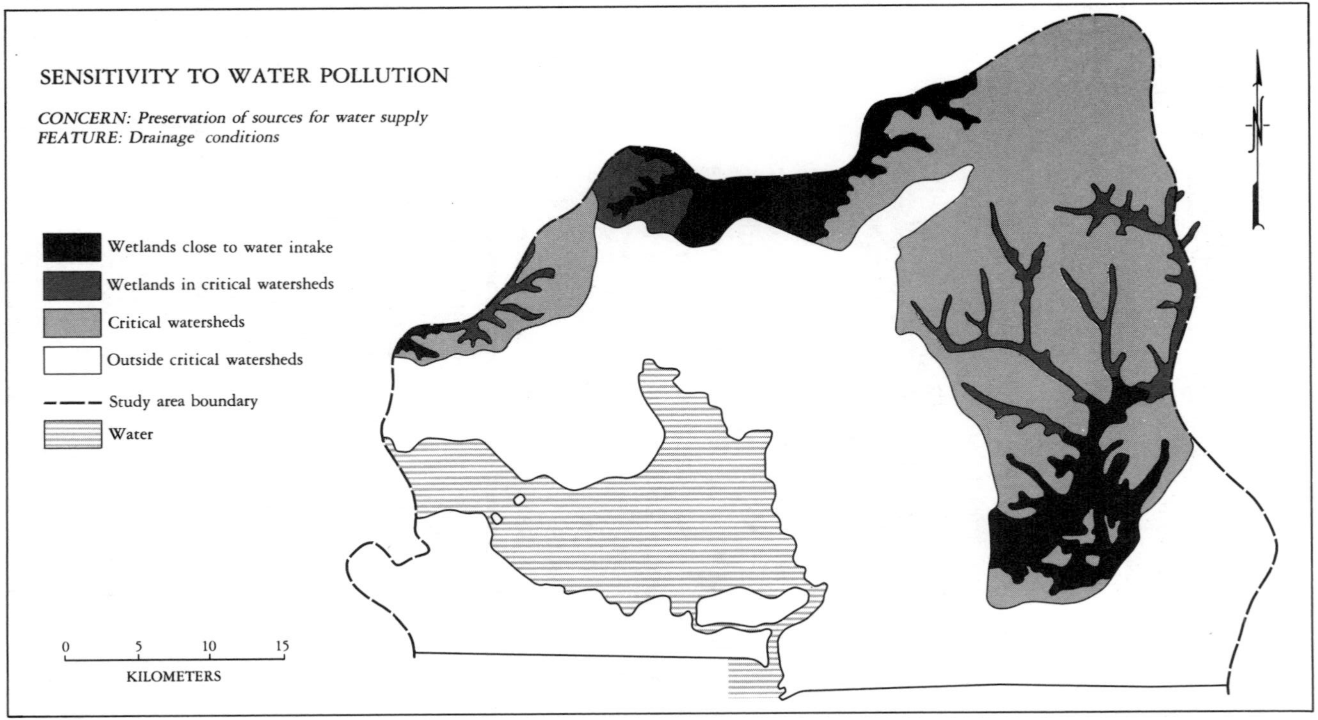

SENSITIVITY TO WATER POLLUTION

CONCERN: *Preservation of sources for water supply*
FEATURE: *Drainage conditions*

Wetlands close to water intake
Wetlands in critical watersheds
Critical watersheds
Outside critical watersheds
Study area boundary
Water

0   5   10   15
KILOMETERS

Figure 7-3. *Example of a Matrix Relating Environmental Constraints to Implications of a Project*

	Disturbance of ecosystem	Removal of vegetation	Erosion	Grading, leveling	Reclamation: landfill	Reclamation: drainage	Storm water runoff (quality, quantity)	Sewage disposal	Solid waste disposal	Emissions (air pollution)	Provision of access (exposure)	Creation of barrier (preemption)	Visual impacts (identity, blockage of vistas)	Sensitivity to flooding	Requiring high foundation loads	Requiring low foundation loads	Requiring roads and utility lines	Sensitivity to noise	Sensitivity to air pollution	Sensitivity to water pollution	
Preservation of water supply																					
Critical watersheds	·	•	•				•	●	•												
Wetlands in critical watersheds	•	•	•	•	•	•	•	●	●		•										
Critical wetlands close to intake	●	•	•	●	●	●	●	●			•										
Critical aquifer recharge areas	•	•		●	●	•	•	•													
Preservation of marginally dry land																					
Sensitive watersheds (runoff quantity)	•			●	●	●															
Preservation of fishing potential																					
Critical channels (migration routes)	•	•			●	●	•	•	•												
Critical wetland (nursery grounds)	●	●			●	●	●	●	●		•										
Preservation of agricultural potential																					
Suitable soils		•	•			•	•	•				·									
Existing subsistence farming		•	•			•	•	•				●									
Existing modern farming/forest reserve		•	•				•				·	●									
Preservation of recreational opportunities																					
Scenic areas	•	•	•	•	•	·	•	•	·		•	●	●								
Areas in natural state	•	•	•	•	•	•	●	●	•		●	•	●								
Scenic areas in natural state	●	•	•	•	•	•	●	•	●		•	●	●								
Seashore and urban waterfronts		•					•	•	•			●	●								
Preservation of air quality																					
Urban airshed	•			•	•			•	•	●											
Avoidance of flooded areas																					
Flood plains														•	•	•	•				
Areas with reclamation constraints														●	●	•	•				
Avoidance of unconsolidated land																					
Old consolidated dunes															•						
Alluvial plains															•		•				
Unconsolidated dunes		●	●	●											•	•	•				
Avoidance of unstable soils																					
Moderate foundation constraints															•						
Severe foundation constraints															●	•	•				
Avoidance of slope constraints																					
Slope stability (too steep)															●	•	•				
Runoff constraint (too flat)															•		●				
Avoidance of existing noise pollution																					
25–30 noise exposure factor																		•			
Over 30 noise exposure factor																		●			
Avoidance of existing air pollution																					
Air pollution impact areas																			●	•	
Avoidance of existing water pollution																					
Polluted water bodies																			•	●	

Note: Size of circle denotes seriousness of the consideration.

Figure 7-4. *Example of an Environmental Zoning Map*

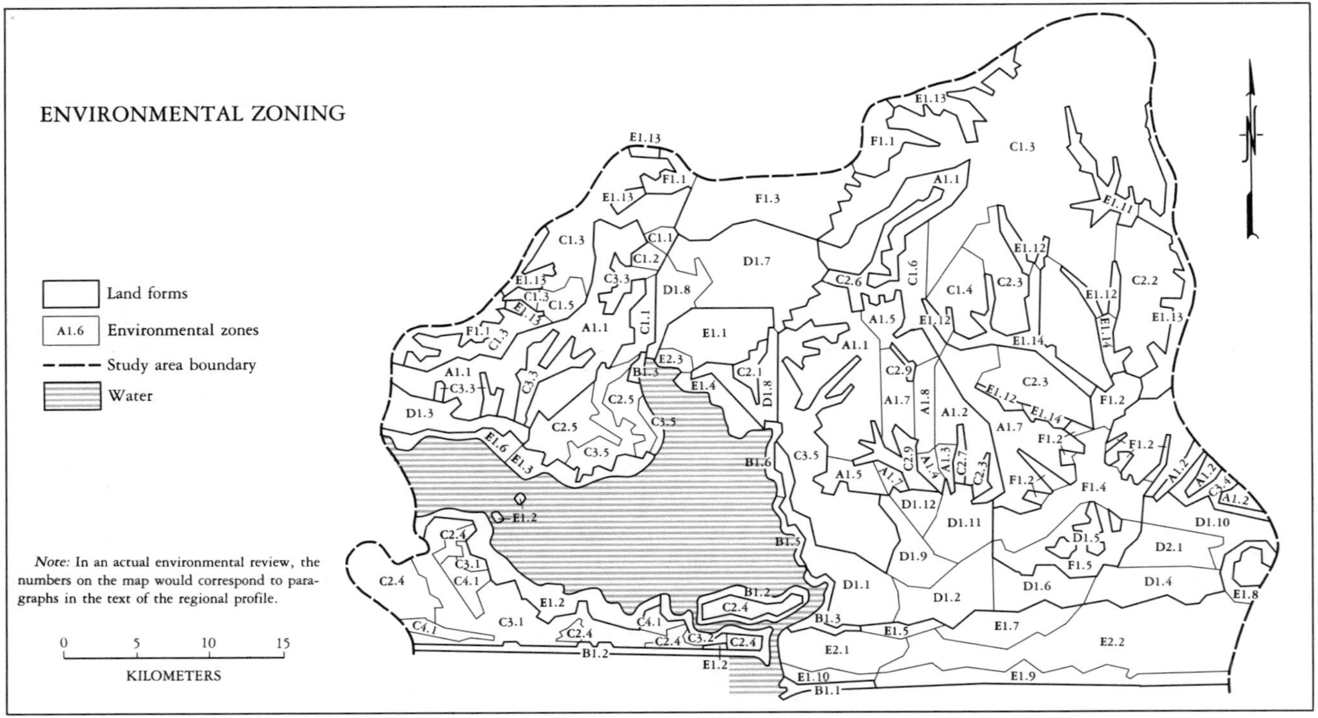

ENVIRONMENTAL ZONING

Land forms

A1.6   Environmental zones

— — —   Study area boundary

▓▓▓   Water

Note: In an actual environmental review, the numbers on the map would correspond to paragraphs in the text of the regional profile.

0   5   10   15

KILOMETERS

ment project affects environmental sensitivities (resources), and environmental hazards in turn affect the sensitivities or requirements of the project. Each map can be accompanied by a description of the environmental constraints and their relationships to the implications of the project. The text is structured by the matrix and covers the following issues for each environmental constraint:

- Its significance for health and safety, socioeconomic or cultural well-being, construction costs, and so on
- Its characteristics (such as location, indicators, interdependencies, and sensitivity)
- Policy issues and administrative provisions
- Ranking and mapping (explanation of map)
- Information (requirements, availability, bibliography)
- Nature and significance of the project's implications that are a source of potential conflict (one chapter for each dot in the matrix)
- Methods of controlling these implications.

To provide a guide to the information, the constraint maps are aggregated into environmental zoning maps (figure 7-4). The result is that the area being studied is divided into geographic zones, each with a specific set of environmental constraints. The zones are coded to identify their environmental setting, and these codes also refer to the relevant chapters and paragraphs in the text. This systematic disaggregation of the body of information on environmental compatibility into a limited number of elements permits selective updating and expansion of the data base, including adjustment of standards and regulations. Most important, it allows maximum reuse of the information for different regions and different types of projects.

As illustrated in figure 7-5, the procedure for establishing a sectoral profile corresponds closely to that for a regional profile. The sectoral profile, however, describes a specific type of project and its relation to a generic environment. The sectoral profile addresses implications of various development options, potential conflicts with environmental constraints, and policies, standards, and design recommendations for dealing with these conflicts.

The sectoral profile makes use of the same matrix as the regional profile, but since the sectoral profile does not relate to a specific

Figure 7-5. *Example of an Urban Growth Pattern, Based on an Environmental Zoning Map*

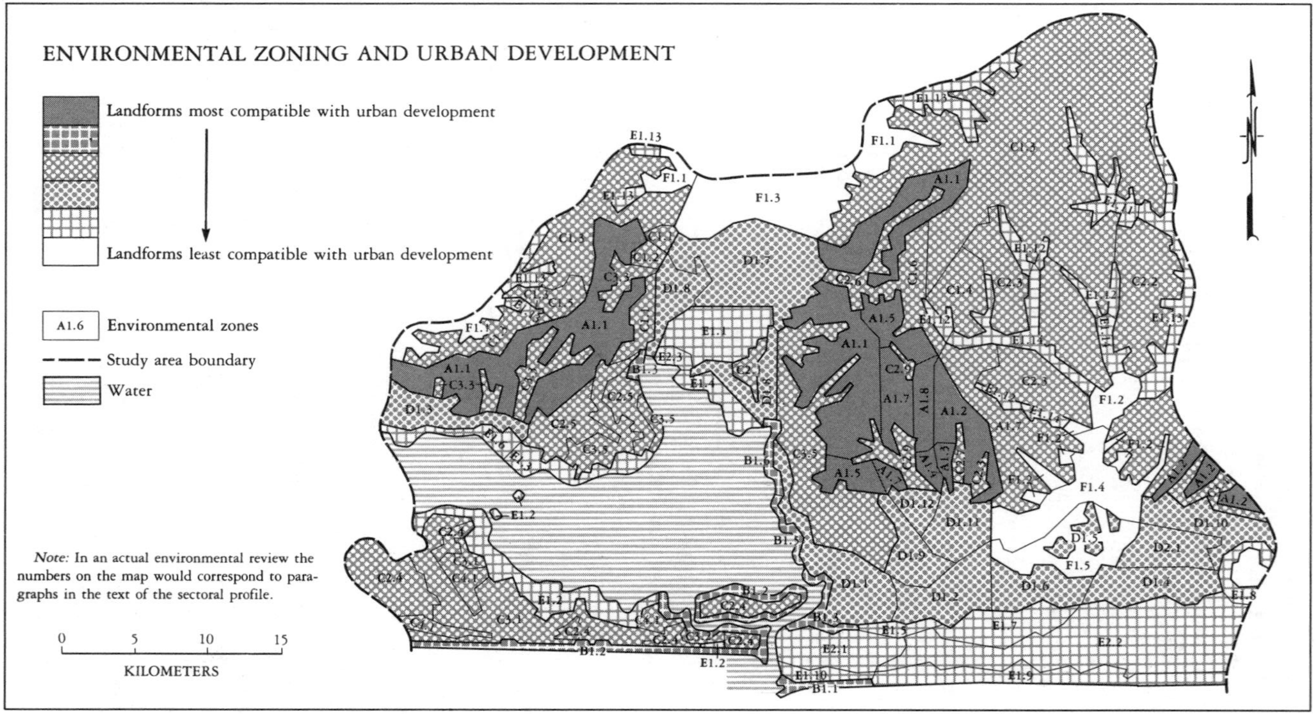

ENVIRONMENTAL ZONING AND URBAN DEVELOPMENT

Landforms most compatible with urban development

Landforms least compatible with urban development

A1.6 Environmental zones

Study area boundary

Water

Note: In an actual environmental review the numbers on the map would correspond to paragraphs in the text of the sectoral profile.

0   5   10   15

KILOMETERS

176

geographic region, there are no constraint maps. The description of environmental constraints takes the form of a generic discussion.

ESTABLISHING ENVIRONMENTAL POLICIES. Analysts can identify environmental features that are relevant to the efficiency and equity of urban development, and they can determine potential conflicts between these features and development activities. To deal with these potential conflicts, however, policies and strategies must be developed and coordinated. Decisionmakers need to be made aware of the issues (for example, threats to fisheries as a result of development) and of the alternatives, consequences, and rough costs of policies. Once policies are established (for example, to protect wetlands in order to preserve fisheries), constraint maps can be updated, and specific development limitations and administrative provisions can be added to the text. Policies and strategies can and should be periodically adjusted to reflct changes in the socioeconomic and physical context and in the awareness of problems and solutions.

DEVELOPING PLANS AND PROJECTS. For project activities having direct consequences for the environment, the information-gathering procedure described above provides access to facts and regulations about isolated issues (for example, conflicts between the use of insecticides on a specific plot of land and the municipal water supply) without requiring long-range, cross-sectoral, and areawide studies and decisionmaking for every project.

The simplest way of using the accumulated information is to evaluate the compatibility of a given development scheme with a given location. Such an analysis can be used by local development officials to ensure that a proposed project adheres to established environmental policies (for example, that a proposed landfill does not block water flow). The analysis can also help private and public planners evaluate the environmental effects of projects (as in environmental assessments, which show how significant issues have been considered in the project design). In addition, the analysis will enable development agencies to identify existing environmental problems (for example, flooding caused by improper landfill) that require remedial action (the construction of drainage channels).

A regional development pattern is defined on the basis of a sectoral profile for general urban development and a regional profile of the entire area under consideration. The purpose of this analysis is to identify a spatial pattern that minimizes conflicts between general urban or regional development and its environmental setting. This analysis can be used in forming policy. Its results provide the framework for strategic public investment (for example, in roads and water supply), which in turn stimulates and guides private activities. The procedure begins by identifying implications for general urban development. Next, potential conflicts with the environmental constraints (figure 7-3) of each zone of the environmental zoning map (figure 7-4) are identified and ranked. A map is then produced on which each area is shaded to correspond to its rank of compatibility. Figure 7-5 presents an example of such a map showing a pattern of urban development that minimizes costs (of overcoming environmental hazards) and maximizes benefits (of using environmental resources). The eventual pattern of development will, of course, vary depending on policies and information derived from other sectors with regard to transport, land prices, employment, and residential locations.

Other uses of accumulated information include the selection of a compatible site for a project and recommendations for ways in which the project design can overcome potential incompatibilities between the project and its location. In all cases, the environmental information base identifies all known environmental constraints, the established policies for the treatment of these constraints, and reusable design solutions for overcoming potential environmental conflicts.

Conclusion

The rapid population growth in the urban areas of developing countries has strained the already overburdened existing municipal services. The task of the planners is to remedy the inadequacies as best as possible to improve solid waste disposal, sewage treatment, and the supply of drinking water as well as to provide adequate housing.

At the same time, the planners have an opportunity to begin to guide future development and growth through the adoption of comprehensive regional and urban plans. Because most developing countries have an inadequate data base at present, the first task is to begin to amass the data with which to formulate comprehensive plans for the management of growth. This data can also serve in the analysis of specific projects while the comprehensive plans are being developed.

Careful attention to impact analysis and siting considerations for each project, as well as sound planning of tranport networks and urban infrastructure, could provide the means for more balanced growth and permit the developing nations to begin to put order into their urban and regional development.

Notes

1. World Bank, *Urbanization*, Sector Working Paper (Washington, D.C., 1972).

2. Johannes F. Linn, *Cities in the Developing World: Policies for Their Equitable and Efficient Growth* (New York: Oxford University Press, 1983).

3. John L. Taylor and David G. Williams, eds., *Urban Planning Practice in Developing Countries* (Elmsford, N.Y.: Pergamon, 1981).

4. Data indicate that the rates of mortality, morbidity, and malnutrition among urban slum dwellers can be as bad as or worse than among rural populations in the same country. S. Basta, "Nutrition and Health in Low Income Areas of the Third World," *Ecology of Food and Nutrition*, vol. 6 (1977).

5. For every $1 invested in a water supply system, approximately $3 is needed for a separate piped system to take away sewage.

6. World Health Organization, *Surveillance of Drinking Water Quality*, Monograph Series no. 63 (Geneva, 1976).

7. See Sandra J. Cointreau, *Environmental Management of Urban Solid Wastes in Developing Countries: A Project Guide* (Washington, D.C.: World Bank, 1982).

8. Ibid.

9. See World Bank, Environment, Science and Technology Unit, "Environmental Requirements of the World Bank" (Washington, D.C., 1982), table 3.

10. See Maritime Transportation Research Board Commission on Sociotechnical Systems, *Port Development in the U.S.*, Panel on Future Port Requirements of the U.S. (Washington, D.C., 1976).

11. See J. L. McHarg, *Design with Nature* (New York: Doubleday, 1969).

Appendix A
Checklist of Environmental Considerations for Project Analysis

This appendix contains checklists of questions that should be routinely considered in assessing the environmental effects of various development projects. The checklists are arranged by topic in the following order:

- Agriculture
- Energy resource systems, including specific considerations for oil and natural gas, coal, hydroelectric, and alternative energy projects
- Industrial development
- Sewerage and sewage treatment
- Transport, including specific considerations for airports, ports and harbors, and roads and highways

AGRICULTURE

Agricultural Development

Development of Natural Resources

- Is this a climax ecosystem (such as an undisturbed tropical forest) or has it undergone earlier man-induced changes?
- If new water sources are to be tapped, what is known about their extent and replenishment?
- Are changes in population density or life style brought about by the project likely to create environmental, health, or social problems?

Project Design and Construction

- Will the measures necessary to protect the environment and health be incorporated in the design and construction of the project?

- How will sheet erosion or gully erosion caused by the removal of trees and other vegetation be controlled?
- If ponds, canals, or other surface waters are involved, can a fishery be established?
- How will the downstream water supply and quality be affected by the project?
- Will stored agricultural products be targets of insect and rodent pests? If so, what control measures will be taken?
- Will wildlife or fish populations and their migratory routes be affected? What will be done to protect them?
- Will pesticides and fertilizers be employed? If so, what steps will be taken to minimize their undesirable effects?

Operations

- How will the project be monitored to gauge its effects on the environment, human health, and social welfare?
- Will extension services be provided? Can they be used to detect and counteract any adverse effects that arise?
- Will those responsible for continuing management and supervision of the project be on the alert for environmental problems? Do they know where to seek advice and assistance?

Sociocultural Factors

- If the project involves settlement or relocation of people, has a plan for their removal and settlement been prepared, approved, or reviewed by qualified social scientists?
- Will the people to be resettled be fully briefed and oriented to their new environmental setting and the changes to be expected in their life styles, living arrangements, and occupation?
- Will the affected people need to acquire new skills and techniques for successful adaptation? Does the project plan provide for the necessary education and training?
- Will the project also provide for training in the techniques of erosion control, water management, forest and range management, and so forth?
- Will indigenous, primitive people be affected? What provisions will be made for their future?

Health Impacts

• Will human diseases associated with agriculture result from this project? If so, how will they be controlled?
• If the project involves colonizing new areas, will the settlers be given medical examinations and treatment to control the introduction of new diseases?
• Will the settlers be informed about the health hazards to be expected and the methods of control?
• Will a system of health care delivery be included in the project?

Long-term Considerations

• Does the project preempt any future resource options by its presence or operation?
• Will the project so alter the environment as to preclude its future use for other activities, including other agricultural uses?
• Will waterlogging or soil salinity become a problem? Can the process of soil laterization be expected; if so, what will be its consequences?
• If large areas of indigenous vegetation (for example, tropical forests) are to be removed, can mesoscale climatic changes be expected?

Irrigation Systems

Development of Natural Resources

• What will be the ecological consequences of changes in land use patterns and population distribution? Will future resource uses be preempted?
• Will undesirable population crowding occur as villages expand to make way for or to take advantage of the irrigated areas?
• Are major components of the ecosystem known? How will the project affect them?
• Will changes in population density upset ecological balances?
• What will be the impact of the project on the biota in the water system?

- Will the diversion of water to cultivated areas seriously degrade the capabilities of the original water system to support valuable biological species?
- Will important wildlife migration routes be permanently disrupted?

Design and Construction

- Is there a consolidated construction plan for the development that takes account of ecological factors?
- Are road patterns, land excavations, fill sites, refuse disposal activities, and the like planned to minimize environmental damage?
- What provisions have been made for restoring borrow pits and other scarred sections of the construction area by filling, grading, and reseeding to prevent erosion?
- Will precautions be taken to protect management and construction crews from introducing new diseases or redistributing endemic diseases?

Operations

- What steps are being taken to preserve fish and wildlife resources in the area?
- Will water diversions be screened to prevent the destruction of fish?
- Will runoff water contain residues, such as pesticides and fertilizers, that contaminate downstream waters?
- Will there be problems of sedimentation, salinity, and erosion?
- How will waterlogging and salt accumulation be controlled? Will aquatic weeds be a serious problem?
- How does the irrigation network interact with sources of drinking water?
- Will irrigation permit the cultivation of new crops to which exogenous pests might be attracted?
- What provision has been made for monitoring the effects of the development on the environment and people?

Sociocultural Factors

- Will the introduction of water mean new crops, new farming methods, or population increases that will be detrimental to important social or cultural practices?
- Will the construction or operation of the system adversely affect other agricultural, economic, or commercial practices in the area?
- Will construction of the system or new cultivation cause people to relocate in search of new opportunities? If so, what steps will be taken to ensure orderly and productive resettlement?

Health Impacts

- To what extent will the project introduce new public health problems? Will health care services be included in the project?
- Will food, wastes, or water cycles aggravate sanitation and disease problems? Has provision been made for adequate environmental sanitation?
- Will changes in water velocities, temperatures, and depth create a more favorable environment for insect pests and disease-bearing organisms?
- Will changes in water patterns introduce disease-bearing organisms into previously unaffected areas?

Long-term Considerations

- What undesirable long-range changes in population or the environment may accompany the development of the irrigation system?
- Will related development projects planned for the future introduce new possibilities for adverse environmental effects?

ENERGY RESOURCE SYSTEMS

Oil and Natural Gas

Development of Natural Resources

- To what degree will oil and gas development affect terrestrial or aquatic life in the vicinity?
- Were environmental factors considered in selecting the transport mode for the oil and gas?
- Have pipeline routes been planned to minimize disturbance of environmentally fragile or sensitive areas?
- Have alternative tanker-loading locations been evaluated—for example, offshore monobuoys as opposed to nearshore fixed berths?
- If oil and gas development is taking place in more than one locality, can integrated planning reduce the number of pipelines, tanker terminals, and staging areas?
- Will pipeline construction affect natural drainage or disturb wetlands?
- Will the oil and gas operations cause subsidence? How will this be mitigated?

Project Design and Construction

- Have the location and phasing of oil and gas development been designed to supply energy at minimum environmental risk?
- Have the probable fate and effects of spilled oil from offshore development sites been evaluated? If there is a choice of development sites, which ones will minimize the expected environmental impacts of spilled oil?
- How will air and water pollution emissions be minimized?
- Have environmental control technologies and practices been incorporated into the project design?
- Are training programs planned to ensure good operating practices and work safety?

- Have the potential impacts of offshore oil and gas operations on commercial fishing been evaluated?
- Are there adequate navigational aids for the increased tanker traffic that may result from oil and gas development?
- Will collision warning devices be installed on offshore platforms?
- Have dikes and berms been constructed to minimize the impact of spills on the shore?
- Have shoreside ballast treatment facilities for tankers been provided?
- Will subsurface safety valves, controlled remotely from the surface, be installed in offshore production wells?
- Have local conditions--such as the possibility of earthquakes, hurricanes, and severe storms--been considered in the design of drilling, production, storage, and transport systems?
- If natural gas is exported in liquid form, will the loading terminal be in a remote location? Are vessel traffic controls planned for ports used by tankers carrying liquid natural gas?

Operations

- Will inspections, including testing of safety equipment, be made on a regular basis?
- Has an emergency response program been established? Does it contain a contingency plan for responding to oil spills?
- If dispersants are used to clean up offshore oil spills, have they been selected to minimize toxicity to marine life?
- How will wastewater from the drilling operation be disposed of?
- How will drill cuttings, spent drilling mud, and other solid wastes be disposed of?
- How will the environmental effects of the operations be monitored?
- What plans have been made to monitor spills, evaluate their causes, and make recommendations for changes?
- Have procedures been established to prevent discharge of oily ballast water?
- Could this project have environmental impacts on other coun-

tries? Have agreements been made that resolve any problems in advance?

Socioeconomic Factors

- Is the oil and gas development likely to transform the economic structure and substantially change the life style and environment in the area?
- Will the oil and gas operations attract workers from other industries and thus create labor shortages?
- Are plans being made to house temporary construction workers?
- Have steps been taken to provide for a possible influx of population? How will housing and essential community facilities and services be provided?
- Are zoning or land use regulations in force in the locality of the project to preserve areas of natural beauty, historic or cultural interest, or recreational value?
- Will local residents be affected by the operations (by noise, odors, or water runoff, for example)?

Health Impacts

- Are emissions from or chemicals used in oil and gas operations toxic?
- Will any of the disposal practices create health problems?
- Are there plans to set up a health care system adequate for the population increase resulting from the development?
- Are there adequate emergency facilities in case of explosions or fires?
- Will construction personnel be exposed to unique local health problems? Will they introduce disease?

Long-term Considerations

- Is the site adequate for enhanced recovery operations?
- Has the possibility of downstream projects, such as refineries, petrochemical plants, and fertilizer plants, been considered? Is the project site suited to future downstream development?

- Does the production plan for oil or gas afford the maximum recovery of the resource?

Coal

Development of Natural Resources

- Have plans for the future use of the land surface been incorporated into the mining and reclamation plan?
- Have environmental factors been considered in selecting coal transport systems?
- Have the impacts on fish, wildlife, and vegetation been considered?
- Will coal mining operations interrupt local water supplies? Have provisions been made to supply local users from alternative sources?
- If the mining takes place beneath populated areas, will surface subsidence cause damage to homes and buildings? Can measures be taken to prevent subsidence?

Project Design and Construction

- Is acid mine drainage a potential problem? What measures will be taken to minimize the potential for acid mine drainage both during operations and after mining has ceased?
- Will coal haul roads be planned to minimize sedimentation?
- Will patterns of underground water flow and surface runoff be adversely affected?
- Will adequate sediment control structures and catch basins be constructed?
- Will methane drained from underground mines be recovered and used as a resource?
- Will monitoring wells be drilled around the mine site to detect groundwater contamination?

Operations

- Will regrading and reclamation be carried out during mining operations?

- Will topsoil be segregated for reuse on regraded spoils?
- Will local residents be disturbed by noise from blasting and mining machinery? What steps will be taken to minimize these disturbances?
- What measures will be taken to prevent ignition of coal mine wastes?
- Are the plant species selected for revegetation suitable? Are they native?
- Will revegetated lands require long-term management, such as irrigation and applications of fertilizer?
- At the conclusion of underground mining operations, will the mine be sealed or flooded to minimize the risk of acid mine drainage?
- Will wastes be disposed of in underground or surface coal mines? If so, might these wastes cause water problems, and what steps will be taken to prevent such problems?

Socioeconomic Factors

- Will the mining operations require that towns and villages be moved? What will be done to relocate the people?
- Will the mining operations cause an increase in population near the mine? What provisions have been made to accommodate an increase?
- Will mining operations threaten important archaeological deposits or cultural practices?

Health Impacts

- When mines are planned for remote areas, will there be adequate health care facilities for miners and their families?
- Will there be educational and training programs to ensure good safety practices?
- Will settling ponds attract insects or create potential disease problems?

Long-Term Considerations

- What is the long-term effect on local water supplies of pumping water during mining operations to lower the groundwater table?

- Will the mining operation attract additional development such as power plants, coal gasification plants, industrial development based on coal, and so on? Are such resources as water, land, and clean air available for additional development?

Hydroelectric Projects

Project Design and Construction

- Does the project design take into account local weather patterns, soil conditions, topography, vegetation, and the seasonal flow rate of neighboring waterways?
- Have all possible effects of large-scale flooding of the impoundment area been taken into account in project planning? Have measures been devised to mitigate these effects (for example, by partially clearing the impoundment area before flooding)?
- Have the likely degree of sedimentation and the associated impacts been fully considered, particularly in reservoirs built on steep slopes and in heavily farmed or eroding areas? What measures have been planned to minimize these effects?
- Have project planners developed a watershed management program for the entire catchment area?
- Will fish ladders be used to enable fish to swim upstream over the dam? Where lotic fish species are involved, have fish hatcheries been considered, particularly if ladders may not be effective?
- Has there been a comprehensive seismic investigation in the early stages of site selection?

Operations

- Are there plans to monitor the effects of the dam on the river downstream?
- How will impacts on local fish populations be dealt with?
- Will equipment be inspected regularly?
- Can the spillway be opened more frequently than planned if

there is a high incidence of decomposition and eutrophication in the reservoir?
- What plans are there to reduce levels of sedimentation if they are higher than anticipated?
- Are there contingency plans in case of downstream flooding?

Socioeconomic Factors

- How will worker migration into the project areas affect the local inhabitants and local patterns of life?
- Have plans been made to provide temporary construction workers with housing, food, and medical services?
- Will flooding of the impoundment area and dam construction require large-scale resettlement of native inhabitants? Can the project be modified to reduce the amount of resettlement necessary? What plans have been made to minimize the impacts of resettlement?
- How will flooding of the impoundment area affect the local economy? Will local inhabitants dependent on farming, fishing, or hunting be put out of work? What plans have been made to reduce these effects?

Health Impacts

- What plans have been made to eliminate vectors of human disease and their hosts?
- Have plans been made to eliminate water weeds?
- Will reservoir water be protected from contamination by untreated sewage and by fertilizer and pesticide runoff?
- Will access to the reservoir be strictly controlled, and how?
- Have plans been made for strict medical supervision of all workers at the dam site?
- What plans have been made to prevent infected workers or local residents from introducing a disease to other parts of the country?

Long-term Considerations

- Will the project produce any irreversible changes in local ecosystems?

- Has the project been designed to ensure the longest possible life for the reservoir?

Alternative Energy Projects

General Considerations

- If a conventional fossil fuel project is under consideration, have alternative energy projects that use renewable resources also been considered?
- What are the economic benefits of a conventional project as opposed to an alternative energy project?
- Is any renewable resource present in sufficient quantities to make the project viable?
- Have the environmental and resource conservation benefits of renewable resource projects been fully taken into account?

Wind Power

- Have plans been made to minimize the interference of access roads and transmission lines with animal grazing and agricultural operations?
- Will the windmills reduce the beauty of a particularly remote and scenic area?
- Have the effects of potential changes to the microclimate during windmill operation been fully studied?
- Will there be an adequate buffer zone around the towers to protect individuals from thrown blades in the event of mechanical failure?
- Have the effects of windmill noise on neighboring residents been taken into account in selecting the site for the wind farm?

Solar Power

- Will the system use a heat transfer or storage medium containing toxic additives?
- Are there plans to inspect the system regularly to spot any cracks in the storage tank or other mechanical problems that might result in leakage of the toxic additives?

Small Hydro

- How will the project minimize interference with the upstream migration of spawning fish?
- Has the project's effect on the downstream aquatic ecology been taken into account?
- Have the cumulative impacts of other existing or planned hydro projects on the same river been fully considered?
- Will the natural drainage pattern be maintained, to prevent erosion?

Biomass

- Will use of biomass as a fuel significantly deplete the food supply in a local community?
- Is it feasible to use the biomass at or near its source?
- What plans have been made to mitigate the air emissions and water effluents likely to be produced by the biomass combustion or conversion project under consideration?
- Are there plans to recycle the effluents?
- Are the effects of biomass removal on the local ecology completely understood? How will these effects be kept to a minimum?

INDUSTRIAL DEVELOPMENT

Development of Natural Resources

- Does the project conform with regional plans for the development and use of natural resources?
- How will the natural resources affected by the project be managed to avoid exploitation and overuse of existing supplies and reserves?
- Does the development plan adequately link requirements for raw materials, utilization of by-products, and shipping and transport facilities, both within the project and in relation to other industries and markets?

- Will the project cause an excessive demand, now or in the future, on the region's energy resources, and what measures are proposed to minimize the effects of such demand?
- How will raw materials be transported, handled, and stored to safeguard workers and the environment?

Site Selection and Project Design

- Have the characteristics and components of alternative sites been identified?
- What hydrological, geological, seismological, and meteorological studies have been made at each site for estimating and minimizing environmental damage from the project?
- How will the impact of the project change with time?
- What environmental impacts will future urban growth, new industries, and other new developments have on project operations?
- Is the proposed site adequate for expansion of project operations in both the short and the long term?
- What are the estimated local and regional economic effects of this project?
- Do the project planning and design staffs include environmental and industrial pollution specialists?
- What effluent control limitations and technologies have been incorporated in the final plans for construction and operation of the project? What alternatives were considered?
- Do effluent limitations and standards conform to the laws and regulations of the country or locality in which the project is located? If not, what are the differences?
- Will the design include measures for preventing or minimizing air, water, and solid waste pollution and their effects on human settlements, agriculture, and other resources?
- Will upstream water users be affected if water close to them is used in industrial processing?
- Will future industrial growth in the region require more stringent and costly emissions control?
- How will installations situated downwind or downstream from the project be affected by the waste disposal measures?

- Are provisions being made for process control, recovery, or final disposal of solid wastes resulting from the application of environmental control measures?
- Are the potential synergistic or antagonistic effects of project wastes combined with other wastes or chemicals in the surrounding media being considered?

Operations

- Before operations begin on the project, what baseline data on the chemical and physical quality of the local environment will be collected to assist in evaluating project effects?
- Will the physical configuration and proposed process allow for future expansion or modification of pollution control facilities with a minimum of difficulty?
- What provisions will be made for initial and continued training of personnel responsible for pollution control and emergencies?
- What is the detailed plan for monitoring effluents after start-up of project operations?
- How will pollution control facilities be inspected, maintained, and repaired on a continuing basis?
- What safeguards will be applied to minimize the environmental effects of supporting activities, such as drilling, dredging, farming, transport, and loading?
- Will undesirable activities or conditions develop around the project, and how will such situations be handled?

Socioeconomic Factors

- What consideration has been given to the direct effects of the project on the locality and to the secondary effects on urban and regional activities?
- What environmental factors and local land use patterns are being considered in selecting the site, the technology, the scale of operations, and other related elements?
- What serious urban problems will be created by the influx of new residents as a result of the project?
- What measures will be taken to provide adequate housing, transport, health services, educational facilities, water supply,

and other community services for families that will be displaced or attracted by the project?

- Will the project's presence or operation preempt or interfere with other important land uses such as population redistribution, housing, tourism, agriculture, fisheries, and wildlife?
- What consideration will be given to disruptions in social and cultural patterns and practices caused by the project?
- Does the project design harmonize with the landscape? Are aesthetic considerations included in the landscaping and architectural plans?
- What measures are provided for preservation and management of historic, religious, geological, and archaeological sites and artifacts that could be adversely affected?
- Is the tourism industry important to the region, or will it be in the future? Are its interests likely to be affected by the project?

Health Impacts

- What health and sanitation problems will be created by the project?
- What measures are proposed for providing plant safety, industrial hygiene, and occupational health programs?
- Are health and safety measures and facilities for production workers incorporated in the overall project design and in construction?
- What measures will be taken to prevent exposure of construction workers and local inhabitants to undue health and safety risks?
- What warning systems are planned in the event of spills, accidents, and other emergencies?
- How will toxic materials resulting from accidental release or natural catastrophes be identified and handled?
- What provisions have been made to monitor and maintain safety equipment in working condition at all times?
- What provisions have been made to prevent contamination of groundwater from leakages or spills of toxic substances?
- What disease problems could be created by insect pests and other carriers as a result of waste-handling facilities?

- What provisions are being made for supplying potable water and disposing of human wastes?
- What health care systems will be available to the workers and their families during construction and after operations start? Can such systems be broadened to include the local population?
- Will health care facilities and staff meet acceptable standards for serving existing or future tourist needs?

Long-Term Considerations

- Are the plans for project location, level of operations, and long-term expansion compatible with overall long-range local and regional development plans?
- What provisions are made in the design to expand pollution control facilities in the event of major expansion of operations or stricter effluent limitations?
- Will this project attract additional development projects? Are the local environmental media capable of assimilating additional projects?

SEWERAGE AND SEWAGE TREATMENT

Development of Natural Resources

- Will the selection of the site and the choice of available technology include environmental considerations, such as effects on water quality and the resulting impact on the area's residents, fish, wildlife, and vegetation?
- Will alternative sites and alternative orientations on the selected site be considered?
- Have schemes been considered to recycle water for irrigation or industrial cooling purposes, or sludge for fertilizer?
- Has the plant been designed to serve as a regional resource, with thought given to expansion?

Project Design and Construction

- Will the project provide a system for domestic and industrial wastes separate from that for storm water? If separate systems are provided, what provision has been made for storm water drainage? If combined, what effects can be anticipated if the system overloads?

- Can the system be economically designed to accommodate or eliminate overloading problems, perhaps by means of storage or pumping or by separating the sewage and storm water components?
- Will the sewage system create new health problems by transporting and concentrating wastes at new locations?
- What effects will the sewage system have on the water supply?
- Is there a consolidated construction plan for the plant that takes into account urban plans as well as ecological factors?
- Are road patterns, land excavations, fill sites, and refuse disposal planned to minimize damage to the natural environment?
- What provisions have been made for restoring scarred sections of the construction area by filling, grading, and reseeding to prevent erosion?

Operations

- Will gases, odors, insects, and disease vectors be a problem?
- Will the proposed types of waste treatment equipment (for example, incinerators or digesters) cause air pollution?
- Are adequate air pollution controls provided?
- What type of sewage will the plant process—domestic, industrial, or mixed? What percentage of the waste in each category will be processed, and how effective will the treatment be for each type?
- What types of toxic materials, such as heavy metals, oils, and hydrocarbons, can be expected in raw sewage inputs?
- Will the plant be designed to remove toxic materials?
- What sewage ordinances are provided to protect the system and personnel from explosives and other dangerous material?
- What provisions have been made for the effective monitoring of plant effluents?
- What are the present and projected uses of the waterways into which the project effluent will be discharged? Will the level of treatment provided be compatible with these uses?

- Will sewage outfalls create additive or synergistic effects?
- What effect will the effluent have on the dissolved oxygen content of the receiving waters?
- What effects will the effluent have on the aquatic biota in the vicinity of the plant and downstream?
- Have seasonal variations in water flow, temperature, and level been considered?
- Will the project lead to thermal pollution of the waterway?
- What provisions have been made for training professional, technical, and operating manpower in the environmental aspects of the system's operation?
- What types of maintenance will be required? Will funds be available?
- Is jurisdictional responsibility clearly established to ensure the operation of the system in a manner that will protect or enhance the environment?

Socioeconomic Factors

- Has the site for the sewage treatment plant been selected to minimize impact on important cultural assets or on land use and economic activities of local residents?

Health Impacts

- How will waterborne diseases and vectors be controlled?
- What effect will the location of outfalls have on domestic and agricultural uses of the watercourses?
- Will the effluent be satisfactorily disinfected?
- What provision has been made for the disposal of sludge in a manner that will not adversely affect public health and welfare or the environment?

Long-Term Considerations

- Is the project designed so that the plant can be expanded in a manner consistent with protection of the environment?

TRANSPORT

Airports

Development of Natural Resources

- How will airport construction or expansion and attendant operations affect local residents and plant and animal life of the area?
- To what extent will the natural habitat of valuable species of fish and wildlife be affected? How can any such losses be mitigated?
- What effects will the airport and related uses of adjacent land have on the water table in the area?
- How will regional water drainage patterns be affected?
- Will increased water runoff from heavy rain or snow clog sewerage systems or drainage ditches?
- Will the disruption of natural water and drainage patterns complicate the operation of public water or sewer systems?

Project Design and Construction

- Are road patterns, land excavations, fill sites, refuse disposal activities, and so on planned so as to minimize damage to the environment?
- Will topsoil be stored for respreading?
- What provisions have been made for restoring scarred sections of the construction area by filling, grading, and reseeding to prevent erosion?
- Can the health of construction personnel be protected?
- Is there a danger that the work force will introduce new health hazards into the project area?

Operations

- What disposition will be made of airport wastes, including sewage, petroleum, and solid wastes?
- If dumped into ground "sinks," will wastes percolate into wells or aquifers?

- Will surface disposal degrade streams or wetlands as a result of leaching and runoff?
- Have monitoring criteria been established for key variables?
- How will waste disposal be monitored?
- What levels of noise can be expected from aircraft operations? How will this impact increase if the airport eventually expands?
- How can the disruptive effects of aircraft noise on local residents, schools, hospitals, and offices be held to acceptable levels?

Socioeconomic Factors

- Will management be provided to preserve and protect historic, religious, geological, or archaeological sites and artifacts?
- What provisions have been made for adequate housing for residents forced to resettle by the development?

Health Impacts

- Will there be monitoring and control of possible foreign disease vectors?
- Has a plan been prepared for controlling the introduction of animal and plant diseases?
- Have plans been made for the management and control of airport sanitation?

Long-Term Considerations

- Is the airport likely to attract industry and housing to adjacent areas? What impact would such developments have on the natural environment?
- What future projects have been planned for the area, and how will they interact with environmental factors?

Ports and Harbors

Development of Natural Resources

- What modifications of the landscape, waterways, and offshore geology will result from the development?

- Will these changes adversely affect fish and wildlife resources? If so, what measures are planned to mitigate the impact?
- What impact will the changes have on existing or projected sewerage or waste disposal systems?
- Will stagnant pools develop that will trap pollutants?
- Will stream discharge patterns be adversely affected?
- Is the project part of a coherent plan for the development of the region?

Project Design and Construction

- What are the existing patterns of coastal or waterway sedimentation?
- How will wave and current action be modified?
- Will the development interrupt sediment transport needed to replenish adjacent beach areas?
- Might induced tidal wash and currents cause beach and coastal erosion?
- If the development is on a river, how will it affect flooding and the upstream and downstream environment?
- What will be the source of landfill and rock materials, and what are the likely effects on the environment, both at the source and at the point of deposition?
- What provisions will be made for reclamation of quarry and borrow areas?

Operations

- What cargoes are likely to be handled, and what are the potential dangers to the environment from accidental or deliberate spills or dumping?
- Have accident contingency plans been formulated?
- Are measures available to handle emergencies or accidents such as spills or collisions?
- What safeguards and contingency plans will be available to contain and clean up hazardous chemicals and oils or wastes from normal operations?
- To what extent will land-filling and dredging operations be necessary?

- How will redredged spoils be disposed of, and with what ecological impacts?
- Will increased shipping and industrial production create significant air pollution because of the direction of prevailing winds?
- How will ship and harbor sewage and other effluents be handled?

Socioeconomic Factors

- What consideration has been given to providing adequate housing and essential community services, such as sewage and transport facilities, in preparation for the expected increase in population as a result of port and industrial development?
- Will port construction or operations adversely affect local cultural or economic values, such as scenic beauty and local fishing and other economic enterprises?
- Have steps been taken to provide for possible population influxes?
- Will historic, religious, archaeological, and geological artifacts be preserved?

Health Impacts

- Will air or water pollution associated with the port adversely affect local workers or adjacent populations?
- Will water supplies and sewage treatment facilities be adequate to meet increasing demands?
- Will health care services be adjusted to fit new requirements?
- Have plans been formulated for protecting people, animals, and plants from introduced diseases and for controlling these diseases?

Long-Term Considerations

- Have the environmental consequences of future area projects been considered in the design and operation of port facilities?

Roads and Highways

Development of Natural Resources

- Will environmental factors be incorporated into the selection of the road or highway route?
- Are the character, quality, and major components of the affected ecosystems known?
- Will access provided by the road open unsettled or previously inaccessible areas to human, animal, or plant communities?
- Will the road's impact on agricultural, industrial, commercial, or other urban land use patterns be considered?
- Does the project complement land use patterns developed for urban or regional programs?
- Will the road have adverse effects on important domestic livestock, wildlife, or vegetation?
- Will wildlife migration routes be disturbed?
- Will squatter settlements along the highway route be controlled?

Project Design and Construction

- Is there a consolidated construction plan for the project that takes into account ecological factors?
- Are forest conservation principles being incorporated into design and construction activities in forested areas?
- Will natural drainage patterns be damaged?
- Do plans include provisions for preventing despoilment of the landscape and vegetation during construction?
- Will clearing, grubbing, and burning be limited, to the extent practicable?
- Will the size and number of quarry, borrow, and disposal sites be controlled?
- Will topsoil be stored for respreading?
- Will soil stabilization measures such as reseeding be taken during construction to minimize erosion by wind or water?
- Do plans include provisions for preventing water pollution by spillage and runoff during construction or use of the roadway?

- Will water impoundments create health hazards?
- Will wastes from machinery, asphalt and concrete plants, and construction camps and shops be controlled to prevent water pollution?
- Will air pollution by smoke, fumes, and sprays originating from construction operations be a problem?
- Will air pollution by dust from unsurfaced roads or construction operations have a deleterious effect on the environment or on human welfare?
- Does the roadway traverse a scenic area? If so, are steps being taken to protect and enhance areas of aesthetic and tourist value?
- If a large work force is to be assembled from various locations, will applicants for employment be given medical screening and employees examined periodically to prevent the introduction or spread of endemic diseases?

Operations

- Will the road serve purposes other than transport?
- Will road shoulders and aprons provide space for strip urbanization or vendors?
- Will heavy traffic produce congestion, pollution, or noise, with adverse consequences to surrounding human, animal, or plant communities?
- Will traffic preempt or disrupt use of agricultural land?
- Will there be an adverse effect on the habitat and migration of wildlife?
- Will facilities be available to monitor traffic and its impact on important elements of ecosystems such as population settlements, migration patterns, diseases, surface water, and erosion?
- What will be the environmental effects of herbicides and pesticides if they are used?

Socioeconomic Factors

- Will the roadway disrupt existing cultures or affect archaeological sites or other unique resources?

• Has provision been made for adequate living conditions for populations that are displaced by construction activity and those that are attracted to newly opened areas?

Health Impacts

• Will the roadway and related construction activity open up new pathways for disease vectors affecting people, plants, or animals (for example, hoof and mouth disease)?

Long-Term Considerations

• Have the ecological and environmental effects of the project been examined in the context of local and regional plans for development?
• Have the effects of future highway or transport development on the ecology of the area been considered?

Appendix B
Information and Data Resources

Although the powerful role of information in all aspects of research and human endeavor is widely recognized, persons working in multidisciplinary fields have difficulty in gaining access to information because the sources are so diverse and scattered. The intrinsic value of information for the efficient use of production and acquisition processes and of human resources is often ignored. Organizations seldom include the cost of acquiring or distributing information in their budgets. Even when available, data accumulated in files, reports, and information systems are often underutilized or wasted. Thus, the search for relevant, timely, and cost-effective information can be complex.

This chapter is a guide to sources of data and information for development projects. The references include scientific, technological, socioeconomic, and legal information of interest to a variety of disciplines and professions. In addition, this chapter identifies some characteristic trends and problems of information retrieval and use. Since references change rapidly as new publications become available, these observations are intended to help in locating new sources in the future.

Definitions

Because problems with terminology can be a barrier to the understanding and easy use of diversified systems, it may be helpful to reexamine a few basic terms. *Data* (as in "data base") are the numeric or bibliographic descriptions of basic facts. *Numeric data bases* or *data banks* may include computerized indexes to and abstracts of journal articles, monographs, reports, legislation, and other documentary sources. Often, full texts of the sources are available. *Information* may be thought of as the total complex or any part of the data that people receive from the outside world and that contribute to their knowledge and understanding. Information may also mean the process by which people learn about themselves or each other.

Scientific and technical as well as socioeconomic information develops in the following stages:

- Generation of new data and research results by specialists in various fields
- Publication of primary reports, conference papers, or journal articles
- Review and synthesis, usually in the form of state-of-the-art papers
- Interpretation and application of new knowledge to a specific problem
- Evaluation of the application and the new development, usually in the context of the subjective opinion of a special interest group or of supporters of a particular policy
- Identification of further research needs and problems.

Trends in Information Access

Awareness of some trends can help in identifying the most appropriate sources for solving a particular problem.

- There has been a sharp increase in development research on social problems; scientific and technological factors are now being considered in the context of concern for the quality of life.
- This trend has been accompanied by the proliferation of information systems and services in multidisciplinary areas (for instance, coal research, nutrition research, and road research).
- Current emphasis is on transmitting research findings to the decisionmaker and practitioner and on sharing specialized information with members of other disciplines and professions. Consequently, the number of publications that present research findings in nontechnical language is growing.
- New technologies have opened up new possibilities for providing information. Many government agencies, private sector companies, and libraries offer computer-based literature searches. In addition, it is recognized that emphasis on communication and information-sharing networks must parallel technological developments. Brochures, bibliographies, user training programs, and the extension of use privileges are offered by most information providers.

- All kinds of international organizations—intergovernmental, nongovernmental, scientific, professional, commercial, and special interest—engage in disseminating information. Guides to their activities, their information services, and persons to contact are important resources in any part of the world.
- Large-scale diversification of information and data needs and sources has led to new types of intermediary services. In Washington, D.C., and many other locations, private information companies and brokers offer customized service for a fee. If time is limited, this resource might be used for building the necessary foundation for project planning.

Information Needs

In their efforts to plan, operate, and evaluate development projects, program officers, project managers, consultants, and others concerned with the environmental impact of the projects need data and information of various types—for example, specific facts; general background information about relevant processes, institutions, and policies; or continuous support from a personal intelligence network of sources. Because the information will be used to assess a range of environmental effects and to identify alternative solutions to a problem, the network of sources normally must span many fields of knowledge. It must cover scientific and technological developments and their social impact, and it should yield relevant and timely information in appropriate depth or convenient summary.

A personal intelligence network of sources normally includes:

- Information sources in print or other recorded form, usually located in libraries or obtainable from publishers or information distribution centers
- Information retrieval systems that can be accessed directly by the user or through an intermediary institution or organization
- Institutional resources in the public and private sectors (for example, agencies, corporations, task forces, commissions, interest groups)
- Personal expertise available through a formal referral service or informal channels.

Strategies for developing and using resources depend on the location of the information seeker and the constraints inposed by his or her circumstances. Ideally some of the data and information should be gathered from diverse sources in the literature during the prefeasibility phase of a project. Not all the intelligence needed can be acquired at headquarters, however. Once on the site the program officer or consultant will need specific information about the cultural, economic, and social characteristics of the site and its population, but the abundant and complex information resources mentioned earlier will not be available in the field. It is therefore important to know in advance what institutional information sources exist in published or unpublished form in the developing country or region in question.

Difficulties in Acquiring Information

A number of practical problems in identifying and obtaining information are characteristic of the multidisciplinary fields of development and environmental impact. Most important, it is difficult to identify relevant subdisciplines and determine the type of knowledge required to solve a problem. Several organizations that generate and collect developmental literature offer assistance with this problem. The International Development Research Center, Ottawa, Canada, has constructed a classification scheme for development literature. The United Nations Centro Latinamericano de Documentatión Económica y Social (CLADES) in Santiago, Chile, publishes PLANINDEX, in which reports and documents are selected and grouped by subject. The *United Nations Document Index* (UNDOC) contains country and subject indexes. The World Bank includes in its formal assessment process an evaluation of the environmental, health, and social implications of its projects on the ecology and cultural heritage of borrowing countries.

Other difficulties in gathering and using information may arise.

- It is not always possible to determine the source of information. Many program planning and evaluation reports have been produced by teams and do not show whether the emphasis of the report was provided by, for example, a water supply engineer, a public health expert, an economist, or an ecologist.

- Information that applies to several disciplines or sectors is often embedded in the literature of particular disciplines or sectors (for example, demography, biology, engineering, population and nutrition, tourism, or water supply and sewerage). Scientific and technical experts who focus on the resources of their own fields miss much relevant interdisciplinary literature.
- Documents often reflect the subjective perceptions and priorities of sponsoring organizations and authors. Reviews are invaluable aids in gaining a broader perspective (for example, *Advances in Ecological Research, Critical Reviews in Environmental Control,* or *Environmental Impact Assessment Review*).
- It is easier to identify a reference than to obtain the document itself. In the United States directories such as *Library and Reference Facilities in the Area of the District of Columbia* (White Plains, N.Y.: Knowledge Industry Publications, Inc., 1979) can lead one to special environmental or legal collections, maps, or statistical data. Many suppliers of computerized data bases, such as the Environment Information Center, Inc. (New York, N.Y.), supplier of ENERGYNET, ENVIROLINE, and ENERGYLINE, provide full texts of documents on microfiche. In developing countries, informal networks or resource people and agencies (planning and technical ministries, research institutes) are indispensable pathways to information. *The Register of Development Research Projects in Africa* (Paris: Organisation for Economic Co-operation and Development, 1979) is an example.
- The proliferation of new studies, research reports, and technical papers in the environmental field makes it hard to stay abreast of the latest developments. A current-awareness service is useful here; for example, the weekly *Current Contents: Agriculture, Biology and Environmental Sciences* and the bimonthly *Environmental Periodicals Bibliography* reprint the tables of contents of relevant journals; the *Hazardous Materials Intelligence Report* records regulations, spills, accidents, and new developments; and *Water Pollution Control* reports on policy and practice.
- Difficulties in obtaining information usually do not become obvious without first-hand experience in searching. Consequently, project plans hardly ever include enough funds and time for accessing complex environmental impact–related information.

Types of Information Resources

Resources include *recorded information* (documents, data sets, maps, drawings, patents, and so on); *institutional resources* (governments, intergovernmental organizations, research institutes, or industrial companies); and *human resources* (such as consultants, researchers, technical experts, and educators).

A strategy for identifying relevant knowledge will assist in building technical background for project planning, management, and evaluation. Two kinds of guides are available to the project planner and manager: guides describing methods of primary data collection, and sources leading to secondary publications such as technical reports, documents, journal articles, conference papers, and books. In the first category are Molly Hageboeck and others, *Manager's Guide to Data Collection* (Washington, D.C.: Practical Concepts, Inc., 1979); D. R. Mickelwait and others, *Information for Decision Making in Rural Development*, 2 vols. (Washington, D.C.: Development Alternatives, Inc., 1978); and the United Nations Industrial Development Organization, *Guide to Practical Project Appraisal* (New York: UNIPUB, 1978). The second category includes such sources as J. M. Morris and E. A. Elkins, *Library Searching: Resources and Strategies with Examples from the Environmental Sciences* (New York: Jeffrey Norton Publishers, 1978), and Vladimir Slamecka, ed., *Scientific and Technical Information Services for Socioeconomic Development* (Washington, D.C.: Information Science and Technology Institute, Inc., 1979).

An overview of multidisciplinary relationships may be gained from *Environmental Classification System* (Illinois Institute for Environmental Quality, 1977, available from the National Technical Information Service in Springfield, Va., as PB 266-113-AS). Next, it may be useful to consult the nearest national focal point of INFOTERRA (formerly International Referral System) of the United Nations Environment Programme (UNEP). This decentralized global network of information sources was mandated by the Governing Council of UNEP in 1972 to facilitate information exchange. National focal points of member nations have been making inventories of the environmental information sources in their own countries. The Programme Activity Centre (PAC) in Nairobi, Kenya, enters sources in a computerized directory that is regularly updated and sent to focal points, which can then refer queries to the sources. The U.S. national focal point, at the Environmental Protection Agency, has published the *Environmental Information Systems Directory*, an indexed listing of special collections and expertise in the United States. The United Nations publishes a *Directory of U.N. Information Systems and Services.*

Several sources published serially by the U.S. federal government supply information on other countries and their institutions. *Country Demographic Profiles* (U.S. Bureau of the Census) covers primarily developing countries and includes data on industry, labor, education, and other social and economic features. *The National Basic Intelligence Factbook* (U.S. Central Intelligence Agency) is a semiannual compilation of information on the economy, land, and water of all countries. *Area Handbooks* (U.S. Army) may be used for background information on national cultures, history, and social and economic conditions. *Post Reports* (U.S. Department of State), available on microfiche only, give information on government institutions, climate, and local social conditions.

Examples of other information sources found in libraries and information centers are listed below, by category. The same types of publications and services are available, to a lesser degree, in the libraries and documentation centers of most developing countries. (Computerized systems are gradually being introduced in the higher-income developing countries.) Many of the listed publications are obtainable directly from the sponsoring organization, the publisher, or the distributor.

Bibliographies

The most up-to-date lists of publications can serve as guides to recent research and to methodologies and findings on impact evaluation. Vance Bibliographies (P.O. Box 229, Monticello, Ill. 61856) are compiled by experts and cover many specialized topics related to environmental impact. Recent examples include reclamation of surface coal mines, development of the international oil industry, and transfer of technology.

Bibliographies published at regular periods include the monthly *World Transindex: Announcing Translations in all Fields of Science and Technology* (International Translations Centre, 101 Doelenstraat, Delft, Netherlands), and *EPA Reports Bibliography Quarterly*

(National Technical Information Service, Springfield, Va.). Many international journals carry bibliographies of recent publications, for example, the quarterly *Interdisciplinary Science Reviews* (Heyden and Son, Inc., 247 South 41 Street, Philadelphia, Pa. 19104); *Development Dialogue*, a journal of international development cooperation (Dag Hammarskjöld Foundation, Ovre Slottsgatan 2, 752 20 Uppsala, Sweden); and the *International Journal of the Environment* (Pergamon Press, Elmsford, N.Y.).

Indexing and Abstracting Services

These analytic reference sources report on recent monographs, journal articles, conference proceedings, environmental impact statements, and other primary publications. *Applied Science and Technology Index, Biological Abstracts, Biological and Agricultural Index, British Technology Index, Chemical Abstracts, Energy Index, Engineering Index, Environment Abstracts*, and *Index Medicus* may be found in the large research libraries of most countries. *Irrigation and Drainage Abstracts, Rural Development Abstracts*, and other specialized services of the Commonwealth Agricultural Bureau are marketed by UNIPUB (345 Park Avenue South, New York, N.Y. 10010).

Some of the more specialized tools are difficult to locate in the collections of developing countries. If they are expected to be needed in the environmental assessment of a development project, it is advisable to use them before the project mission to the developing country begins. Examples are *Air Pollution Abstracts, Applied Ecology Abstracts, EIS: Digests of Environmental Impact Statements*, PLANINDEX, *Pollution Abstracts, Selected Water Resources Abstracts*, and *The World Bank Research Program Abstracts of Current Studies*. (A more complete list appears in *Ulrich's International Periodicals Directory*.)

Bibliographic Data Bases

Most of the indexing and abstracting services listed above are available in machine-readable form for a fee. The information industry includes organizations and companies that produce bibliographic data bases, distributors whose computer systems can be contacted from a computer terminal, and suppliers who combine data-base compilation and distribution.

Many libraries act as intermediaries and offer the assistance of experienced literature searchers. New data bases, search capabilities, and costs are provided in Martha Williams, *Computer-readable Databases: A Directory and Data Sourcebook* (White Plains, N.Y.: Knowledge Industry Publications, 1979), a source that is frequently updated. Lists and descriptions of data bases and terms of search are available from most libraries that offer the service.

Another useful publication is *Online Review*, which provides descriptions of new data bases. Examples of data bases are AGRICOLA (National Agricultural Library), APILIT (American Petroleum Institute), ENERGYLINE, ENVIROLINE, and ENERGYNET (Environment Information Center, Inc.), ENVIRONMENTAL IMPACT STATEMENTS (Information Resources Press), GEOREF (American Geological Institute), NTIS Bibliographic Data File (National Technical Information Service), SSIE (Smithsonian Science Information Exchange), and SWIRS (Solid Waste Information Retrieval System). The following data bases are especially useful for development projects: ECONOMICS ABSTRACTS (Netherlands Ministry of Economic Affairs), AIR ECOLOGY SYSTEM (U.S. Environmental Protection Agency), AGRICULTURAL ECONOMICS (U.S. Department of Agriculture), INTERNATIONAL LABOUR DOCUMENTATION (International Labour Office), and POLLUTION ABSTRACTS (Data Courier, Inc.). On-line data bases may be accessed by several commercial systems, for example, BRS (Bibliographic Retrieval Services, Inc.), DIALOG (Lockheed Information Systems), and ORBIT (System Development Corporation).

Information Dissemination Systems and Institutional Resources

Recognizing the need for information coordination and dissemination in support of development objectives, several international governmental and nongovernmental organizations have established multipurpose information systems. Based on the cooperation of national centers, each responsible for identifying and recording relevant documents in its own territory, these international systems have developed large-scale data bases on such topics as agriculture, technical cooperation, the peaceful uses of nuclear science, science policy, and transnational corporations. Information has been disseminated by distributing data bases to cooperating countries, by publishing technical findings, by answering queries, by compiling directories of experts, and by organizing workshops and seminars. For example, AGRIS (the International Information System for the Agricultural Sciences and Technology, established by the FAO) covers, among other topics, food and nutrition, forestry, natural resources, and pollution; and *Agrindex*, a monthly bulletin issued by the FAO, highlights documents contributed by participating countries. Similarly INIS, the International Nuclear Information System, was set up in Vienna by the International Atomic Energy Agency, and Unesco sponsored SPINES, the Information Exchange System on Science Policies.

The following systems disseminate information for development projects or link development specialists in cooperative networks:

- The African Bibliographic Center is a nonprofit organization in Washington, D.C., funded by the U.S. Agency for International Development (AID). Its goal is to meet information needs on African affairs abroad and in the United States. SADEX (Southern Africa Development Information/Documentation Exchange) is an index to publications.

- The American Society for Public Administration, Section on International and Comparative Administration (ASPCA/SICA), Africa Committee, has established a network of individuals with skills in areas of special need.

- The Development Reference Service (DRS) is operated by the Society for International Development in Rome. The question-and-answer service operates through a worldwide network of correspondents, some of whom themselves act as relays within their own national or professional networks.

- The Development Resources Information System (DEVSIS) of the International Development Research Centre includes bibliographic records of the economic and social development literature. Regional centers are in various phases of development.

- The Energy for Rural Development Network (ERDINET) proposes to link eight countries for research cooperation, information exchange, and information resource sharing. The plan is sponsored by the East-West Center, Honolulu, Hawaii. Participating countries are Bangladesh, India, Indonesia, Nepal, the Philippines, Sri Lanka, Thailand, and the United States.

- The International Irrigation Information Centre (IIIC) in Bet Dagan, Israel, has an effective publication program and serves as a clearinghouse for experts and projects.

- The Land Tenure Center of the University of Wisconsin, Madison, funded by AID, engages in research, formal education and short-term workshops, publication and library programs, consulting and technical assistance, and formation of linkages with other organizations.

- PLANINDEX is published twice yearly by the United Nations Economic Commission for Latin America (ECLA/CEPAL) and is produced by CLADES. The index provides summaries of studies, plans, and research on the subject of development planning in the region. Copies of documents referenced may be obtained from CEPAL/CLADES, Casilla 179-D, Santiago, Chile.
- The AID-supported Program for Advanced Studies in Institution Building and Technical Assistance Methodology (PASITAM) at Indiana University, Bloomington, publishes various information packages: Design Notes, Design Studies, and Papers.
- The Sahel Institute's RESADOC, in Bamako, Mali, is a scientific and technical documentation and information network under the sponsorship of the Permanent Interstate Committee for Drought Control in the Sahel (CILSS). The network, sponsored by AID, links sectoral centers, the documentation services of administrative offices, research and training institutions, and specialized regional centers.
- Servicio Interamericano de Información sobre Desarrollo Urbano (SINDU) of Bogotá, Colombia, has developed a data base and printed directory of Latin American development agencies, research centers, and university departments. It emphasizes urban development, but it also lists references to rural development organizational expertise.
- The Technical Assistance Information Clearinghouse (TAICH), developed by the American Council of Voluntary Agencies for Foreign Service with assistance from AID, has announced a referral service, INTERDEX, which provides information on private voluntary organizations in the United States.
- Technical Cooperation among Developing Countries (TCDC), a special unit of the United Nations Development Programme (UNDP), has established a data base on the technical capacities of developing countries through its information referral system.
- Volunteers in Technical Assistance (VITA) responds to questions through its inquiry and documentation services and searches the literature for users in developing countries; with a grant from Control Data Corporation, VITA computerizes abstracts of inquiries it has answered correctly.

While the specialized agencies of the United Nations and other large intergovernmental organizations have been developing cooperative information systems in interdisciplinary areas, a number of governmentally or privately subsidized regional and national organizations provide access to more narrowly focused information. Activities range from in-house compilations of research and data through technical workshops to the dissemination of information products. Institutional resources are listed at the end of this chapter. Several directories of organizations and information systems, listed in this guide, will assist the searcher in identifying potentially interesting institutional resources.

Distance and time limitations may adversely influence the usefulness of information. Program officers and other development specialists most often look for promptly available information in making environmental decisions at each part of the project cycle. Large-scale international information systems, scattered around the world, may not always prove responsive to these immediate needs. The decisionmaker may therefore want to break information gathering into two stages.

In the phases of project identification, preparation, and appraisal, the decisionmaker can contact organizations in the United States that operate information exchange networks. The Center for Research in Water Resources at the University of Texas in Austin, for example, has developed exchange relationships with the International Hydrology Program, the International Association of Hydrological Centers, the International Water Resources Association, and others. Thus, documents of several widely scattered organizations may be obtained from a single source. The directory published by the U.S. national focal point of UNEP at the U.S. Environmental Protection Agency serves as a link to sources with networking capabilities.

Once work begins at the project site, the team of specialists will find that the search for information resources in the United States and other industrialized countries is too time-consuming and the information they offer is irrelevant to local conditions. Yet data are critically needed to make adjustments in project planning, operations, or evaluation. Local agencies and organizations in developing countries that might provide information include government agencies, regional planning bodies, development banks, scientific and technological information centers, industrial documentation centers, and scientific societies. Sometimes technical assistance projects are evaluated by local agricultural, medical, and scientific research centers that also study particular problems of the area. Such centers may have data files and unpublished documents that are not yet obsolete.

As increasing sociocultural understanding of the impact of development on the local population and environment has become necessary, planning and development documentation centers have been established in many countries. The Consejo Nacional Desarrollo Económico y Social in Peru and the Institute of Social and Economic Research of the University of the West Indies in Jamaica attest to this trend. Special missions sent to examine conditions in a certain sector should contact the relevant sectoral planning and research institutes to gather information. World Bank missions such as those in Abidjan and Nairobi are likely links to indigenous data sources. The national focal point of UNEP should be contacted as a first step to identify nearby environmental information collections. In addition, the official gazette issued by most central governments is a source for locating records and documents of government agencies even if they have not been disseminated through the traditional literature. The Library of Congress publishes bibliographies of official publications of various countries which help to identify government agencies that issue documents. International lists of journals and bulletins may lead to institutions engaged in industrial development and environmental protection. Examples of such journals and their publishing agencies are: *Mineral Wealth*, Directorate of Geology and Mining, Government of Gujarat, India; *African Journal of Ecology* (formerly *East African Wildlife Journal*), East African Wildlife Society; *Coal and Steel*, Indian Mine Managers' Association, India; *Monthly Bulletin*, Ministry of Mines and Hydrocarbons, Venezuela; *Monthly Bulletin*, Ministry of Petroleum and Mines, West Indies; *Nigerian Mining and Geo-Sciences Society Journal*.

Sources on Evaluating Scientific, Technical, and Socioeconomic Data

Although descriptive reports, monographs, and other textual sources are useful in gathering information for the support of development projects, the staff will need primary data indicating the demographic, economic, sociocultural, environmental, and health conditions of a population. It has often been stated in the literature that defining and measuring the quality of human life and the changes in quality introduced by project interventions are among the most difficult tasks in the development process. At its best, the assessment effort draws on the conceptual approaches and methodologies of several disciplines. Members of an interdisciplinary team may improve their communication with each other initially by collecting scientific glossaries and handbooks to clarify nomenclature, measurement concepts, and techniques that do not pertain to their primary discipline. The *Environmental Impact Statement Glossary* (New York: Plenum, 1979), for example, gives multiple definitions of terms. Then, as the team prepares to specify the objectives of the project, it will need sources to assist in identifying indicators for measuring the impact of intervention. A further need for information sources arises as decisions have to be made on appropriate data collection techniques to be used to identify local conditions. The project staff could also use some basic sources to locate repositories of local scientific, technical, and socioeconomic data.

Problems of environmental measurements and indicators have been recognized as conceptual, methodological, and cultural. Discussions in the literature range from L. W. Milbrath's broad descriptive approach in "Policy-relevant Quality of Life Research" (*American Academy of Political and Social Science Annals*, vol. 444, 1979) to the specific observations in C. L. G. Bell and P. B. R. Hazell, "Measuring the Indirect Effects of an Agricultural Investment Project on its Surroundings" (*American Journal of Agricultural Economics*, vol. 62, no. 1, 1980). It is essential to distinguish between two kinds of publications on indicators: those pertaining to the measurement of conditions of a particular area, population, or impact, and those describing general approaches to theoretical and methodological problems. An example of the latter is *Indicators of Environmental Quality and the Quality of Life* (Paris: Unesco, 1978).

The collection, evaluation, and dissemination of scientific, technical, and socioeconomic data have spawned a literature so extensive that observers comment more frequently on information overload than on accessibility of data. A few key sources will assist the user in cutting through the maze. The Committee on Data for Science and Technology (CODATA) of the International Council of Scientific Unions in Paris publishes *CODATA Bulletin*, each issue of which is devoted to the data requirements and resources of a specific scientific field. The *CODATA Newsletter* announces new techniques, data centers, and publications as they become available.

The organization works to improve the quality of critical evaluation, standardization, and dissemination methods through data centers and networks.

In the United States, the recently established International Association for Impact Assessment endeavors to bridge the interests of data users in the scientific and technical fields and in the social sciences. Plans include publication of a bulletin and information exchange among members. *Environment Impact Assessment Review*, published quarterly by Plenum Press, includes scientific papers, summaries of research reports, and announcements of new organizations concerned with data sources for impact evaluation.

Other types of information resources related to numeric data are:

- Handbooks, manuals, and monographs dealing with the collection, analysis, and evaluation of data, for example, Robert Rosen, *Fundamentals of Measurement and Representation of Natural Systems* (New York: Elsevier North-Holland, Inc., 1978)

- Specialized sources on the development of indicators in particular sectors and under specific circumstances, for example, *Indicators for Evaluating Transport Output* (Paris: OECD, 1979), and *Urban Environment Indicators* (Paris: OECD, 1978)

- Sources on national and international environmental standards and their applications, for example, *Guidelines for Assessing Industrial Environmental Impact and Environmental Criteria for the Siting of Industry* (Nairobi: UNEP, 1980)

- Project reports describing methods for including local participation in planning and evaluation, for example, Michael M. Cernea, *Measuring Project Impact: Monitoring and Evaluation in the PIDER Rural Development Project—Mexico* (Washington, D.C.: World Bank, 1979)

- Case studies of the use of data systems to support management and decisionmaking, for example, those in D. R. Mickelwait and others, *Information for Decision Making in Rural Development*

- Registries of development research projects which lead to the identification of specialized expertise and experience in various countries, including the *Register of Development Research Projects in Africa* (Paris: OECD, 1979)

- Directories of data centers, data banks, and numeric data bases that may be accessed in the United States and other countries, for example, *Information Systems for Soil and Related Data* (1981), and *Factual Data Banks in Agriculture* (1978), both issued by the Centre for Agricultural Publishing and Documentation (PUDOC), Wageningen, Netherlands.

Guides to Current Developments

Information is not only for the specific task of solving problems or making decisions but also to help development specialists keep abreast of research in their fields. In the face of rapid changes in scientific knowledge and technology, however, development specialists find it increasingly difficult to keep up to date even in their own specializations. Research has shown that the following types of sources have been most effective for maintaining at least a modest degree of currency in new developments in a field.

- The informal exchange of information among peers in the same discipline as well as in related areas has long been a favorite mode of communication. Its widespread practice has been demonstrated by such publications as S. G. Barry, *Indexes to Expertise: An Examination of Practical Systems* (London: British Library, 1976).
- State-of-the-art reviews synthesize and evaluate, usually annually, new theories, methods, practices, and policy issues. *Advances in Environmental Sciences and Technology* (New York: Wiley-Interscience) is an example.
- Several publications reproduce the tables of contents of key journals; for instance, the weekly *Current Contents: Agriculture, Biology and Environmental Sciences* (Philadelphia: Institute for Scientific Information), and the quarterly *International Bibliography Information Documentation* (New York: UNIPUB). The latter covers mainly periodicals and series of international organizations.
- Various newsletters, bulletins, and announcement services bring summaries of research reports, conferences, and new technical publications to the scientist's desk. Some are available by paid subscription; others are free of charge upon request. *Issue Alert* (New York: Environment Information Center) highlights the most significant references in *Environment Abstracts* and also sells full-size or microfiche copies of the highlighted documents. *Reports* (International Development Research Centre) is being used worldwide for development news.

- Summaries of lengthy documents are available by subscription. *EIS: Digests of Environmental Impact Statements* (Arlington, Va.: Information Resources Press) abstracts and indexes impact statements issued by the federal government. Full and microfiche copies may be purchased from the same source.
- Some information systems provide abstracts of research in progress, organized by topic. The abstracts of the Smithsonian Science Information Exchange (SSIE) are available in machine-readable form. Examples of more narrowly focused research inventory files include *Current Agricultural Research for Developing Countries (CARIS)* and the *World Survey of Current Research and Development on Roads and Road Transport*. An overview of such systems and their publications can be found in *Information Services on Research in Progress: A Worldwide Inventory* (Smithsonian Science Information Exchange and Unesco, 1978).
- Organizations, associations, and publishers maintain large mailing lists and announce free of charge the availability of new publications and other information resources. For example, a leaflet of the American Society for Testing and Materials lists all forty-eight volumes of the *1981 Annual Book of ASTM Standards*.

Cartographic Sources

Developmental work and impact assessment may require topographic, geologic, soil, vegetation, weather, or thematic-statistical maps. Maps may be purchased or acquired free of charge directly from the producing organization, or they may be used in libraries. The World Bank's map collection is an excellent source, and the Library of Congress houses a collection of 3.5 million maps and charts. The *World Directory of Map Collections* (The Hague: International Federation of Library Associations and Institutions, 1976) and *Map Collections in the United States and Canada*, 2d ed. (New York: Special Libraries Association, 1976) will lead to other, often highly specialized, collections. Sources that describe worldwide mapping activities and technical aspects of working with cartographic materials include the annual *World Cartography*, issued by the United Nations, and G. C. Dickinson, *Maps and Air Photographs*, 2d ed. (New York: Halsted Press, 1979).

Maps may be purchased from federal agencies. The *Guide to U.S. Government Maps* (Document Index, Box 195, McLean, Va. 22101), available by annual subscription, can be used for identification. The Defense Mapping Agency (DMA) (U.S. Naval Observatory, Bldg. 59, Washington, D.C. 20305) publishes medium-scale topographic maps of foreign areas and also makes map collections available in its depository libraries. Another source is the National Ocean Survey (Riverdale, Md. 20840).

Still useful as a guide to direct acquisition of cartographic sources in other countries is the *Worldwide Directory of National Earth-Science Agencies*, U.S. Geological Survey Circular 716 (Washington, D.C., 1975).

Acquiring documents and other resources directly from the producer or distributor is often the most efficient way to construct collections for project support. Orders for publications may be placed from the United States or abroad; charges will include out-of-country postage, if applicable. Distributors of UN documents are found all over the world; the UN publications offices in New York and Geneva can provide lists. The next section gives a brief list of useful sources.

Institutional Resources

This section contains addresses and, where available, telephone numbers and cable addresses for sources for relevant publications and other forms of information. Notes on special services are included. In addition, the *Yearbook of International Organizations* (published biennially by the Union of International Associations, Brussels, and distributed by Gale Research Company, Book Tower, Detroit, Mich. 48226) is an excellent source for addresses and descriptions of international organizations, both governmental and nongovernmental.

International Organizations

ARCT   African Regional Centre for Technology, BP 2435, Dakar, Senegal; telephone: 22 77 12, 22 17 13; cables: CRATEX SG—DAKAR

CHEC   Commonwealth Human Ecology Council, 63 Cromwell Road, London, S.W. 7, United Kingdom; telephone: 373 6761; cables: CHEC LONDON SW 7

CIEI   Center for International Environment Information, c/o UNA–USA, 345 East 46 Street, New York, N.Y. 10017; telephone: (212) 697-3232

ECA   Economic Commission for Africa, P.O. Box 3001, Addis Ababa, Ethiopia; telephone: 44 72 00; cables: ECA ADDIS ABABA

ECE   Economic Commission for Europe, Palais des Nations, CH-1211 Geneva 10, Switzerland; telephone: 34-60-11, 31-02-11; cables: UNATIONS GENEVA

ECLA   Economic Commission for Latin America, Edificio Naciones Unidas, Avenida Dag Hammarskjöld 3030, Vitacura, Santiago, Chile; telephone: 40-04-31; cables: UNATIONS SANTIAGO

ECOSOC   Economic and Social Council, United Nations, New York, N.Y. 10017; telephone: (212) 754-3354; cables: UNATIONS NEW YORK

ESCAP   Economic and Social Commission for Asia and the Far East, Sala Santitham, Rajadamnern Avenue, Bangkok 2, Thailand; telephone: 2829161–200; cables: ESCAP BANGKOK

FAGS   Federation of Astronomical and Geophysical Sciences, Royal Greenwich Observatory, Hailsham, East Sussex, BN27 1RP, United Kingdom

FAO   Food and Agriculture Organization, Via delle Terme di Caracalla, 1-00100 Rome, Italy; telephone: 57971; cables: FOODAGRI ROME

GATT   General Agreement on Tariffs and Trade, Villa la Fenêtre, Palais des Nations, CH-1211 Geneva 10, Switzerland; telephone: 34-60-11, 32-02-11; cables: GATT GENEVA

HABITAT   United Nations Center for Human Settlements, P.O. Box 30030, Nairobi, Kenya; telephone: 332383; cables: UNITERRA

IAEA   International Atomic Energy Agency, Kärntnerring 11, A-1010 Vienna 1, Austria; telephone: Vienna 2360-0; cables: INATOM VIENNA

IAMBE   International Association for Medicine and Biology of the Environment, 115, rue de la Pompe, F-75116 Paris, France; telephone: 553-45-04; cables: ECOMEBIO PARIS

IARC	International Agency for Research on Cancer, 150 cours Albert Thomas, F-69372 Lyon, France; telephone: 875 81 81; cables: UNICANCER
IAWL	International Association for Water Law, Via Montevideo 5, 1-00198 Rome, Italy; telephone: 845-7685
IAWPR	International Association on Water Pollution Research, c/o Institut für Hydrobiologie, Olbersweg 24, 2 Hamburg-50, Federal Republic of Germany; telephone: 04-11-39107
ICAO	International Civil Aviation Organization, International Aviation Square, 1000 Sherbrooke Street, West Montreal, Canada; telephone: 285 8219; cables: ICAO MONTREAL
ICEF	International Committee for Research and Study of Environmental Factors, Ave. Franklin Roosevelt 50, C.P. 196, B-1050 Brussels, Belgium; telephone: 649 00 30, ext. 2511
ICEL	International Council of Environmental Law, Adenauerallee 214, D-5300 Bonn, Federal Republic of Germany; telephone: 49 22 21
ICSU	International Council of Scientific Unions, Via Cornelio Celso 7, 00161 Rome, Italy
IDRC	International Development Research Centre, P.O. Box 8500, Ottawa K 1G 3H9, Canada; telephone: (613) 996-2321; cables: RECENTRE. Regional offices: P.O. Box 30677, Nairobi, Kenya; B.P. 11007, C.D. Annexe, Dakar, Senegal; Tanglin P.O. Box 101, Singapore 9124, Republic of Singapore; Apartado Aereo 53016 Bogotá D.E., Colombia; P.O. Box 14 Orman, 40E1 Messaha St. Dokki-Giza, Cairo, Egypt. With an extensive research, development, and publication program, the center serves as an effective contact point in several regions.
IFS	International Foundation for Science, Box 5073, Stockholm 5, Sweden; telephone: 08-22-0760
IIED	International Institute for Environment and Development, 10 Percy St., London W1P ODR, United Kingdom; telephone: 580 7656; cables: EARTHSCAN LONDON W1

IIIC	International Irrigation Information Centre, P.O. Box 49, Bet Dagan, Israel; telephone: 03 940356; cables: IRRICENTER
IITA	International Institute of Tropical Agriculture, Oyo Road, PMB 5320, Ibadan, Nigeria; telephone: 23741; cables: TROPFOUND IKEJA
ILO	International Labour Organisation, 4 Route de Morillons, CH-1211 Geneva 22, Switzerland; telephone: 99 61 11; cables: INTERLAB GENEVA
IMO	Inter-Governmental Maritime Organization (includes Maritime Environmental Protection Committee), 101-104 Piccadilly, London W1V OAE, United Kingdom; telephone: 01 499 9040; cables: INMARCOR LONDON W1
IOC	Intergovernmental Oceanographic Commission, 7, Place de Fontenoy, F-75700 Paris, France; telephone: 577 16 10, ext. 2456
ISES	International Solar Energy Society, National Science Centre, 191 Royal Parade, P.O. Box 52, Parkville, Melbourne, Victoria 3052, Australia; telephone: 347 4941; cables: ENGRESEARCH
ISTE	International Society for Tropical Ecology, Department of Botany, Banaras Hindu University, Varanasi 221005, India
ITC	International Institute for Aerial Survey and Earth Sciences, 350 Boulevard 1945, P.O. Box 6, Enschede, Netherlands; telephone: 053-320220; cables: AERSUR-ENSCHEDE
IUBS	International Union of Biological Sciences, 51, Bd. de Montmorency, F-75016 Paris, France; telephone 525 00 09; cables: ICSU 630553 F
IUCN	International Union for the Conservation of Nature and Natural Resources, Ave. du Mont-Blanc, CH-1196 Gland, Switzerland; telephone: (022) 64 32 54; cables: IUCNATURE GLAND
IUFRO	International Union of Forestry Research Organizations, Norwegian Forest Research Institute, Aas NLH, Norway

OAS	Organization of American States, Pan American Union Building, 17th St. and Constitution Avenue, N.W., Washington, D.C. 20006; telephone: (202) 789-3000; cables: OAS WASHINGTON
OECD	Organisation for Economic Co-operation and Development, 2, rue André Pascal, F-75116 Paris, France; telephone: 524-82-00; cables: DEVELOPECONOMIE. Publications and Information Center: Suite 1207, 1750 Pennsylvania Ave. N.W., Washington, D.C. 20006; telephone: (202) 724-1857. Publications list is available free of charge.
PAHO	Pan American Health Organization, 525 23rd Street, N.W., Washington, D.C. 20037; telephone: (202) 861-3200; cables: OFSANPAN WASHINGTON
UN	United Nations. Publications, United Nations, Room A-3315, New York, N.Y. 10017; telephone: (212) 754-3354; cables: UNATIONS NEW YORK. Geneva office: Palais des Nations, CH-1211 Geneva 10, Switzerland; telephone: 34-60-11, 31-02-11; cables: UNATIONS GENEVA
UNCTAD	United Nations Conference on Trade and Development, Palais des Nations, CH-1211 Geneva 10, Switzerland; telephone: 34-60-11, 31-02-11; cables: UNATIONS GENEVA
UNDP	United Nations Development Programme, 866 United Nations Plaza, New York, N.Y. 10017; telephone: (212) 754-1234; cables: UNDEVPRO NEW YORK
UNEP	United Nations Environment Programme, P.O. Box 30552, Nairobi, Kenya; telephone: 333930; cables: UNITERRA NAIROBI; telex: 22068 UNITERRA. Includes Environment Programme Information Centre, Global Environmental Monitoring System (GEMS), International Centre for Industry and the Environment (ICIE), and International Referral System for Sources of Environmental Information (INFOTERRA). All referral services are free of charge.
Unesco	United Nations Educational, Scientific, and Cultural Organization (includes Intergovernmental Oceanographic Commission, IOC), 7, Place de Fontenoy, F-75700 Paris, France; telephone: 577 16 10; cables: UNESCO PARIS

UNESOB   United Nations Economic and Social Office in
          Beirut, United Nations Building, Beirut, Lebanon;
          telephone: 27-29-27, 27-29-28, 27-30-25; cables:
          UNATIONS BEIRUT

UNIDO   United Nations Industrial Development Organiza-
          tion, Vienna International Centre, P.O. Box 300,
          A-1400 Vienna, Austria; telephone: 26 310; cables:
          UNIDO VIENNA

UNIPUB   345 Park Avenue South, New York, N.Y. 10010.
          Commercial distributor for FAO, UNDP, Unesco,
          UNIDO, UNITAR, WHO, and other intergovernmental
          organizations, each of which has a separate docu-
          ment dissemination system. Publishes *International
          Bibliography, Information, Documentation* (IBID), which
          lists monographs and tables of contents of periodicals
          of intergovernmental organizations.

UNITAR   United Nations Institute for Training and Research,
          801 United Nations Plaza, New York, N.Y. 10017;
          telephone: (212) 754-8621; cables: UNINSTAR NEW
          YORK

WEC   World Environment Center, 605 Third Avenue,
          17th floor, New York, N.Y. 10158; telephone: (212)
          986-7200

WHO   World Health Organization. Headquarters: CH 1211
          Geneva 27, Switzerland; telephone: 91 21 11; cables:
          UNISANTE GENEVA. Regional Office for Africa: P.O.
          Box No. 6, Brazzaville, People's Republic of the
          Congo; telephone: 813860

WMO   World Meteorological Organization, 41, avenue
          Giuseppe-Motta, CH-1211 Geneva, Switzerland;
          telephone: 34-64-00; cables: METEOMOND
          GENEVA

WWF   World Wildlife Fund, Ave. du Mont-Blanc,
          CH-1196 Gland, Switzerland; telephone:
          (022) 64 19 24

U.S. Sources

U.S. Department of State, Agency for International Development, Washington, D.C. 20523. Addresses of missions and overseas offices are listed in the *United States Government Manual*.

U.S. Department of State, Office of Public Communications, Bureau of Public Affairs, Room 5821, 2201 C Street, N.W., Washington, D.C. 20520. The series *Background Notes* and *Area Handbooks* are useful for information about other countries. They are also available for purchase from the Superintendent of Documents, U.S. Government Printing Office.

U.S. General Accounting Office, Distribution Section, Room 1518, Washington, D.C. 20548. Reports listed in the *Monthly List of GAO Reports* are available free of charge.

U.S. Government Printing Office, Superintendent of Documents, Washington, D.C. 20402. Requests should include sponsoring agency, title of document, and stock number (S/N), if available. Prepayment is required.

U.S. International Environmental Referral Center (USIERC), U.S. Environmental Protection Agency, PM-213, 401 M Street, S.W., Room 2902 WSM, Washington, D.C. 20460; cables: EPAWSH; telex: 892758. Serves as the U.S. national focal point for INFOTERRA.

U.S. National Technical Information Service (NTIS), U.S. Department of Commerce, 5285 Port Royal Road, Springfield, Va. 22161; telephone: (703) 487-4600. Central source for government-sponsored research and development reports. Selling agent for EPA technical documents. Offers both printed abstracting services and the computerized NTIS data base.

U.S. Smithsonian Science Information Exchange (SSIE), 1730 M Street, N.W., Room 300, Washington, D.C. 20036. Collects, indexes, and disseminates information about ongoing research in all areas of the physical and life sciences. Literature searches are conducted for a fee. The SSIE data base is also available commercially.

Bibliography

The general and topical source materials listed here indicate the kinds of publications available rather than the full scope of the vast literature that touches on environmental assessment. Citations are organized alphabetically within the following categories:

- General references
- Agriculture
- Development and environment
- Energy resources
- Industry
- Legal sources
- Pollution
- Public health
- Sewerage and sewage treatment plants
- Standards and measurement
- Technology transfer and appropriate technology
- Transport
- Urban development
- Utilities
- Water resources

Note: Inquiries about documents issued by the Environment, Science, and Technology Unit, the Office of Environmental and Health Affairs, the Office of Environmental Affairs, and the Office of Environmental and Scientific Affairs should all be directed to the Office of Environmental and Scientific Affairs of the World Bank, the current name of that unit.

General References

Bibliographies

Agricultural Research Index. 2 vols. Guernsey, U.K.: Francis Hodgson, 1979.
Agriculture: An Annotated Bibliography. Philadelphia, Pa.: Heyden, 1981.

Berry, J. K. "Spatial Information Systems: 'Instant' Maps for Analyzing Natural Resources Data." *Special Libraries*, vol. 72, no. 3 (July 1981), pp. 261–69.

Bibliographic Guide to Government Publications: Foreign, 1980. 2 vols. Boston, Mass.: G. K. Hall & Co., 1981.

Bibliographic Guide to Latin American Studies: 1980. 3 vols. Boston, Mass.: G. K. Hall & Co., 1981.

Bibliographic Guide to Law: 1980. 2 vols. Boston, Mass.: G. K. Hall & Co., 1981.

Bibliographic Guide to Technology: 1980. 2 vols. Boston, Mass.: G. K. Hall & Co., 1981.

Bloch, C. C. *Coal Information Sources and Data Bases.* Park Ridge, N. J.: Noyes Data Corporation, 1980.

Clark, B. D., and others. *Environmental Impact Assessment, A Bibliography with Abstracts.* New York: Bowker, 1980.

Cutright, N. J., and D. P. Kibbe. *A Partial Bibliography on Rare and Endangered Species.* Woodstock, Vt.: Vermont Institute of Natural Science, 1978.

Gilmartin, K. J., and others. *Annotated Bibliography of Current Literature on Social Indicators.* New York: Garland STPM Press, 1980.

Hallaron, S. A. *Urbanization in the Developing Nations: A Bibliography.* Monticello, Ill.: Council of Planning Librarians, 1976.

Institute of Development Studies and the Latin American Social Science Council. *Bibliography of Selected Latin American Publications on Development.* Brighton, U.K.: University of Sussex, 1978.

Ives, J. H. *International Occupational Safety and Health Resource Catalogue.* New York: Praeger, 1981.

Knight, A. W., and M. A. Simmons, eds. *Water Pollution.* Man and the Environment Information Guide Series. Detroit, Mich.: Gale, 1980.

Matthews, W. H. *Resource Materials for Environmental Management and Education.* Cambridge, Mass.: MIT Press, 1976.

Meshenberg, M. J. *Environmental Planning.* Man and the Environment Information Guide Series. Detroit, Mich.: Gale, 1976.

Middlebrooks, E. J., N. B. Jones, M. F. Torpy, and J. H. Reynolds. *Lagoon Information Source Book.* Ann Arbor, Mich.: Ann Arbor Science Publishers, Inc., 1978.

Orr, James F., and Judith L. Wolfe. *Technology Transfer and the Diffusion of Innovations: A Working Bibliography with Annotations.* Public Administration Series 232. Monticello, Ill.: Vance Bibliographies, 1979.

Rudd, R. L., ed. *Environmental Toxicology.* Man and the Environment Information Guide Series. Detroit, Mich.: Gale, 1977.

Rybczynski, Witold, Chongrak Poprasert, and Michael McGarry. *Low-Cost Technology Options for Sanitation: A State-of-the-Art Review and Annotated Bibliography.* Ottawa: International Development Research Centre, 1978.

Schwartz, M. D. *Environmental Law: A Guide to Information Resources.* Detroit, Mich.: Gale, 1977.

Tchobanoglous, George, and others, eds. *Wastewater Management: A Guide to Information Sources.* Man and the Environment Information Guide Series, vol 2. Detroit, Mich.: Gale. 1976.

Trzyna, Thaddeus C., ed. *International Environmental Affairs: A Guide to the Literature.* Claremont, Calif.: Public Affairs Clearinghouse/Center for California Public Affairs, 1978.

U.K. Foreign and Commonwealth Office, Overseas Development Administration. *Overseas Development and Aid: A Guide to Sources of Information and Material.* London, 1979.

United Nations Industrial Development Organization. *Information Sources on Bioconversion of Agricultural Wastes.* New York: United Nations, 1979.

U.S. Department of Commerce. *Coastal Zone Management: An Annotated Bibliography.* Washington, D.C., 1980.

U.S. Energy Information Administration. *Publications Directory: A Guide.* Washington, D.C., 1981.

U.S. Environmental Protection Agency. *Current Views on Solid Waste Management.* Washington, D.C., 1978.

———. Office of Pesticides and Toxic Substances. *Chemical Information Resources Handbook.* Washington, D.C., 1981.

Water Resource Management: An Annotated Bibliography. Philadelphia, Pa.: Heyden, 1981.

White, A. G. *Project Management—Pulling It Together: A Selected Bibliography.* Public Administration Series 281. Monticello, Ill.: Vance Bibliographies, 1979.

Wolf, C. P. *Quality of Life, Concept and Measurement: A Preliminary Bibliography.* Public Administration Series 249. Monticello, Ill.: Vance Bibliographies, 1979.

World Bank. "The Environment—A Useful Bibliography." Washington, D.C., Office of Environmental and Scientific Affairs, 1980.

———. *World Bank Research in Water Supply and Sanitation: Summary of Selected Publications.* Washington, D.C., 1980.

———. *An Annotated Bibliography of Environmental Economics.* Washington, D.C., 1981.

Data Collection Methods

Cochrane, Glynn. *The Cultural Appraisal of Development Projects.* New York: Praeger, 1979.

Delp, Peter, and others. *Systems Tools for Project Planning.* Bloomington, Ind.: Program of Advanced Studies in Institution Building and Technical Assistance Methodology (PASITAM), 1977.

Gittinger, J. Price. *Economic Analysis of Agricultural Projects*. 2d ed. Baltimore, Md: Johns Hopkins University Press, 1982.

Hageboeck, Molly, and others. *Manager's Guide to Data Collection*. Washington, D.C.: Practical Concepts Incorporated, 1979.

Heaslip, G. B. *Environmental Data Handling*. New York: Wiley, 1975.

Hursh-Cesar, Gerald, and Prodipto Roy, eds. *Third World Surveys: Survey Research in Developing Nations*. New Delhi: Macmillan Company of India, 1976.

Jorgensen, S. E., ed. *Handbook of Environmental Data and Ecological Parameters*. Environmental Sciences and Applications, no. 6. Elmsford, N.Y.: Pergamon, 1979.

Kalbermatten, John M., DeAnne S. Julius, and Charles G. Gunnerson. *Appropriate Sanitation Alternatives: A Technical and Economic Appraisal*. Baltimore, Md: Johns Hopkins University Press, 1982.

Kearl, Bryant, ed. *Field Data Collection in the Social Sciences: Experiences in Africa and the Middle East*. New York: Agricultural Development Council, 1976.

Kulp, E. M. *Designing and Managing Basic Agricultural Programs*. Bloomington, Ind.: International Development Institute, 1977.

Mickelwait, D. R., and others. *Information for Decision Making in Rural Development*. 2 vols. Washington, D.C.: Development Alternatives, Inc., 1978.

Perry, Roger, and Robert Young. *Handbook of Air Pollution Analysis*. New York: Wiley, 1977.

Rush, W. H. *Application of Comprehensive Computerized Surveys in the Collection and Analysis of Farm Data in Developing Countries*. Washington, D.C.: American Technical Assistance Corporation, 1977.

Shaner, W. W. *Project Planning for Developing Economies*. New York: Praeger, 1979.

United Nations Industrial Development Organization (UNIDO). *Guide to Practical Project Appraisal*. New York: United Nations, 1978.

United Nations Institute for Training and Research (UNITAR). *Planning in Developing Countries: Theory and Methodology*. New York: United Nations, 1980.

Weisel, P. F., and D. R. Mickelwait. *Designing Rural Development Projects: An Approach*. Washington, D.C.: Development Alternatives, Inc., 1978.

Directories

Africa–Middle East Petroleum Directory. Tulsa, Okla.: Penn Well Books, 1981.

Ann Arbor Science Special Task Group. *Solar Energy and Research Directory*. Ann Arbor, Mich.: Ann Arbor Science Publishers, Inc., 1977.

Asia-Pacific Petroleum Directory. Tulsa, Okla.: Penn Well Books, 1981.

Bauly, J. A., and C. B. Bauly, eds. *World Energy Directory: A Guide to Organizations and Research Activities in Non-Atomic Energy*. Guernsey, U. K.: Francis Hodgson, 1981.

Commonwealth Secretariat. *Appropriate Technology in the Commonwealth: A Directory of Institutions*. London, 1978.

Energy Reference Handbook. 2d ed. Washington, D.C.: Government Institutes, Inc., 1978.

Environment Information Center, Inc. *Federal Government—Executive Branch* (Energy Directory Update Service). New York, 1978.

———. *Energy Directory*. New York, 1980.

Food and Agriculture Organization. *AGRIS Forestry: World Catalogue of Information and Documentation Services*. Rome, 1979.

Huber, E. E., and others. *Inventory of Sources of Computerized Ecological Information*. Publication no. 1265, ORNL-5441. Oak Ridge, Tenn.: U.S. Department of Energy, 1978.

Information Market Place 1978–79: An International Directory of Information Products and Services. New York: Bowker, 1978.

International Irrigation Information Centre, ed. *Irrigation: International Guide to Organizations and Institutions*. Elmsford, N.Y.: Pergamon, 1980.

Meyers, B. E., and others. *Federal Environmental Data: A Directory of Selected Sources*. NTIS PB-275-902. Rockville, Md.: Capital Systems Group, 1977.

National Research Council, U.S. National Committee for Geochemistry. *Geochemistry and the Environment*. 3 vols. Washington, D.C.: National Academy of Sciences, 1978.

Organisation for Economic Co-operation and Development. *Appropriate Technology Directory*. Paris, 1979.

Press, Jacques Cattele, ed. *Energy Research Programs*. New York: Bowker, 1980.

Quigg, P. W., ed. *World Directory of Environmental Education Programs*. Prepared by International Institute for Environmental Affairs in cooperation with the Institute of International Education. New York: Bowker, 1973.

Reeder, P. L. de, ed. *Environmental Programmes of Intergovernmental Organisations*. Elmsford, N.Y.: Pergamon, 1978.

Trzyna, Thaddeus C., ed. *Population: An International Directory of Organizations and Information Resources*. Claremont, Calif.: Public Affairs Clearinghouse/ Center for California Public Affairs, 1976.

———, ed. *World Food Crisis: An International Directory of Organizations and Information Resources*. Claremont, Calif.: Public Affairs Clearinghouse/Center for California Public Affairs, 1977.

Trzyna, Thaddeus C., and Eugene V. Coan, eds. *World Directory of Environmental Organizations*. 2d ed. Claremont, Calif.: Public Affairs Clearinghouse/ Center for California Public Affairs, 1976.

United Nations Development Programme. *The Directory of Services for Technical Co-operation among Developing Countries.* New York, 1978.

———. *International Directory of Technical Cooperation Resources in Developing Countries.* New York, 1978.

U.S. Agency for International Development. *Directory of Development Resources.* Washington, D.C., 1980. Supplement, 1981.

U.S. Department of the Interior, Geological Survey. *Worldwide Directory of National Earth-science Agencies and Related International Organizations,* comp. W. E. Bergquist, E. J. Tinsley, L. Yordy, and R. L. Miller. C 0834. Washington, D.C., 1981.

U.S. Environmental Protection Agency. *Environmental Information Systems Directory: An Inventory of Environmental Information Systems with Indexes.* 2d ed. Washington, D.C., 1977.

U.S. Library of Congress, National Referral Center. *A Directory of Information Resources in the United States: Geosciences and Oceanography.* Washington, D.C., 1981.

Wilson, C. W. I., ed. *World Nuclear Directory: A Guide to Organizations and Research Activities in Atomic Energy.* 6th ed. Guernsey, U.K.: Francis Hodgson, 1981.

Wilson, William K., Morgan D. Dowd, and Phyllis A. Sholtys, comps. *World Directory of Environmental Research Centers.* 2d ed. New York: Oryx Press, 1974.

World Environmental Directory. Silver Spring, Md.: Business Publishing, Inc., 1980.

Glossaries

Abrams, Charles. *The Language of the Cities: A Glossary of Terms.* New York: Viking Press, 1971.

Butler University, Holcomb Research Institute, Institute of Ecology. *An Ecological Glossary for Engineers and Resource Managers.* Indianapolis, Ind., 1973.

Cagnacci-Schwicker, A., ed. *International Dictionary of Metallurgy, Mineralogy, Geology and the Mining and Oil Industries.* Wiesbaden, Federal Republic of Germany: Bauverlag, 1970.

Clason, W. E. *Elsevier's Dictionary of Measurement and Control.* New York: Elsevier North-Holland, Inc., 1977.

Conseil International de la Langue Francaise. *Glossary of the Environment.* New York: Praeger, 1977.

Frick, G. W., ed. *Environmental Glossary.* Washington, D.C.: Government Institutes, 1980.

Landy, Marc. *Environmental Impact Statement Glossary.* New York: Plenum, 1979.

Lewis, W. H., ed. *Ecology Field Glossary: A Naturalist's Vocabulary.* Westport, Conn.: Greenwood Press, 1977.

Meinck, F., and K. Mohle. *Dictionary of Water and Sewage Engineering.* New York: Elsevier North-Holland, Inc., 1977.

Tver, D. F., ed. *Dictionary of Dangerous Pollutants, Ecology and Environment.* New York: Industrial Press, 1981.

Information and Data Systems

Atherton, Pauline. *Handbook for Information Systems and Services.* Paris: Unesco, 1977.

Centre for Agricultural Publishing and Documentation (PUDOC). *Factual Data Banks in Agriculture.* Proceedings of a Symposium, 1977. Wageningen, Netherlands, 1978.

Directory of Online Information Resources. 8th ed. Kensington, Md.: CSG Press, 1981.

Dosa, M. L. "Environmental Information Systems." In *Information for Economic Planning and Development for the African Region, Proceedings of a Seminar, Accra, Ghana, 1978,* ed. C. O. Kisiedu. Vol. 1. Legon, Ghana: University of Ghana, 1980.

———. *Information Systems for Soil and Related Data.* Proceedings of the Second Australian Meeting of the ISSS Working Group on Soil Information Systems, Canberra, Australia, 19–21 February 1980. Wageningen, Netherlands, 1981.

Hall, J. L., and M. J. Brown. *On-Line Bibliographic Data Bases: An International Directory.* Detroit, Mich.: Gale, 1981.

Karen, Carl, and Larry Harmon. "Information Services Issues in Less Developed Countries." In *Annual Review of Information Science and Technology.* Vol. 15. White Plains, N.Y.: Knowledge Industry Publications, 1980.

Kruzas, A. T., ed. *Encyclopedia of Information Systems and Services.* 4th ed. Detroit, Mich.: Gale, 1981.

Moore, A. W., and S. W. Bie, eds. *Users of Soil Information Systems.* Wageningen, Netherlands: Centre for Agricultural Publishing and Documentation (PUDOC), 1977.

Morris, J. A., and E. A. Elkins. *Library Searching: Resources and Strategies with Examples from the Environmental Sciences.* New York: Jeffrey Norton Publishers, 1978.

Organisation for Economic Co-operation and Development. *Workshop on Information Systems for Rural Development Projects.* Paris, 1978.

Sadovsky, A. D., and S. W. Bie, eds. *Developments in Soil Information Systems.*

Wageningen, Netherlands: Centre for Agricultural Publishing and Documentation (PUDOC), 1978.

Slamecka, Valdimir, ed. *Scientific and Technical Information Services for Socioeconomic Development*. Washington: D.C.: International Science and Technology Institute, Inc., 1979.

U.S. National Oceanic and Atmospheric Administration. *Guide to NOAA's Computerized Information Retrieval Services*. Rockville, Md., 1979.

Woolston, John, ed. *International Cooperative Information Systems*. Proceedings of a Seminar in Vienna, July 9–13, 1979. Ottawa: International Development Research Centre (IDRC), 1980.

Resource Persons

Barbaro, Ronald, and F. L. Cross, Jr., eds. *National Directory: Environmental Impact Experts, Consultants, Regulatory Aspects*. Westport, Conn.: Technomic Publishing Company, 1974.

Barry, S. G. *Indexes to Expertise: An Examination of Practical Systems*. British Library Research and Development Report 5314. London: British Library, 1976.

Environment Information Center, Inc. *User's Guide to Searchers [of ENERGYNET]*. New York, 1981.

Industry Analysts in the Federal Government. Washington, D.C.: Washington Researchers, 1978.

Institute for Ecology. *Directory of Environmental and Life Scientists*. Prepared for the U.S. Army Corps of Engineers. 9 vols. Washington, D.C.: U.S. Government Printing Office, 1974.

Organisation for Economic Co-operation and Development. *Register of Development Research Projects in Africa*. Paris, 1979.

Who's Who in Ocean and Fresh Water Science. Guernsey, U.K.: Francis Hodgson, 1978.

World Environmental Center. *Contact: Toxics, A Guide to Specialists on Toxic Substances*. New York, 1981.

Agriculture

Alvim, Paulo de T., and T. T. Kozlowski, eds. *Ecophysiology of Tropical Crops*. New York: Academic Press, 1977.

Andreou, Paris. "Some Handicaps in Mechanized Farming in Bangladesh." *Journal of Administration Overseas*, vol. 18, no. 3 (July 1979), pp. 209–13.

Bartsch, W. H. *Employment and Technology Choice in Asian Agriculture*. New York: Praeger, 1977.

Bates, Robert H., and Michael F. Lofchie. *Agricultural Development in Africa.* New York: Praeger, 1980.

Bene, J. G., H. W. Beall, and A. Cote. *Trees, Food, and People: Land Management in the Tropics.* Ottawa: International Development and Research Centre, 1977.

Biswas, M. R., and A. K. Biswas. *Desertification: Associated Case Studies Prepared for the United Nations Conference on Desertification.* Environmental Sciences and Applications, no. 12. Elmsford, N.Y.: Pergamon, 1980.

Braakhekke, W. G. *On Coexistence: A Casual Approach to Diversity and Stability in Grassland Vegetation.* Wageningen, Netherlands: Centre for Agricultural Publishing and Documentation (PUDOC), 1980.

Bromley, Daniel W. *Improving Irrigated Agriculture: Institutional Reform and the Small Farmer.* World Bank Staff Working Paper no. 531. Washington, D.C.: World Bank, 1982.

Brown, A. W. A. *Ecology of Pesticides.* Somerset, N.J.: Wiley-Interscience, 1978.

Brown, Lester. *The Worldwide Loss of Cropland.* Washington, D.C.: Worldwatch Institute, 1978.

Buckett, M. *An Introduction to Farm Organization and Management.* Elmsford, N.Y.: Pergamon, 1981.

Buringh, P. *Introduction to the Study of Soils in Tropical and Subtropical Regions.* 3d ed. Wageningen, Netherlands: Centre for Agricultural Publishing and Documentation (PUDOC), 1979.

Cannell, G. H., and others, eds. *Agriculture in Semi-Arid Environments.* New York: Springer-Verlag, 1979.

Carruthers, Ian, and Roy Stoner. *Economic Aspects and Policy Issues in Groundwater Development.* World Bank Staff Working Paper no. 496. Washington, D.C.: World Bank, 1981.

Cernea, Michael M. *Land Tenure Systems and Social Implications of Forestry Development Programs.* World Bank Staff Working Paper no. 452. Washington, D.C.: World Bank, 1981.

Cox, G. W., and M. D. Atkins. *Agricultural Ecology.* San Francisco, Calif.: Freeman, 1979.

Davis, Ted J., ed., *Increasing Agricultural Productivity: Proceedings of the Third Annual Agricultural Sector Symposium.* Washington, D.C.: World Bank, 1982.

Deboeck, Guido, and Bill Kinsey. *Managing Information for Rural Development: Lessons from Eastern Africa.* World Bank Staff Working Paper no. 379. Washington, D.C.: World Bank, 1980.

Donaldson, Graham, and others. *Forestry.* World Bank Sector Policy Paper. Washington, D.C.: World Bank, 1978.

Emmerson, Donald K. *Rethinking Artisanal Fisheries Development: Western Concepts, Asian Experiences.* World Bank Staff Working Paper no. 423. Washington, D.C.: World Bank, 1980.

Feder, Gershon, Richard Just, and David Zilberman. *Adoption of Agricultural Innovations in Developing Countries: A Survey.* World Bank Staff Working Paper no. 542. Washington, D.C.: World Bank, 1982.

Food and Agriculture Organization. *Poultry Feeding in Tropical and Subtropical Countries.* FAO Agricultural Development Paper no. 82. Rome, 1975.

————. *Production, Trade and Utilization of Seaweeds and Seaweed Products.* Rome, 1976.

————. *Review and Analysis of Agrarian Reform and Rural Development in the Developing Countries since the Mid 1960s.* Rome, 1978.

————. *Economic Analysis of Forestry Projects: Case Studies.* Rome, 1979.

————. *Yield Response to Water.* Rome, 1979.

————. *Farm Management Research for Small Farmer Development.* Rome, 1980.

————. *Forestry for Rural Communities.* Rome, 1980.

————. *Public Forestry Administrations in Latin America.* FAO Forestry Paper no. 25. Rome, 1981.

————. *The State of Food and Agriculture 1980.* Rome, 1981.

Grimwood, B. E. *Coconut Palm Products: Their Processing in Developing Countries.* Agriculture Development Paper no. 91. Rome: Food and Agriculture Organization, 1975.

Hall, D. W. *Handling and Storage of Food Grains in Tropical and Subtropical Areas.* Agricultural Development Paper no. 90. Rome: Food and Agriculture Organization, 1975.

Hamilton, L. S. *Tropical Rainforest Use and Preservation: A Study of Problems and Practices in Venezuela.* New York: Sierra Club International Earthcare Center, 1976.

Harrison, James Q., Jon A. Hitchings, and John W. Hall. *India: Demand and Supply Prospects for Agriculture.* World Bank Staff Working Paper no. 500. Washington, D.C.: World Bank, 1981.

Henzel, E. F. "What Can Australia Do to Increase Food Production in the Tropics?" *Search,* vol. 7 (1976), p. 119.

Herzka, A., ed. *Post-harvest Food Crop Conservation.* Elmsford, N.Y.: Pergamon, 1981.

Hook, Donald D., and R. M. M. Crawford. *Plant Life in Anaerobic Environments.* Ann Arbor, Mich.: Ann Arbor Science Publishers, Inc., 1978.

International Agricultural Development Service. *Agricultural Development Indicators.* New York: International Development Service, 1978.

International Food Policy Research Institute. *Food Needs for Developing Countries: Projections of Production and Consumption to 1990.* Washington, D.C., 1978.

Janzen, D. H. "Tropical Agroecosystems." *Science,* vol. 182 (1973), pp. 1212–19.

Juke, Thomas H. "Nutrition and the Food Supply: Controversies and Prospects." *American Biology Teacher*, vol. 38 (1976), p. 162.

Korten, Frances F. *Building National Capacity to Develop Water Users' Associations: Experience from the Philippines.* World Bank Staff Working Paper no. 528. Washington, D.C.: World Bank, 1982.

Laur, Timothy Michael. "The World Food Problem and the Role of Climate." *American Geophysical Union Transactions*, vol. 57 (1976), p. 189.

Lenihan, John, and William W. Fletcher, eds. *Environment and Man.* Vol. 2, *Food, Agriculture and the Environment.* New York: Academic Press, 1976.

Loosli, J. K., and I. K. McDonald. *Nonprotein Nitrogen in the Nutrition of Ruminants.* FAO Agricultural Studies no. 75. Rome: Food and Agriculture Organization, 1976.

Marstrand, P., J. Gribbin, and H. Rush. "Knowledge Intensive Agriculture—the Need for Science in Labor Intensive Agriculture." *Food Policy*, vol. 3 (1978), p. 272.

National Academy of Sciences. *Making Aquatic Weeds Useful: Some Perspectives for Developing Countries.* Washington, D.C., 1976.

Pacey, Andre. "Technology Is Not Enough: The Provision and Maintenance of Appropriate Water Supplies." *Aqua*, vol. 19 (1977), p. 1.

Pinstrup-Andersen, Per. *Nutritional Consequences of Agricultural Projects: Conceptual Relationships and Assessment Approaches.* World Bank Staff Working Paper no. 456. Washington, D.C.: World Bank, 1981.

Pollnac, Richard B. *Sociocultural Aspects of Developing Small-Scale Fisheries: Delivering Services to the Poor.* World Bank Staff Working Paper no. 490. Washington, D.C.: World Bank, 1981.

Slater, L. E., and S. K. Levin, eds. *Climate's Impact on Food Supplies, Strategies and Technologies for Climate-Defensive Food Production.* American Association for the Advancement of Science, Selected Symposia Series no. 62. Boulder, Colo: Westview Press, 1981.

Smith, R. C. G., and H. C. Harris. "Environmental Resources and Restraints to Agricultural Production in a Mediterranean-type Environment." *Plant and Soil*, vol. 58 (1981), p. 31.

Thompson, J. R. *Advances in Research and Technology of Seeds.* Wageningen, Netherlands: Centre for Agricultural Publishing and Documentation (PUDOC), 1980.

United Nations Educational, Scientific, and Cultural Organization. *Development of Arid and Semi-arid Lands: Obstacles and Prospects.* Program on man and the Environment Technical Report no. 6. New York: United Nations, 1977.

United Nations Institute for Training and Research. *Alternative Strategies for Desert Development and Management.* 4 vols. Elmsford, N.Y.: Pergamon, 1980.

U.S. General Accounting Office. *Need to Concentrate Intensive Timber Management on High Productive Lands.* Washington, D.C., 1978.

Van den Bosch, R. *The Pesticide Conspiracy.* New York: Doubleday, 1980.

World Bank. *Fishery.* Sector Policy Paper. Washington, D.C., 1982.

Wortman, Sterling, and Ralph Cummings, Jr. *To Feed This World: The Challenge and the Strategy.* Baltimore, Md.: Johns Hopkins University Press, 1978.

Emissions and Controls

Allen, G. R. "The World Fertilizer Situation." *World Development*, vol. 5, nos. 5–7 (May–July 1977), pp. 525–36.

Bolin, Bert, and Erik Arrhenius. "Nitrogen—An Essential Life Factor and a Growing Environmental Hazard: Report from Nobel Symposium No. 38." *Ambio*, vol. 6, nos. 2–3 (1977), pp. 96–106.

Darmansyah, I. "Problems of Pesticide Management and Safety Programs in Southeast Asia." In *Pesticide Management and Insecticide Resistance*, ed. D. L. Watson and A. W. A. Brown. New York: Academic Press, 1977.

Davies, J. E. "Pesticide Management Safety—From a Medical Point of View." In *Pesticide Management and Insecticide Resistance*, ed. D. L. Watson and A. W. A. Brown. New York: Academic Press, 1977.

Gustafsson, Ynagve. "Variations in Rainfall as a Natural Constraint on Agriculture." *Ambio*, vol. 6 (1977), p. 34.

International Atomic Energy Agency. *Trace Contaminants of Agriculture, Fisheries and Food in Developing Countries.* Vienna, 1976.

Loehr, Raymond C. *Food Fertilizer and Agricultural Residues.* Ann Arbor, Mich.: Ann Arbor Science Publishers, Inc., 1977.

———. *Pollution Control for Agriculture.* New York: Academic Press, 1977.

Muthod, M. K. "Economic Evaluation of the Environmental Effects of Erosion." *Agriculture and Environment*, vol. 3 (1976), p. 21.

Olsen, R. A. "Fertilizers for Food Production vs. Energy Needs and Environmental Quality." *Ecotoxicology and Environmental Safety*, vol. 1 (1977), p. 322.

Ormrod, D. P. *Pollution in Horticulture.* New York: Elsevier North-Holland, Inc., 1978.

Quraishi, M. Sayeed. *Biochemical Insect Control: Its Impact on Economy, Environment, and Natural Selection.* New York: Wiley-Interscience, 1977.

Impact

Cabrea, S. de, C. Rolz, J. P. Menchu, J. Valladares, R. Garcia, and F. Aguire. *A Review on the Utilization of Agricultural Wastes in Central America.* Rome: Food and Agriculture Organization, 1978.

Food and Agriculture Organization. *Impact Monitoring of Residues from the Use of Agricultural Pesticides.* FAO Report no. 1975. Rome, 1975.

———. *Fertilizers and Their Use: A Pocket Guide for Extension Officers.* 3d ed. Rome, 1978.

———. *Soil and Plant Testing as a Basis of Fertilizer Recommendations.* Rome, 1980.

———. *Pesticide Residues in Food.* Rome, 1981.

Ilemobade, A. A. *The Problem of Pesticide Residues and Environmental Pollution in Tropical Countries and Veterinary Education.* Rome: Food and Agriculture Organization, 1978.

Khan, S. U. *Pesticides in the Soil Environment.* Fundamental Aspects of Pollution Control and Environmental Science, vol. 5. New York: Elsevier North-Holland, Inc., 1980.

Murdock, M. S. *The Impact of Agricultural Development on a Pastoral Society: The Shukrija of the Eastern Sudan.* Albany, N.Y.: State University of New York Research Foundation, 1979.

Ohsaka, Akira, and others, eds. *Animal, Plant, and Microbial Toxins.* Proceedings of the Fourth International Symposium on Animal, Plant and Microbial Toxins, September 8–13, 1974. 2 vols. New York: Plenum, 1976.

Pimentel, David, and J. H. Perkins. *Pest Control: Cultural and Environmental Aspects.* American Association for the Advancement of Science, Selected Symposia Series no. 43. Boulder, Colo.: Westview Press, 1980.

Thomas, M. L. "Pesticides in Developing Countries—Significance of Chlorinated Hydrocarbon Residues in Human Milk from Central America." In *International Conference on Environmental Sensing and Assessment.* Vol. 1. New York: Institute of Electrical and Electronics Engineers, 1976.

Irrigation Systems

Agarwal, Anil. "Coaxing the Barren Deserts Back to Life." *New Scientist,* vol. 75, no. 1069 (1977), pp. 674–75.

Bergman, Hellmuth, and Jean-Marc Boussard. *Guide to the Economic Evaluation of Irrigation Projects.* Washington, D.C.: OECD Publications and Information Center, 1976.

Caprihan, S. P. "Pilot Integrated Irrigation Projects for Policy Formulation for Removing Food Shortage in Developing Countries." *Indian Journal of Power and River Valley Development* (August 1975), pp. 256–60.

Clayton, Eric. "Monitoring, Management and Control of Irrigation Projects; The Example of Mwea, Kenya (Survey Report, Wye College, U.K.)." *Water Supply and Management,* vol. 5, no. 1 (1981), p. 107.

Coward, E. W., Jr. "Principles of Social Organization in an Indigenous Irrigation System." *Human Organization,* vol. 38, no. 1 (Spring 1979), pp. 28–36.

Davis, Leonard S. *Irrigation and Water Systems in Africa: An Introductory Survey.* Monticello, Ill.: Council of Planning Librarians, 1977.

Davy, E. G. *An Evaluation of Climate and Water Resources for Development of Agriculture in the Sudano-Sahelian Zone of West Africa.* Geneva: World Meteorological Organization, 1977.

Eckholm, Erick, and Lester R. Brown. "The Deserts Are Coming." *Futurist,* vol. 11, no. 6 (1977), p. 361–69.

El-Sherbini, A. A. "Problems in Arid Agriculture in West Asia." *World Development,* vol. 5 (1977), p. 441.

Hagan, R. M., C. E. Houston, and S. U. Allison. *Successful Irrigation: Planning, Development, Management.* Rome: Food and Agriculture Organization, 1975.

Johl, S. S., and C. de Clero, eds. *Irrigation and Agricultural Development.* Elmsford, N.Y.: Pergamon, 1980.

Maass, Arthur, and Raymond L. Anderson. *And the Desert Shall Rejoice: Conflict, Growth, and Justice in Arid Environments.* Cambridge, Mass.: MIT Press, 1978.

Mabbutt, J. A. "The Impact of Desertification as Revealed by Mapping." *Environmental Conservation,* vol. 5 (1978), p. 45.

McGarry, Michael G., and Jill Stainforth, eds. *Compost, Fertilizer, and Biogas Production from Human and Farm Wastes in the People's Republic of China.* Ottawa: International Development Research Centre, 1978.

National Research Council. *Climate and Food.* Washington, D.C.: National Academy of Sciences, 1976.

———. *Leucaena: Promising Forage and Tree Crop for the Tropics.* Washington, D.C.: National Academy of Sciences, 1977.

———. *Supporting Papers: World Food and Nutrition Study.* Vol. 2, *Study Team 4, Resources for Agriculture; Study Team 5, Weather and Climate.* Washington, D.C.: National Academy of Sciences, 1977.

———. *Analytical Studies for the U.S. Environmental Protection Agency.* Vol. 7, *Pesticide Decision Making.* Washington, D.C.: National Academy of Sciences, 1978.

Pillsbury, A. F. *Sprinkler Irrigation.* Agricultural Development Paper no. 88. Rome: Food and Agriculture Organization, 1975.

Revelle, Roger. "The Resources Available for Agriculture." *Scientific American,* vol. 235, no. 3 (1976), pp. 164–74.

Shalhevet, J., and others, eds. *Irrigation of Field and Orchard Crops under Semi-Arid Conditions.* Elmsford, N.Y.: Pergamon, 1979.

Stepanov, I. N., and E. I. Chembarisov. "Irrigation Effect on the Mineralization of River Waters." *Water, Air and Soil Pollution,* vol. 9 (1978), pp. 397–401.

Streutker, A. "The Development of Permanent Crop Production on Efficient

Irrigation and Drainage at the Vaalharts Government Water Scheme." *Water S.A.*, vol. 3, no. 2 (1977), pp. 90–103.

Tolba, M. K., Y. Rebeyrol, L. Voskresenski, and J. H. Bland. "Desertification." *World Health* (July 1977), pp. 2–23.

Walton, J. D., Jr., A. H. Roy, and S. H. Bomar, Jr. *A State of the Art Survey of Solar Powered Irrigation Pumps, Solar Cookers, and Wood Burning Stoves for Use in Sub-Sahara Africa.* Atlanta, Ga.: Georgia Institute of Technology Engineering Experiment Station, 1978.

Ward, Barbara. "Ariadne's Liquid Thread." *Economist*, vol. 262, no. 6962 (1977), pp. 39–42,

Wiener, Aaron. "Coping with Water Deficiency in Arid and Semiarid Countries through High-Efficiency Water Management." *Ambio*, vol. 6, no. 1 (1977), pp. 77–82.

―――. "Rural Water Management in Developing Countries." *Natural Resources Forum*, vol. 1, no. 2 (1977), pp. 111–17.

Worthington, E. Barton. The Greening of the Desert: What Cost to Farmers? *Civil Engineering ASCE*, vol. 48, no. 8 (1978), pp. 60–63.

Zonn, I. S. "Irrigation of the World's Arid Lands." *World Crops*, vol. 29, no. 2 (1977), pp. 72–73.

Development and Environment

Applebaum, George D. "Controlling the Environmental Hazards of International Development." *Ecology Law Quarterly*, vol. 5 (1976), p. 321.

Barbour, I. G. *Technology, Environment and Human Values.* New York: Praeger, 1980.

Baum, Warren C. *The Project Cycle.* Washington, D.C.: World Bank, 1983.

"Case Studies in Environmental Disruption and Eco-management: A Global Survey." In *Global Perspectives on Ecology*, ed. Thomas C. Emmell. Part 2. Palo Alto, Calif.: Mayfield, 1977.

Chan, George, and B. S. Saini, "Strategy for Ecodevelopment of an Island Community." *Ekistics*, vol. 40 (1975), p. 232.

Clausen, A. W. *Address to the Board of Governors by A. W. Clausen, President, World Bank and International Finance Corporation.* Washington, D.C.: World Bank, 1982.

Craik, Kenneth, and Ervin H. Zube. *Perceiving Environmental Quality: Research and Applications.* New York: Plenum, 1976.

Deutsch, K. W., ed. *Eco-socio Systems and Eco-politics: A Reader on Human and Social Implications of Environmental Management in Developing Countries.* Paris: Unesco, 1977.

Dworkin, D. M., and P. E. Dascher. *Environmental Sciences in Developing Countries.* Scientific Committee on Problems of the Environment of the International Council of Scientific Unions, SCOPE Report 8. New York: Wiley, 1974.

Edington, John M., and M. Ann Edington. *Ecology and Environmental Planning.* New York: Halstead Press, 1978.

"Environment and Development." *Environment International,* vol. 1 (1978), pp. 141–46.

Ghai, D. P., A. R. Khan, E. L. H. Lee, and T. Alfthan. *The Basic-Needs Approach to Development.* Geneva: International Labour Office, 1978.

Goldstein, Joan. *Environmental Decision Making in Rural Locales.* New York: Praeger, 1981.

Goodland, Robert. *Tribal Peoples and Economic Development: Human Ecologic Considerations.* Washington, D.C.: World Bank, 1982.

Gour-Tanguay, R., ed. *Environmental Policies in Developing Countries.* Beitrage zur Umweltgestaltung Bd. A27. Stuttgart: Brockhaus, 1977.

"A Growing Worry: The Consequences of Development." *Conservation Foundation Letter* (January 1978).

Hall, A. V. "Endangered Species in a Rising Tide of Human Population Growth." *Royal Society of South Africa Transactions,* vol. 43 (1978), p. 37.

James, Jeffrey. "Growth, Technology and the Environment in Less Developed Countries: A Survey." *World Development,* vol. 6 (1978), p. 937.

Johnson, D. "Land-State Alternatives for Planning and Management, Task Force on Natural Resources and Land-Use Information and Technology." *Journal of the American Institute of Planners,* vol. 43 (1977), pp. 96–98.

Knight, Peter T., ed. *Implementing Programs of Human Development.* World Bank Staff Working Paper no. 403. Washington, D.C.: World Bank, 1980.

Kormondy, E. J., and J. F. McCormick. *Handbook of Contemporary Developments in World Ecology.* Westport, Conn.: Greenwood Press, 1981.

Krasner, Leonard, ed. *Environmental Design and Human Behavior: A Psychology of the Individual in Society.* Elmsford, N.Y.: Pergamon, 1979.

Marstrand, P. K. "Ecological and Social Evaluation of Industrial Development." *Environmental Conservation,* vol. 3, no. 4 (Winter 1976), pp. 303–09.

McEvoy, James, III, and Thomas Dietz. *Handbook for Environmental Planning: The Social Consequences of Environmental Change.* Somerset, N.J.: Wiley-Interscience, 1977.

Mitchell, Harold P. "Challenges in a Changing World." *Environmental Conservation,* vol. 5, no. 1 (1978), pp. 3–10.

Müller, P., ed. *Ecosystem Research in South America.* Stuttgart: Brockhaus, 1977.

Myers, Norman. "China's Approach to Environmental Conservation." *Environmental Affairs,* vol. 5 (1976), p. 33.

National Academy of Sciences, Committee on Remote Sensing for Development. *Resource Sensing from Space: Prospects for Developing Countries.* Washington, D.C., 1977.

Naveh, Z. "The Role of Landscape Ecology in Development." *Environmental Conservation*, vol. 5 (1978), pp. 57–63.

Okwuosa, E. A. *New Direction for Economic Development in Africa.* New York: Africa Books, 1976.

Pearson, C., and A. Pryor. *Environment: North and South: An Economic Interpretation.* New York: Wiley, 1978.

Polunin, Nicholas. *Growth without Ecodisasters? Proceedings of the Second International Conference on Environmental Future, Reykjavik, Iceland, 1977.* New York: Wiley, 1979.

Rabie, Andre. *South African Environmental Legislation.* Environmental Protection Agency—International Environment Document Report. Washington, D.C., 1976.

Richards, Paul. "What Environmental Crisis Means in Africa." *Nature*, vol. 259, no. 5541, p. 258.

Rondinelli, D. A., and Kenneth Ruddle. *Urbanization and Rural Development: A Spatial Policy for Equitable Growth.* New York: Praeger, 1978.

Sagasti, Francisco. *Science and Technology for Development.* Ottawa: International Development Research Centre, 1978.

Wall, Albert. *Environment and Development.* Washington, D.C.: World Bank, 1979.

World Bank. *Water Supply and Waste Disposal.* Washington, D.C., 1980.

Energy Resources

Bassan, Elizabeth, ed. *Global Energy in Transition: Environmental Aspects of New and Renewable Sources for Development.* New York: Sierra Club International Earthcare Center, 1981.

Brown, Norman, ed. *Renewable Energy Resources and Rural Application in the Developing World.* Boulder, Colo.: Westview Press, 1978.

Cleveland, Harlan. *Energy Futures of Developing Countries.* New York: Praeger, 1980.

Dorf, Richard C. *The Energy Factbook.* New York: McGraw-Hill, 1981.

El-Hinnawi, E. E. *Energy and Environment.* New York: Elsevier North-Holland, Inc., 1978.

Fallen-Bailey, Darrel G., and Trevor A. Byer. *Energy Options and Policy Issues in Developing Countries.* World Bank Staff Working Paper no. 350. Washington, D.C.: World Bank, 1979.

Foster, John, and others. *Energy for Development*. Prepared for the North-South Roundtable of the Society for International Development and the Overseas Development Council. New York: Praeger, 1981.

Gentemann, Karen M., ed. *Social and Political Perspectives on Energy Policy*. New York: Praeger, 1981.

Hill, Richard F., ed. *Energy Technology: Expanding Energy Supplies*. Papers presented at the Seventh Energy Technology Conference and Exposition. Washington, D.C.: Government Institutes, 1980.

Institution of Electrical Engineers (U.K.). *Future Energy Concepts*. London: Peter Peregrinus Ltd., 1981.

Lenihan, John, and W. W. Fletcher, eds. *Energy Resources and the Environment. Environment and Man*. Vol. 1. New York: Academic Press, 1976.

Mangone, G. J., ed. *Energy Policies of the World*. Vol. 1. New York: Elsevier North-Holland, Inc., 1976.

National Academy of Sciences, *Energy and Climate*. Studies in Geophysics. Washington, D.C., 1977.

National Research Council of Thailand. *Energy for Rural Development, Implementation Plan for Inter-Country Research Activities, 1980–1983*. Honolulu: East-West Resource Systems Institute, 1980.

National Resource Council, Board on Science and Technology for International Development. *Proceedings: International Workshop on Energy Survey Methodologies for Developing Countries, January 21–25, 1979, Jekyll Island, Georgia*. Washington, D.C., 1980.

Organisation for Economic Co-operation and Development. *Energy Production and Environment*. Washington, D.C.: OECD Publications and Information Center, 1977.

Simon, Andrew L. *Energy Resources*. Elmsford, N.Y.: Pergamon, 1975.

Somers, W. E., L. Kurylko, J. R. Stone, and M. L. Hughen. *Energy Use and Energy Conservation Opportunities in Copper Refining—A Case Study*. Transactions Paper Selection no. A81-17. Warrendale, Pa.: Metallurgical Society of the American Institute of Mining, Metallurgical, and Petroleum Engineers, 1981.

Stunkel, K. R. *National Energy Profiles*. New York: Praeger, 1981.

Sullivan, Thomas F., ed. *Energy Reference Handbook*. 2nd ed. Washington, D.C.: Government Institutes, 1977.

Theodore, Louis, Anthony J. Buonicore, and Edmund J. Rolinski. *Energy and the Environment: Interactions*. 2 vols. Boca Raton, Fla.: CRC Press, Inc., 1980.

World Bank, *Annual Report 1982*. Washington, D.C., 1982.

———. *The Energy Transition in Developing Countries*. Washington, D.C., 1983.

Alternative Sources of Energy

Braunstein, H. M., E. D. Copenhaver, and H. A. Pfuderer, eds. *Environmental, Health, and Control Aspects of Coal Conversion: An Information Overview.* Woburn, Mass.: Ann Arbor Science Publishers, Inc., 1981.

De Renzo, D. J., ed. *Wind Power.* Park Ridge, N.J.: Noyes Data Corporation, 1979.

El-Hinnawi, Essam E. *Nuclear Energy and the Environment.* Elmsford, N.Y.: Pergamon, 1980.

Fernandes, John H. "Alternative Energy Technologies, A Blueprint for Progress." *Combustion,* vol. 52, no. 7 (January 1981), pp. 8–16.

Halacy, D. S., Jr. *Earth, Wind, Sun and Water: Our Energy Alternatives.* New York: Harper and Row, 1977.

Hartnett, James P., ed. *Alternative Energy Sources.* New York: Academic Press, 1976.

Hughart, David P. *Prospects for Traditional and Non-conventional Energy Sources in Developing Countries.* World Bank Staff Working Paper no. 346. Washington, D.C.: World Bank, 1979.

Kreith, Frank, and Ronald E. West. *Economics of Solar Energy and Conservation Systems.* 3 vols. Boca Raton, Fla.: CRC Press, Inc., 1980.

National Academy of Sciences. *Energy for Rural Development: Renewable Resources and Alternative Technologies for Developing Countries.* Washington, D.C., 1976.

———. *Methane Generation from Human, Animal and Agricultural Wastes.* Washington, D.C., 1977.

———. *L'energie et le Developpement Rural: Ressources Renouveables et Options Techniques pour les Pays en Developpement.* Washington, D.C.: U.S. Agency for International Development, 1978.

National Resource Council, Board on Science and Technology for International Development. *Firewood Crops: Shrub and Tree Species for Energy Production.* Washington, D.C., 1980.

National Science Foundation. *Proceedings of the Second Workshop in Wind Energy Conversion Systems, June 9–11, 1975.* Washington, D.C., 1975.

Organisation for Economic Co-operation and Development, Nuclear Energy Agency. *Safety of the Nuclear Fuel Cycle.* A State-of-the-Art Report by a Group of Experts of the NEA Committee on the Safety of Nuclear Installations. Paris, 1981.

Probstein, Ronald F., David Goldstein, and Harris Gold. *Water in Synthetic Fuel Production: The Technology and Alternatives.* Cambridge, Mass.: MIT Press, 1978.

Ramsey, J. B. *The Economics of Exploration for Energy Resources*. Greenwich, Conn.: JAI Press, Inc., 1981.

Ridgeway, James, and Bettina Conner. *New Energy: Understanding the Crisis and a Guide to Alternative Energy Systems*. Boston, Mass.: Beacon Press, 1975.

Tanzania National Scientific Research Council. *Workshop on Solar Energy for the Villages of Tanzania, August 11–19, 1977*. Dar es Salaam, 1978.

United Nations Industrial Development Organization. *Technology for Solar Energy Utilization*. Development and Transfer of Technology Series no. 5. New York, 1978.

U.S. General Accounting Office. *Unique Helium Resources Are Wasting: A New Conservation Policy Is Needed*. Washington, D.C., 1979.

Veziroglu, T. Nejat, ed. *Alternative Energy Sources: An International Compendium*. Washington, D.C.: Hemisphere Publishing Co., 1978.

Wahl, E. F. *Geothermal Energy Utilization*. New York: Wiley, 1977.

"Wave Energy." *Oceans*, vol. 8, no. 5 (1975).

World Bank. *Alcohol Production from Biomass in the Developing Countries*. Washington, D.C., 1980.

———. *Mobilizing Renewable Energy Technology in Developing Countries: Strengthening Local Capabilities and Research*. Washington, D.C., 1980.

———. *Renewable Energy Resources in the Developing Countries*. Washington, D.C., 1980.

———. *Emerging Energy and Chemical Applications of Methanol: Opportunities for Developing Countries*. Washington, D.C., 1982.

Worldwatch Institute. *Rivers of Energy: The Hydropower Potential*. Worldwatch Paper 44. Washington, D.C., 1981.

———. *Wind Power: A Turning Point*. Worldwatch Paper 45. Washington, D.C., 1981.

Industry

Andriamananjara, Rajowna. "Relating Industrialisation in Africa to People's Needs." *International Labor Review*, vol. 117, no. 6 (1978), pp. 757–61.

Balassa, Bela. *The Process of Industrial Development and Alternative Development Strategies*. World Bank Staff Working Paper no. 438. Washington, D.C.: World Bank, 1980.

Food and Agriculture Organization. *Report of the Fourth Session of the African Forestry Commission*. Rome, 1976.

Gillies, M. T. *Potable Water from Wastewater*. Park Ridge, N.J.: Noyes Data Corporation, 1981.

Myers, Norman. "China's Approach to Environmental Conservation." *Environmental Affairs*, vol. 5, no. 1 (1976), pp. 33–63.

Organisation for Economic Co-operation and Development. *Pollution Control Costs in the Primary Aluminum Industry.* Paris, 1977.

Polimeros, George. *Energy Cogeneration Handbook: Criteria for Central Plant Design.* New York: Industrial Press, 1981.

Sittig, Marshall. *Handbook of Toxic and Hazardous Chemicals.* Park Ridge, N.J.: Noyes Data Corporation, 1981.

Sontag, J. M. *Carcinogenesis in Industry and the Environment.* New York: Marcel Dekker, 1981.

Steel, W. F. *Small-Scale Employment and Production in Developing Countries.* New York: Praeger, 1980.

Turner, Louis, and James Bedore. *Middle East Industrialization.* New York: Praeger, 1980.

United Nations. *Industrial Processing of Natural Resources.* New York, 1981.

United Nations Industrial Development Organization. *Manual for the Preparation of Industrial Feasibility Studies.* New York: United Nations, 1978.

Wall, Nelson C. *Small-Scale Industry Development in South Santa Catarina, Brazil: A Case History.* Atlanta, Ga.: Georgia Institute of Technology International Development Data Center, Office of International Programs, 1976.

Westphal, Larry E. *Korea's Experience with Export-Led Industrial Development.* World Bank Staff Working Paper no. 249. Washington, D.C.: World Bank, 1977.

World Bank. *Environmental Considerations for the Industrial Development Sector.* Washington, D.C., 1978.

World Bank, Office of Environmental Affairs, "Environmental Guidelines"
Foreword, 1982
Aluminum Industry, 1983
Cane Sugar Industry, 1982
Cement, 1983
Chlor-Alkali Industry, 1983
Dairy Products Industry, 1983
Dust Emissions, 1983
Effluents, Disposal of Industrial Wastes, 1983
Effluents, Liquid, Land Disposal and Treatment, 1983
Electrostatic Precipitators (ESPs), 1983
Ethanol Production, 1983
Fertilizer Manufacturing Wastes, 1983
Fish and Shellfish Processing, 1983
Fruit and Vegetable Processing, 1983
Geothermal Development, 1983
Glass Manufacturing, 1983

Iron and Steel Industry—General Considerations, 1983

Iron and Steel Industry—Blast Furnace, 1983

Iron and Steel Industry—By-product Coke Ovens, 1983

Iron and Steel Industry—Ore Preparation, Sintering and Pelletizing, 1983

Iron and Steel Industry—Rolling and Finishing Operations, 1983

Iron and Steel Industry—Steel Making Process, 1983

Lead Sampling and Analyses, 1982

Leather Tanning and Finishing, 1983

Meat Processing and Rendering, 1983

Mining—Strip Surface Mining Operations (Sediment and Erosion Control–Land Reclamation), 1982

Mining—Underground (Coal), 1983

Nitrogen Oxide Emissions, 1982

Nitrogen Oxide Sampling and Analyses, 1982

Noise, 1983

Non-ferrous Metals Industry—Aluminum, 1983

Non-ferrous Metals Industry—Copper and Nickel, 1983

Non-ferrous Metals Industry—Lead and Zinc, 1983

Non-ferrous Metals Industry—Silver, Tungsten, Columbium and Tantalum, 1983

Offshore Hydrocarbon Exploration and Production Projects, 1983

Oil Pipelines, 1983

Palm Oil Industry, 1982

Pesticide Manufacture—Safety and Ecology, 1983

Pesticides—Guidelines for Use, 1983

Petroleum Refining, 1983

Plating and Electroplating, 1983

Plywood Manufacturing, 1983

Poultry Processing, 1983

Pulp and Paper Industry, 1983

Rodenticides, 1983

Rubber Production (Crumb), 1983

Secondary Environmental Effects, 1983

Slaughterhouses I—Industrial Waste Disposal, 1983

Slaughterhouses II—Design Arrangement, 1983

Sulfur Dioxide Ambient Levels, 1984

Sulfur Dioxide Emission Standards, 1984

Sulfur Dioxide Sampling and Analyses, 1982

Pesticides—Guidelines for Use, 1983

Pesticides—Manufacturing, 1983

Pesticides—Packaging and Labeling, 1983

Pesticides—Transportation and Distribution, 1983

Plywood Mills, 1984

Power Plants, Coal and Fuel Oil, 1984

Pulp and Paper Industry, 1984

PVC Processing (Polyvinyl Chloride), 1984

Rodenticides, 1983

Sawmills, 1984

Slaughterhouses, 1984

Steel Plants, 1984

Sulfuric Acid Plants, 1983

Tanneries, 1984

Tea Processing, 1984

Textiles, 1984

Emission and Control

Al-Layla, M. A., and others. *Handbook of Waste Water Collection and Treatment, Principles and Practices.* New York: Garland STPM Press, 1980.

Bouscaren, R. "Planning Resources in the Emission of Pollutants from Industrial Sources." *Public Health in Europe*, vol. 8 (1977), pp. 81–86.

Cairns, J. R., K. L. Dickson, and E. E. Hendricks. *Recovery and Restoration of Damaged Ecosystems.* Charlottesville, Va.: University of Virginia Press, 1977.

Calleley, A. G., C. F. Forster, and D. A. Stafford, eds. *Treatment of Industrial Effluents.* London: Hodder and Stoughton, 1977.

Dyer, J. C. *Handbook of Industrial Wastes Pretreatment.* New York: Garland STPM Press, 1980.

Fishbein, Lawrence. *Potential Industrial Carcinogens and Mutagens.* Studies in Environmental Science, no. 4. Amsterdam: Elsevier Scientific Publishing, 1979.

Fung, R., ed. *Protective Barriers for Containment of Toxic Materials.* Park Ridge, N.J.: Noyes Data Corporation, 1980.

Gardner, B. D. "The Chemical and Biological Recovery of an Organically Polluted Sandy Beach in Natal, South Africa following the Diversion of Effluents to an Offshore Pipeline." *Water S.A.*, vol. 3 (1977), pp. 12–16.

Jenkins, S. H., ed. *Marine, Municipal and Industrial Waste-water Disposal.* Sorrento Conference, 1975. Elmsford, N.Y.: Pergamon, 1978.

————. *Nitrogen as a Water Pollutant.* Progress in Water Technology, vol. 8, pt. 415. Elmsford, N.Y.: Pergamon, 1978.

Lenihan, John, and W. W. Fletcher, eds. *Reclamation.* Environment and Man, vol. 4. New York: Academic Press, 1976.

Louw, C. W., and J. F. Richards. "Determination of the Volatile Organic Substances in the Air of South African City and Industrial Environments." In *Fourth International Clean Air Conference: Paper Abstracts,* 1977.

Martin, A. E., ed. *Emission Control Technology for Industrial Boilers.* Park Ridge, N.J.: Noyes Data Corporation, 1981.

Middlebrooks, E. J. *Industrial Pollution Control.* New York: Wiley, 1979.

Sittig, Marshall. *Incineration of Industrial Hazardous Wastes and Sludges.* Park Ridge, N.J.: Noyes Data Corporation, 1979.

————, ed. *Pesticide Manufacturing and Toxic Materials Control Encyclopedia.* Park Ridge, N.J.: Noyes Data Corporation, 1980.

U.S. General Accounting Office. *How to Dispose of Hazardous Waste—A Serious Question That Needs to Be Resolved.* Washington, D.C., 1978.

Venter, G. P. N. "Air Pollution in the Planning and Siting of Industries." *South African Institute of Mining and Metallurgy Journal,* vol. 78, no. 1 (1977), pp. 12–16.

Fertilizer Plants

Keshavamurthy, G. S. "Pollution Control in a Modern Fertiliser Plant—A Case Study." *Fertiliser News* (India), vol. 22, no. 12 (December 1977), pp. 72–76.

Organisation for Economic Co-operation and Development. *Emission Control Costs in the Fertilizer Industry.* Washington, D.C.: OECD Publications and Information Center, 1978.

Rai, L. C., and H. D. Kumar. "Studies on the Seasonal Variation in the Algal Communities of Pond Polluted with Fertilizer Factory Effluent." *Indian Journal of Ecology,* vol. 4, no. 2 (July 1977), pp. 124–31.

Sittig, Marshall. *Fertilizer Industry, Processes, Pollution Control and Energy Conservation.* Park Ridge, N.J.: Noyes Data Corporation, 1979.

Impacts—General

Christie, N. D., and A. Moldan. "Effects of Fish Factory Effluent on the Benthic Macrofauna of Saladanha Bay." *Marine Pollution Bulletin,* vol. 8, no. 2 (1977), pp. 41–45.

Crosson, P. R. "Agricultural Inputs and Environmental Impacts." Paper read at meeting of American Association for the Advancement of Science, January 26–32, 1975, New York. Processed.

Organisation for Economic Co-operation and Development. *Environmental Damage Costs.* Washington, D.C.: OECD Publications and Information Center, 1975.

Iron and Steel Mills

Boegman, N. "Air Pollution and the Metallurgical Industry." *South African Institute of Mining and Metallurgy Journal,* vol. 78, no. 1 (August 1977), pp. 8–11.

Drabkin, Marvin, and Richard Helfand. *A Review of Performance for New Stationary Sources—Iron and Steel Plants/Basic Oxygen Furnace.* MTR-7324, EPA/450/3-78-116. McLean, Va.: Mitre Corporation, November 1978.

Heynike, J. J. C. "Some Aspects of Energy and the Environment in the Steel Industry." *South African Institute of Mining and Metallurgy Journal,* vol. 78, no. 2 (September 1977), p. 24.

National Academy of Sciences. *Iron, Medical and Biologic Effects of Environmental Pollutants.* Washington, D.C., 1977.

Organisation for Economic Co-operation and Development. *Emission Control Costs in the Iron and Steel Industry.* Washington, D.C.: OECD Publications and Information Center, 1977.

Mining Operations

Canada, Department of Energy, Mines and Resources. *Mining to Manufacturing: Links in a Chain.* Ottawa: Supply and Services Canada, Publishing Centre, 1978.

Castilla, J. C. "Marine Environment Impact Due to Mining Activities of El-Salvador Copper Mine, Chile." *Marine Pollution Bulletin,* vol. 9, no. 3 (March 1978), pp. 67–70.

Colorado State University, Fort Collins. Natural Resource Ecology Laboratory. *Environmental Effects of Western Coal Surface Mining. Part II: The Aquatic Macroinvertebrates of Trout Creek, Colorado.* Final report by S. P. Canton and J. V. Ward. Fort Collins, Colo., 1978.

Cunningham, Simon. *Foreign Mining Companies in a Developing Country.* New York: Praeger, 1981.

"Declaration of Policy of the American Mining Congress." *Mining Congress Journal,* vol. 62, no. 11 (1976), pp. 65–74.

"Ergo-tailings Re-treatment on a Massive Scale." *Mining,* vol. 137, no. 4 (1977), pp. 333–37.

Farmer, Eugene E., and Bland Z. Richardson. *Acid Mine Waste Revegetation: Influence on Soil-Water Quality.* Ogden, Utah: U.S. Forest Service, Intermountain Forest and Range Experiment Station, January 1971.

National Academy of Sciences. *Technological Innovation and Forces for Change in the Mineral Industry.* Washington, D.C., 1978.

Radetzki, Marina. "Where Should Developing Countries' Minerals Be Processed? The Country View Versus the Multinational Company View." *World Development,* vol. 5, no. 4 (April 1977), pp. 325–36.

Rowe, J. E. *Coal Surface Mining Reclamation.* Public Administration Series 252. Monticello, Ill.: Vance Bibliographies, 1979.

Takevchi, Kenji, G. E. Thiebach, and Joseph Hilmy. "Investment Requirements in the Non-fuel Mineral Sector in the Developing Countries." *Natural Resources Forum,* vol. 1, no. 3 (April 1977), pp. 263–76.

U.S. Department of the Interior, Mining Enforcement and Safety Administration. *Fault Tree Analysis.* I69.812:8. Washington, D.C., 1978.

Van Der Walt, S. R., R. Van Eldick, and H. G. J. Potgieter. "The Recovery of Fe, Mn, and Al from a Mine Water Effluent." *Water Research,* vol. 9, no. 10 (October 1975), pp. 865–69.

Petroleum and Petrochemical Industries

Council of Economic Priorities, with J. N. Boothe. *Cleaning Up: the Cost of Refinery Pollution Control.* New York: Praeger, 1977.

Farrington, J. W. "Oil Pollution in the Coastal Environment." In *Proceedings of a Conference.* Vol. 2. Washington, D.C.: U.S. Environmental Protection Agency, Office of Water Planning and Standards, 1977.

Hay, K. G. "The Impact of Offshore Petroleum Operations on Marine and Estuarine Areas." In *Proceedings of a Conference.* Vol. 2. Washington, D.C.: U.S. Environmental Protection Agency, Office of Water Planning and Standards, 1977.

Hodges, Michael. *The Development of the International Oil Industry.* Public Administration Series 253. Monticello, Ill.: Vance Bibliographies, 1979.

Kennedy, John L. "Despite Success, Southeast Asia Oil Hunt Just Started." *Oil and Gas Journal,* vol. 73, no. 9 (1975), pp. 69–95.

National Science Foundation. *The Role of Microorganisms in the Recovery of Oil.* NS 1.2:M58. Washington, D.C., 1977.

Nelson-Smith, A. "Biological Consequences of Oil Spills." *Marine Environment,* vol. 5 (1977), pp. 46–69.

Odu, C. T. I. "Fermentation Characteristics and Biochemical Reactions of Some Organisms Isolated from Oil Polluted Soils." *Environmental Pollution,* vol. 25, no. 4 (April 1978), pp. 271–76.

Rigassi, Danilo A. "South America: Brazil Leads the Way in Offshore Drilling." *World Oil,* vol. 181, no. 3 (1975), pp. 66–77.

Sittig, Marshall. *Petroleum Transportation and Production, Oil Spills and Pollution Control.* Park Ridge, N.J.: Noyes Data Corporation, 1978.

"South America Shifts Its Focus Seaward." *Drilling-DCW*, vol. 36, no. 4 (1975), pp. 28–30.

United Nations Environment Programme. *Petroleum Industry and the Environment: Seminar Papers and Documents.* Nairobi, 1977.

U.S. Department of Energy. *Environmental Development Plan: Oil Supply.* E 1.36:0024. Washington, D.C., 1978.

Varshney, C. K. "A Quantitative Assessment of Sulfur Dioxide Emission from Fossil Fuels in India." *Air Pollution Control Association Journal*, vol. 28, no. 11 (November 1978), pp. 1141–42.

Pulp and Paper Mills

Atwell, J. S. "Sludge-Dewatering Techniques Must Meet Pollution Control Requirements." *Pulp and Paper*, vol. 52, no. 11 (October 1978), pp. 180–82.

Council on Economic Priorities. *Paper Profits: Pollution in the Pulp and Paper Industry.* Cambridge, Mass.: MIT Press, 1972.

Ellis, D. V. "Pollution Control Regulations and Monitoring Technology: A Review of Research and Development from the Pulp and Paper Industry." *Progress in Water Technology*, vol. 9 (1977), pp. 673–82.

Food and Agriculture Organization. *World Pulp and Paper Demand, Supply and Trade: Selected Papers of an Expert Consultation held in Tunis, 20–22 September 1977.* FAO Forestry Paper no. 4/1 and 4/2. Rome, 1977.

———. *Pulping and Paper-making Properties of Fast-growing Plantation Wood Species.* Rome, 1978.

Gove, G. W. "Pulp and Paper Industry Effluent Management." *Journal of the Water Pollution Control Federation*, vol. 58, no. 6 (June 1978), pp. 1215–54.

Gove, G. W., A. J. Carlson, and J. J. McKeown. "Development of a Management Strategy for Intermittent Process Loss Control." In *TAPPI Environmental Conference Proceedings April 12–14, 1978.* Atlanta, Ga.: Technical Association of the Pulp and Paper Industry, 1978.

Indian Pulp and Paper Technical Association. *Guidelines for Chemical Recovery and Effluent Disposal in Small Paper Plants.* Saharanpur, India: Institute of Paper Technology, 1975.

Meshramkar, P. M. *Research and Development for the Indian Pulp and Paper Industry.* Saharanpur, India: Institute of Paper Technology, 1977.

Monzie, P. "Outlook for Progress and Technological Methods in a Paper Industry Confronted with Environmental Problems." In *Proceedings of United Nations Economic Commission for Europe. Seminar on Non-waste Technology and Production.* Elmsford, N.Y.: Pergamon, 1978.

Nordstrom, H., L. Widell, and G. Wohlfahrt. "Energy and Environment." In FAO, *World Pulp and Paper Demand, Supply, and Trade: Selected Papers of an*

Expert Consultation Held in Tunis 20–22 September 1977. FAO Forestry Paper no. 4/1. Rome: Food and Agriculture Organization, 1977.

Poole, N. J., R. J. Parkes, and D. J. Wildish. "Reaction of Estuarine Ecosystems to Effluent from Paper and Pulp Industry." *Helgolander Wissenschaftliche Meeresuntersuchung*, vol. 30, no. 1–4 (1977), pp. 622–32.

Poole, N. J., D. J. Wildish, and D. D. Kristmanson. "The Effects of the Pulp and Paper Industry on the Environment." *Critical Reviews in Environmental Control*, vol. 8, no. 2 (1978), p. 153.

Roscio, H. A. del, and M. Davidovsky. "Technical-economic Solution to the Problem of Effluents in an Integrated Papermill." *Asociacion de Tecnicos de la Industria Papeleray Celulosica Argentina, ATIPCA*, vol. 16, no. 4 (1977), pp. 45–59. In Spanish.

Sadawarte, N. S., and A. K. Prasad. "Future Needs in Research and Development in Indian Paper Industry." *Indian Pulp and Paper Technical Association*, vol. 14, no. 2 (1977), pp. 93–99.

Sittig, Marshall. *How to Remove Pollutants and Toxic Materials from Air and Water: A Practical Guide.* Pollution Technology Review no. 32. Park Ridge, N.J.: Noyes Data Corporation, 1977.

———. *Pulp and Paper Manufacture, Energy Conservation and Pollution Prevention.* Park Ridge, N.J.: Noyes Data Corporation, 1977.

Villanueva, E. P., and Escolano, J. O. "Water-polluting Effluent of Alkaline Pulping Processes: Its Nature and Treatment." *Technology Journal* (Philippines), vol. 3, no. 1 (April 1978), pp. 43–49.

World Bank. *Environmental Considerations in the Pulp and Paper Industry.* Washington, D.C., 1980.

Smelting Plants

Branquinho, C. L., and U. J. Robinson. "Some Aspects of Lead Pollution in Rio de Janeiro." *Environmental Pollution*, vol. 10, no. 4 (1976), pp. 287–92.

Jenner, J. C., and others. "Transport and Distribution of Lead from Mining, Milling and Smelting Operations in a Forest Ecosystem." In National Science Foundation, *Lead in the Environment, Report and Analysis of Research at Colorado State University*, ed. William R. Boggess. Washington, D.C.: National Science Foundation, 1977.

Nordenson, I., G. Beckman, L. Beckman, and S. Nordstrom. "Occupational and Environmental Risks in and around a Smelter in Northern Sweden: II Chromosomal Aberrations in Workers Exposed to Arsenic." *Hereditas*, vol. 88, no. 1 (1978), pp. 47–50.

Organisation for Economic Co-operation and Development. *Pollution Control Costs in Primary Aluminum Industry.* Washington, D.C.: OECD Publications and Information Center, 1977.

United Nations Environment Programme. *Environmental Aspects of Aluminum Smelting: A Technical Review.* Industry and Environment Technical Review Series 3. Nairobi, 1981.

U.S. Environmental Protection Agency. *Survey of Legislation and Regulation for the Control of Emissions from Aluminum Reduction Plants, with Particular Reference to Fluorides.* Washington, D.C., 1976.

Textile Mills

Conner, J. R. "Disposal of Concentrated Wastes from the Textile Industry." *Industrial Water Engineering,* vol. 14, no. 4 (July–August 1977), pp. 6–11.

Gardiner, D. K., and B. J. Borne. "Textile Waste Waters: Treatment and Environmental Effects." *Dyers and Color Journal,* vol. 94 (August 1978), pp. 334–49.

MacPhee, J. R. "Effects of Legislation and Environmental Pressure on the Textile Industry." *Textile Institute and Industry,* vol. 16 (November 1978), pp. 344–58.

Shenai, V. A. "Chemical Hazards in Mills." *Textile Asia,* vol. 9 (December 1978), pp. 87–88, 97.

Talbort, R. S. "Textile Wastes in Relation to Water Conservation and Waste Water Management." *Journal of the Water Pollution Control Federation,* vol. 50, no. 6 (June 1978), pp. 1258–60.

Tourism

Burn, Henry Pelham. "Packaging Paradise." *Sierra Club Bulletin,* vol. 60, no. 5 (1975), pp. 25–28.

Canada, Department of Industry, Trade and Commerce. *Design in Tourism: Accommodation.* Ottawa: Supply and Services Canada, Publishing Centre, 1977.

Hutchinson, Alan. "Elephant Survival: Two Schools of Thought." *Wildlife,* vol. 17, no. 3 (1975), pp. 104–07.

Gunn, C. A. *Tourism Planning.* New York: Crane, Russak & Co., 1979.

Marsh, John S. "Tourism and Development: The East African Case." *Alternatives,* vol. 5 (1975), p. 15.

Mountfort, Guy. "Tourism and Conservation." *Wildlife,* vol. 17, no. 1 (1975), pp. 30–33.

Organisation for Economic Co-operation and Development. *The Impact of Tourism on the Environment.* Paris, 1980.

―――. *Tourism Policy and International Tourism in OECD Member Countries, 1981.* Paris, 1981.

Seabrooke, A. K., and J. S. Marsh, eds. *The Environmental Impact of Water-based Recreation: An Annotated Bibliography.* Public Administration Series no. 777. Monticello, Ill.: Vance Bibliographies, 1981.

Tangi, Mohamed. "Tourism and the Environment." *Ambio,* vol. 6, no. 6 (1977), pp. 336–41.

Legal Sources

Arbuckle, J. G., and others. *Environmental Law Handbook.* Washington, D.C.: Government Institutes, 1979.

Emond, D. P. *Environmental Assessment Law.* Toronto: Emond-Montgomery Ltd., 1978.

Food and Agriculture Organization. *Food and Agriculture Legislation.* Annual vols., 1952–. Rome.

————. *Water Law in Selected African Countries.* Rome, 1979.

International Environment Reporter. Monthly series. Washington, D.C.: Bureau of National Affairs, Inc.

International Union for Conservation of Nature and Natural Resources. *Survey of Current Developments in International Environmental Law,* comp. Alexandre Charles Kiss. Gland, Switzerland, 1976.

————. *Guidelines for Protected Areas Legislation.* Environmental Policy and Law Paper no. 16. Morges, Switzerland, 1981.

Organisation for Economic Co-operation and Development. *Legal Aspects of Transfrontier Pollution.* Paris, 1978.

Reuester, B., and B. Semma. *International Protection of the Environment: Treaties and Related Documents.* Dobbs Ferry, N.Y.: Oceana, 1975.

Schneider, Jan. *World Public Order of the Environment: Towards an International Ecological Law and Organization.* Toronto: University of Toronto Press, 1979.

Shah, S. M. "Urban Land Use Controls in Asia and the Far East: Legal and Administrative Framework." *Earth Law Journal,* vol. 2 (1976), p. 111.

Telclaff, L. A. *International Environmental Law.* New York: Praeger, 1974.

United Nations Environment Programme. *Register of International Conventions for Environmental Protection.* Claremont, Calif.: Public Affairs Clearinghouse/ Center for California Public Affairs, 1978.

U.S. Congress, Senate Committee on Commerce, Science and Transportation. *Treaties and Other International Agreements on Fisheries, Oceanographic Resources, and Wildlife Involving the United States.* Washington, D.C., 1977.

U.S. General Accounting Office. *Marine Sanctuaries Program Offers Protection and Benefits Other Laws Do Not.* CED-81-37. Washington, D.C., 1981.

Pollution

Dart, R. K., and R. J. Stretton. *Microbiological Aspects of Pollution Control.* New York: Elsevier North-Holland, 1980.

Deininger, Rolf. *Models for Environmental Pollution Control.* Ann Arbor, Mich.: Ann Arbor Science Publishers, Inc., 1974.

Organisation for Economic Co-operation and Development. *Economics of Transfrontier Pollution.* Washington, D.C.: OECD Publications and Information Center, 1976.

——. *Pollution Changes. An Assessment.* Washington, D.C.: OECD Publications and Information Center, 1976.

——. *Transfrontier Pollution and the Role of States.* Paris, 1981.

Air Pollution

Bassow, Herbert. *Air Pollution Chemistry: An Experimenter's Source Book.* Rochelle Park, N.J.: Hayden Book Co., 1976.

Bladen, W. A., and P. P. Karan. "Perception of Air Pollution in a Developing Country." *APCA Journal*, vol. 26 (1976), p. 139.

DeKoning, H. W., and A. Kohler. "Monitoring Global Air Pollution." *Environmental Science and Technology*, vol. 12 (1978), p. 884.

Koenig, L. R. "A Numerical Experiment on the Effects of Regional Atmospheric Pollution on Global Climate." *Journal of Applied Meteorology*, vol. 14 (1975), pp. 1023–36.

Licht, William. *Air Pollution Control Engineering, Basic Calculations for Particulate Collection.* New York: Marcel Dekker, 1980.

National Academy of Sciences. *Testing for Effects of Chemicals on Ecosystems.* Washington, D.C.: National Academy Press, 1981.

Purves, David. *Trace Element Contamination of the Environment.* Amsterdam: Elsevier Scientific, 1977.

Schneider, T., ed. *Air Pollution Reference Measurement Methods and Systems, Proceedings of the International Workshop of the National Institute of Public Health, Bilthoven, Netherlands, 1977.* Studies in Environmental Science, no. 2. Amsterdam: Elsevier Scientific, 1978.

Smith, V. K. *The Economic Consequences of Air Pollution.* Cambridge, Mass.: Ballinger, 1977.

Smith, W. H., ed. *Air Pollution and Forests, Interactions between Air Contaminants and Forest Ecosystems.* New York: Springer-Verlag, 1981.

Stern, A. C., ed. *Air Pollution.* Vols. 1–4. 3d ed. New York: Academic Press, 1976–77.

Strauss, Werner, ed. *Air Pollution Control*. Part 3. Somerset, N.J.: Wiley-Interscience, 1978.

Thomas, Vinod. *Pollution Control in Sao Paulo, Brazil: Costs, Benefits, and Effects on Industrial Location*. World Bank Staff Working Paper no. 501. Washington, D.C.: World Bank, 1981.

Torrey, S., ed. *Trace Contaminants from Coal*. Park Ridge, N.J.: Noyes Data Corporation, 1978.

Warner, P. O. *Analysis of Air Pollutants*. Somerset, N.J.: Wiley-Interscience, 1976.

World Health Organization and World Meteorological Organization. *Air Monitoring Programme Design for Urban and Industrial Areas*. WHO Offset Publication 33. Geneva: World Health Organization, 1977.

Noise and Surface Pollution

Alexandre, A., and J. P. Barde. "Noise Abatement Policies for the Eighties." *Ambio*, vol. 10, no. 4 (1981), pp. 166–70.

Bassow, Herbert. *Land Pollution Chemistry: Experimenter's Source Book*. Rochelle Park, N.J.: Hayden Book Co., 1976.

Bugliarello, George, and others. *The Impact of Noise Pollution*. Elmsford, N.Y.: Pergamon, 1976.

Cunniff, P. J. *Environmental Noise Pollution*. New York: Wiley, 1977.

May, D. N., ed. *Handbook of Noise Assessment*. New York: Van Nostrand Reinhold, 1978.

Nodig, Carl, and others. *Reassessment of Noise Concerns of Other Nations (1976)*. Vol. 2, *Country-by-Country Reviews*. NTIS PB-259 924. Washington, D.C.: Environmental Protection Agency, 1976.

Stathis, F. C. "Community Noise Levels in Patras, Greece." *Journal of the Acoustic Society of America*, vol. 69, no. 2 (1981).

U.S. Environmental Protection Agency. *Toward a National Strategy for Noise Control*. Washington, D.C., 1977.

U.S. General Accounting Office. *Hazardous Waste Sites Pose Investigation, Evaluation, Scientific and Legal Problems*. CED-81-57. Washington, D.C., 1981.

Water Pollution

Bassow, Herbert. *Water Pollution Chemistry: An Experimenter's Source Book*. Rochelle Park, N.J.: Hayden Book Co., 1976.

Branica, M., and Z. Konrad, eds. *Lead in the Marine Environment, Proceedings of the International Experts Discussion, Rovinj, Yugoslavia, 1977*. Elmsford, N.Y.: Pergamon, 1980.

Butler, G. C. *Principles of Ecotoxicology*. Scientific Committee on Problems of the Environment of the International Council of Scientific Unions, SCOPE Report 12. New York: Wiley, 1978.

Ember, L. R. "Water Reuse Reconsidered." *Environmental Science and Technology*, vol. 9 (1975), p. 708.

Fisheries Research Board of Canada. *Aquatic Environmental Quality: Problems and Proposals*. Ottawa: Supply and Services Canada, Publishing Centre, 1977. English and French.

Food and Agriculture Organization. *Pollutants in Aquatic Environments: Detection, Measurement and Monitoring*. Rome, 1976.

———. *Utilization of Heated Effluents and Recirculation Systems for Intensive Aquaculture*. Technical Paper 39. Rome, 1981.

Fried, J. J. *Ground Water Pollution: Theory, Methodology, Modelling and Practical Rules*. New York: Elsevier North-Holland, Inc., 1975.

Goldberg, E. D. *Strategies for Marine Pollution Monitoring*. New York: Wiley, 1976.

Halasi-Kun, G. J. *Pollution and Water Resources: Columbia University Seminar Series*. Vols. 13-1, 13-2. Elmsford, N.Y.: Pergamon, 1980.

Jenkins, S. H., ed. *Nitrogen as a Water Pollutant*. Elmsford, N.Y.: Pergamon, 1977.

Krenkel, P. A., and Vladimir Novotny. *Water Quality Management*. New York: Academic Press, 1980.

Ravera, O., ed. *Biological Aspects of Freshwater Pollution: Proceedings of the Course Held at the Joint Research Centre of the European Communities, Ispra, Italy, 1978*. Elmsford, N.Y.: Pergamon, 1979.

Sanks, R. M. *Water Treatment Plant Design for the Practicing Engineer*. Ann Arbor, Mich.: Ann Arbor Science Publishers, Inc., 1978.

Simpson, J. R., and R. M. Bradley. "The Environmental Impact of Water Reclamation in Overseas Countries." *Water Pollution Control*, vol. 77 (1978), pp. 222–47.

Suess, M. J., ed. *Examination of Water for Pollution Control: A Handbook for Management and Analysis*. Elmsford, N.Y.: Pergamon, 1981.

Sykora, J. L., and others. *Water Quality in Open Finished Water Reservoirs— Allegheny County, Pennsylvania*. EPA-600/1-81-008. Washington, D.C.: U.S. Environmental Protection Agency, January 1981.

Tu, A. T., ed. *Survey of Contemporary Toxicology*. New York: Wiley, 1980.

U.S. General Accounting Office. *The Debate over Acid Precipitation: Opposing Views, Status of Research*. EMD-81-131. Washington, D.C., 1981.

U.S. National Committee for Representation of the United States to the International Association on Water Pollution. *Developments at the Tenth International Conference on Water Pollution Held at Toronto, Canada, on June*

23–27, 1980. EPA-600/9-81-012. Washington, D.C.: U.S. Environmental Protection Agency, February 1981.

Wolfe, D. A., ed. *Fate and Effects of Petroleum Hydrocarbons in Marine Organisms and Ecosystems.* Elmsford, N.Y.: Pergamon, 1977.

Wood, E. J. Ferguson, and R. E. Johannes, eds. *Tropical Marine Pollution.* Elsevier Oceanography Series 12. New York: Elsevier North-Holland, Inc., 1975.

World Health Organization. *Waste Discharge into the Marine Environment: Principles and Guidelines.* Elmsford, N.Y.: Pergamon, 1981.

Zoeteman, B. C. J. *Sensory Assessment of Water Quality.* Series on Environmental Sciences, vol. 2. Elmsford, N.Y.: Pergamon, 1980.

Public Health

Agrawal, Y. K. "Metal Contents in the Drinking Water of Cambay." *Water, Air, and Soil Pollution,* vol. 9, no. 4 (May 1978), pp. 429–31.

American Physiological Society. *Reactions to Environmental Agents.* Handbook of Physiology, section 9. Baltimore, Md., 1977.

Berg, Gerald. *Indicators of Viruses in Water and Food.* Ann Arbor, Mich.: Ann Arbor Science Publishers, Inc., 1978.

Bradley, D. J. "Health Aspects of Water Supplies in Tropical Countries." In *Water, Wastes and Health in Hot Climates,* ed. R. Feachem, M. McGarry, and D. Mara. London and New York: Wiley, 1977.

Calabrese, E. S. *Nutrition and Environmental Health: The Influence of Nutritional Status on Pollutant Toxicity and Carcinogenicity.* New York: Wiley, 1980.

Canada, Environmental Health Directorate. *Dioxyde D'azoe et Oxyde: Recommendations Relatives aux Exposition Professionnelles.* Ottawa: Direction de l'Hygiène du Milieu, 1977.

————. *Qualité Microbiologique de l'Eau Potable.* Ottawa: Direction de l'Hygiène du Milieu, 1977.

Chandra, S., and S. Mandal. "Occurrence of Allergenic Pollen in the Atmosphere of Calcutta—Another Cause for Organic Environmental Pollution." *Science and Culture* (India), vol. 44, no. 4 (April 1978), pp. 175–77.

Dennis, B., and G. P. Patil. "The Use of Community Diversity Indices for Monitoring Trends in Water Pollution Impacts." *Tropical Ecology* (India), vol. 18, no. 1 (1977), pp. 36–51.

Dick, R. I. "Sludge Treatment, Utilization and Disposal." *Journal of the Water Pollution Control Federation,* vol. 50, no. 6 (June 1978), pp. 1096–1131.

Elinson, Jack, and others, eds. *Health Goals and Health Indicators: Policy, Planning and Evaluation.* American Association for the Advancement of Science, Selected Symposia no. 2. Boulder, Colo.: Westview Press, 1978.

Faruqee, Rashid. *Analyzing the Impact of Health Services: Project Experiences from India, Ghana, and Thailand.*" World Bank Staff Working Paper no. 546. Washington, D.C.: World Bank, 1982.

Feachem, R. G. "Infectious Disease Related to Water Supply and Excreta Disposal Facilities." *Ambio*, vol. 6 (1977), pp. 51–54.

Feachem, Richard G., David J. Bradley, Hemda Garelick, and D. Duncan Mara. *Health Aspects of Excreta and Sullage Management—A State-of-the-Art Review.* Appropriate Technology for Water Supply and Sanitation, vol. 3. Washington, D.C.: World Bank, 1980.

Feachem, R. G., M. McGarry, and D. Mara. *Water, Wastes and Health in Hot Climates.* New York: Wiley, 1977.

Golladay, Fredrick. *Health.* World Bank Sector Policy Paper. Washington, D.C.: World Bank, 1980.

———. *Health Issues and Policies in the Developing Countries.* World Bank Staff Working Paper no. 412. Washington, D.C.: World Bank, 1980.

Graun, Gunther F. "Water Borne Outbreaks." *Journal of the Water Pollution Control Federation*, vol. 49, no. 6 (1977), pp. 1268–79.

Hanchett, E. S. *Community Health Assessment: A Conceptual Tool Kit.* New York: Wiley, 1979.

Hattingh, W. H. J. "Reclaimed Water: A Health Hazard?" *Water S.A.*, vol. 3 (1977), pp. 104–12.

Hill, William F., Walter Jakubowski, W. Elmer, and N. A. Clarke. "Detection of Virus in Water; Sensitivity of the Tentative Standard Method for Drinking Water." *Applied and Environmental Microbiology*, vol. 31, no. 2 (1976), pp. 254–61.

International Development Research Centre. *Sanitation in Developing Countries.* Ottawa, 1981.

International Institute for Environment and Development. "Clean Water for All: A Seminar at HABITAT, the United Nations Conference on Human Settlements." *United Nations Water Conference/Mar del Plata, March 14–25, 1976.* Washington, D.C., 1977.

Isley, R. B. *The Relationship of Accessible Water and Adequate Sanitation to Maternal and Child Health: Looking Forward to the Drinking Water and Sanitation Decade.* Washington, D.C.: Water and Sanitation for Health Project, 1979.

Jolley, R. L. *Water Chlorination: Environmental Impact and Health Effects.* Vol. 1. Ann Arbor, Mich.: Ann Arbor Science Publishers, Inc., 1978.

Jolley, R. L., H. Gorcheu, and D. H. Hamilton, Jr. *Water Chlorination: Environmental Impact and Health Effects.* Vol. 2. Ann Arbor, Mich.: Ann Arbor Science Publishers, Inc., 1978.

Kasperson, R. E. "Public Acceptance of Water Re-use: A State-of-the-Art Analysis." In *Water Re-use and the Cities*, ed. R. E. Kasperson and J. X.

Kasperson. Hanover, N.H.: University Press of New England, 1977.

Kaul, A. K., H. Broeshart, W. Takken, M. Weiss, and J. E. Vercoe. "Beneficial Uses of Radiation in Agriculture and Disease Control." *IAEA Bulletin*, vol. 20, no. 3 (1978), p. 2.

Kielman, Arnfried A., and others. *Child and Maternal Health Services in India: The Narangwal Experiment*. Vol. 1, *Integrated Nutrition and Health Care*. Baltimore, Md.: Johns Hopkins University Press, 1984.

Konchady, D. "The Development of Rural Water Supplies and Sanitation, with Particular Reference to Developing Countries." *Public Health in Europe*, vol. 8 (1977), p. 5.

Koshal, R. K. "Water Pollution and Human Health." *Water, Air, and Soil Pollution*, vol. 5 (1976), pp. 289–97.

Lee, S. D. *Biochemical Effects of Environmental Pollutants*, Ann Arbor, Mich.: Ann Arbor Science Publishers, Inc., 1977.

Lenihan, John, and W. W. Fletcher, eds. *Health and the Environment*. Vol. 3, *Environment and Man*. New York: Academic Press, 1976.

Lopez, Pizarro, E. "Water Pollution: A Problem for Health and Agricultural Development." *Correo Agricola* (Costa Rica), vol. 1, no. 2 (September 15, 1977), pp. 8–10.

McKelvey, John J., Bruce F. Eldridge, and Karl Maramorosch, eds. *Vectors of Disease Agents: Interactions with Plants, Animals, and Man*. New York: Praeger, 1981.

National Research Council, Safe Drinking Water Committee. *Drinking Water and Health*. Washington, D.C.: National Academy of Sciences, 1978.

Nellor, M. A. H. *Health Effects of Water Reuse by Groundwater Recharge*. Austin, Tex.: Center for Research in Water Resources, 1980.

Pojasek, Robert B. *Drinking Water Quality Enhancement through Source Protection*. Ann Arbor, Mich.: Ann Arbor Science Publishers, Inc., 1977.

Purdom, P. E., ed. *Environmental Health*. 2d ed. New York: Academic Press, 1979.

Pyle, D. F. *Voluntary Agency-Managed Project Delivering an Integrated Package of Health, Nutrition and Population Services: The Maharashtra Experience*. New Delhi: Ford Foundation, 1979.

Ramanathan, N. L., and S. Kashyap. "Occupational Environment and Health in India." *Ambio*, vol. 4 (1975), p. 60.

Segal, S. J., and B. Winikoff, eds. *Health and Population in Developing Countries, Selected Papers from the 5th Bellagio Population Conference, 1979*. Elmsford, N.Y.: Pergamon, 1980.

Sharpston, M. J. "A Health Policy for Developing Countries." In *Leading Issues in Economic Development*. New York: Oxford University Press, 1976. World Bank Reprint Series no. 67.

Shelat, R. N., and M. G. Mansuri. "Problems of Village Sanitation in India."
  In *Water, Wastes and Health in Hot Climates*, ed. R. Feachem, M. McGarry,
  and D. Mara. New York: Wiley, 1977.

Shuval, H. I. "Public Health Considerations in Waste Water and Excreta
  Re-use for Agriculture." In *Water, Wastes, and Health in Hot Climates*, ed.
  R. Feachem, M. McGarry, and D. Mara. New York: Wiley, 1977.

Subrahmanyam, D. V. "Community Water Supply and Excreta Disposal in
  the Developing Countries." *Ambio*, vol. 6 (1977), pp. 51–54.

Suckcharoen, S. "Alarming Signs of Mercury Pollution in Fresh Water Area of
  Thailand." *Ambio*, vol. 7, no. 3 (1978), pp. 113–16.

Taylor, Carl E., and others. *Child and Maternal Health Services in India: The
  Narangwal Experiment*. Vol. 2, *Integrated Family Planning and Health Care*.
  Baltimore, Md.: Johns Hopkins University Press, 1984.

Tellegen, A. V. "Elephant and the Tree—Community Health Care in a Rural
  Area." *Tropical and Geographical Medicine*, vol. 28 (1976), pp. 553–83.

Thapalyal, Lalit. "Environmental Health: Source of Life." *World Health* (July
  1976), p. 8.

Tordoir, W. F., and E. A. H. Van Heemstra-Lequin, eds. *Field Worker Exposure
  during Pesticide Application, Proceedings of the 5th International Workshop of the
  Scientific Committee on Pesticides of the International Association on Occupational
  Health, The Hague, Netherlands, 9–11 October 1979*. New York: Elsevier
  North-Holland, Inc., 1980.

U.S. General Accounting Office. *Sporadic Workplace Inspections for Lethal and
  Other Serious Health Hazards*. Washington, D.C., April 1978.

———. *Grain Dust Explosions—An Unsolved Problem*. Washington, D.C.,
  1979.

Water, Health, and Development, London: Tri-Med Books, Ltd., 1978.

Willis, C. A. "Health Physics Problems in Developing Countries." *Health
  Physics*, vol. 31 (1976), p. 538.

World Health Organization. *Lead*. Environmental Health Criteria 3. Geneva,
  1977.

———. *Principles and Methods for Evaluation of the Toxicity of Chemicals. Part 1*.
  Environmental Health Criteria 6. Geneva, 1978.

———. *National Decision-making for Primary Health Care: A Study by the
  UNICEP/WHO Joint Committee on Health Policy*. Geneva, 1981.

Yehaskel, A. *Activated Carbon-Manufacture and Regeneration*. Park Ridge, N.J.:
  Noyes Data Corporation, 1978.

Zerbonia, R., and B. Soraya. "Air Pollution Control in Iran." *Journal of the Air
  Pollution Control Association*, vol. 28, no. 4 (April 1978), pp. 334–37.

Sewerage and Sewage Treatment Plants

Feachem, Richard G., David J. Bradley, Hemda Garelick, and D. Duncan Mara. *Sanitation and Disease: Health Aspects of Excreta and Wastewater Management.* World Bank Studies in Water Supply and Sanitation, no. 3. Chichester, U.K.: Wiley, 1983.

Goddard, M., and M.Butler, eds. *Viruses and Wastewater Treatment, Proceedings of International Symposium at the University of Surrey, Guilford, 1980.* Elmsford, N.Y.: Pergamon, 1981.

Kalbermatten, John M., DeAnne S. Julius, and Charles G. Gunnerson. *Appropriate Sanitation Alternatives: A Technical and Economic Appraisal.* World Bank Studies in Water Supply and Sanitation, no. 1. Baltimore, Md.: Johns Hopkins University Press, 1982.

Kalbermatten, John M., DeAnne S. Julius, Charles G. Gunnerson, and D. Duncan Mara. *Appropriate Sanitation Alternatives: A Planning and Design Manual.* World Bank Studies in Water Supply and Sanitation, no. 2. Baltimore, Md.: Johns Hopkins University Press, 1982.

Leich, H. H. "Sanitation for the Developing Nations." *Compost Science,* vol. 18 (1977), p. 21.

McClelland, N. I. *Individual Onsite Waste Water Systems.* 4 vols. Ann Arbor, Mich.: Ann Arbor Science Publishers, Inc., 1977–1978.

McGarry, M. G. "Sanitary Sewers for Underdeveloped Countries—Necessity or Luxury?" *Civil Engineering ASCE,* vol. 48, no. 8 (1978), pp. 70–75.

Pacey, Arnold. "Technology Is Not Enough: The Provision and Maintenance of Appropriate Water Supplies." *Aqua,* vol. 1, no. 1 (1977), pp. 1–58.

Pickford, John. "Sewerage for Developing Countries," *Effluent and Water Treatment Journal,* vol. 18, no. 3 (March 1978), pp. 119–20, 122–23, 127, 129.

Stander, G. J. "Modern Thinking in Waste Water Management." *Water Technology,* vol. 10 (1978), pp. 9–15.

Emissions and Controls

Atkinson, A. L. "Sewage Treatment Internationally." In *Annual Conference of Pollution Control Association of Ontario: Proceedings.* Ontario: Pollution Control Association, 1976.

Benjes, H. H., Jr. *Handbook of Biological Waste Water Treatment, Evaluation, Performance and Cost.* New York: Garland STPM Press, 1980.

Cointreau, Sandra J. *Environmental Management of Urban Solid Waste in Developing Countries: A Project Guide.* World Bank Technical Paper no. 5. Washington, D.C.: World Bank, 1982.

Connor, M. A. "Modern Technology for Recovering Energy and Materials from Urban Wastes—Its Applicability in Developing Countries, First Recycling World Congress: Proceedings." *Survey Engineer*, vol. 2, no. 14 (1978), pp. i–xii.

DaSilva, E. J., A. C. J. Burgers, and R. J. Olembo. "Waste Bioconversion: Environmental Management for Economic Progress in Developing Countries." In *FAO/UNEP Seminar on Residue Utilization—Management for Economic Progress in Developing Countries, Rome (Italy), 18 January 1977*, pp. 7–20. Rome: Food and Agriculture Organization, 1978.

Elmendorf, Mary Lindsay, and Patricia K. Buckles. *Sociocultural Aspects of Water Supply and Excreta Disposal*. Appropriate Technology for Water Supply and Sanitation, vol. 5. Washington, D.C.: World Bank, 1980.

Golueke, C. G. "The Biological Approach to Solid Waste Management." *Compost Science*, vol. 18, no. 4 (July–August 1977), pp. 4–9.

Hoppe, T. C. "Secondary Effluent without Phosphate Removal Used for Cooling Water Make-up." *Water and Sewage Works*, vol. 68, no. 2 (1976), pp. 62–65.

Kalbermatten, John M., DeAnne S. Julius, and Charles G. Gunnerson. *A Sanitation Field Manual*. Appropriate Technology for Water Supply and Sanitation, vol. 11. Washington, D.C.: World Bank, 1980.

―――. *Technical and Economic Options*. Appropriate Technology for Water Supply and Sanitation, vol. 1. Washington, D.C.: World Bank, 1980.

―――. *A Summary of Technical and Economic Options*. Appropriate Technology for Water Supply and Sanitation, vol. 1a. Washington, D.C.: World Bank, 1980.

―――. *Technical and Economic Options*. Appropriate Technology for Water Supply and Sanitation, vol. 1. Washington, D.C.: World Bank, 1980.

Mara, D. Duncan. *Sanitation Alternative for Low-Income Communities—A Brief Introduction*. Appropriate Technology for Water Supply and Sanitation, vol. 1b. Washington, D.C.: World Bank, 1982.

Mattock, Gerry, ed. *New Processes of Waste Water Treatment and Recovery*. New York: Halsted Press, 1978.

Okun, D. A., and G. Ponghis. *Community Wastewater Collection and Disposal*. Geneva: World Health Organization, 1975.

Pickford, John. "Solid Waste in Hot Climates." In *Water, Wastes and Health in Hot Climates*, ed. R. Feachem, M. McGarry, and D. Mara. New York: Wiley, 1977.

Shuval, Hillel I., Charles G. Gunnerson, and DeAnne S. Julius. *Night-Soil Composting*. Appropriate Technology for Water Supply and Sanitation, vol. 10. Washington, D.C.: World Bank, 1980.

Smith, James K., A. J. Englande, and M. M. McKown. *Characterization of Reusable Municipal Waste Water Effluents and Concentration of Organic Constituents*. Cincinnati, Ohio: U.S. Environmental Protection Agency, 1977.

Stander, G. J., and A. J. Clayton. "Planning and Construction of Waste Water Reclamation Schemes as an Integral Part of Water Supply." In *Water, Wastes and Health in Hot Countries*, ed. R. Feachem, M. McGarry, and D. Mara. New York: Wiley, 1977.

U.S. Environmental Protection Agency. *Land Treatment of Municipal Waste Water Effluents. Case Histories.* Washington, D.C., 1976.

————. *Land Treatment of Municipal Waste Water Effluents. Design Factors.* 2 vols. Washington, D.C., 1976.

————. *Fourth Report to Congress: Resource Recovery and Waste Reduction.* Washington, D.C., 1977.

U.S. General Accounting Office. *Conversion of Urban Waste to Energy: Developing and Introducing Alternate Fuels from Municipal Solid Waste.* Washington, D.C., 1979.

Vargas, V. E. *Some Aspects of the Methods Available for the Detection of Pesticides Residues in Sewage Sludges.* London: Imperial College of Science and Technology, 1976.

Water Research Centre, Medmenham. *Water Purification in the European Economic Community: A State of the Art Review.* Elmsford, N.Y.: Pergamon, 1977.

Impact

Allie, G. C., O. O. Hart, T. R. Davies, and A. J. Hassett. "The Effect of Toxic Loads on Effluent Purification Systems." *Water S.A.*, vol. 3, no. 2 (1977), pp. 83–89.

Bunge, W. D., W. N. Cramer, and E. Epstein. "Destruction of Pathogens in Sewage Sludge by Composting." *Transactions of the ASAE*, vol. 21, no. 3 (May–June 1978), pp. 510–14.

Fratric, I., and E. Parrakova. "Waste Management Problems and Their Impact on the Environment." In *Cornell Agricultural Waste Management Conference 1976, Proceedings.* Ann Arbor, Mich.: Ann Arbor Science Publishers, Inc., 1977.

Hill, B. J. "The Effect of Heated Effluent on Egg Production in the Estuarine Prawn *Upogebia africana*." *Journal of Experimental Marine Biology and Ecology*, vol. 29, no. 3 (1977), pp. 291–302.

Standards and Measurement

Bell, C. L. G., and P. B. R. Hazell. "Measuring the Indirect Effects of an Agricultural Investment Project on Its Surrounding Region." *American Journal of Agricultural Economics*, vol. 62, no. 1 (February 1980), pp. 75–86. World Bank Reprint Series no. 152.

Bendix, Selina. *Environmental Assessment: Approaching Maturity*. Ann Arbor, Mich.: Ann Arbor Science Publishers, Inc., 1978.

Berry, B. J. L., ed. *The Social Burdens of Environmental Pollution: A Comparative Metropolitan Data Source*. Cambridge, Mass.: Ballinger, 1976.

Blake, D. H., W. C. Fredrick, and M. S. Myers. *Social Auditing*. New York: Praeger, 1976.

Bond, Richard G., and Conrad P. Straub. *CRC Handbook of Environmental Control*. Cleveland, Ohio: CRC Press Inc., 1978.

Braden, Spruille, III. *Graphic Standards of Solar Energy*. Boston, Mass.: CRB Publishing Co., 1977.

Calabrese, E. J. *Methodological Approaches to Deriving Environmental and Occupational Health Standards*. New York: Wiley, 1978.

Canter, L. *Introduction to Environmental Impact Analysis*. New York: McGraw-Hill, 1977.

Castagnino, W. "Environmental Monitoring in Latin America and the Caribbean." In *International Conference on Environmental Sensing and Assessment*. Vol. 1. New York: Institute of Electrical and Electronics Engineers, 1976.

Cernea, Michael M. *Measuring Project Impact: Monitoring and Evaluation in the PIDER Rural Development Project—Mexico*. World Bank Staff Working Paper no. 332. Washington, D.C.: World Bank, 1979.

Cheremisinoff, P. N., ed. *Industrial Pollution Control Measurement and Instrumentation*. Westport, Conn.: Technomic Publishing Co., 1976.

————. *Air Pollution Sampling and Analysis Deskbook*. Ann Arbor, Mich.: Ann Arbor Science Publishers, Inc., 1978.

Cheremisinoff, P. N., and A. C. Moresi. *Environmental Assessment and Impact Statement Handbook*. Ann Arbor, Mich.: Ann Arbor Science Publishers, Inc., 1977.

Cohen, J. M., and N. T. Uphoff. *Rural Development Participation: Concepts for Measuring Participation for Project Design, Implementation and Evaluation*. Ithaca, N.Y.: Cornell University Rural Development Committee, 1976.

Commission of the European Communities. *Health Criteria (Exposure/Effect Relationships) for Mercury*. Elmsford, N.Y.: Pergamon, 1979.

Cross, F. L., Jr., ed. *Water Pollution Monitoring*. Environmental Monograph Series, vol. 1. Westport, Conn.: Technomic Publishing Co., 1975.

Dassmann, R. F., and Duncan Poore. *Ecological Guidelines for Balanced Land Use: Conservation and Development in High Mountains*. Gland, Switzerland: International Union for Conservation of Nature and Natural Resources, 1979.

De Chiara, Joseph, and Lee E. Koppelman. *Site Planning Standards*. New York: McGraw-Hill, 1978.

Evans, L. S., and others. *Acid Precipitation: Considerations for an Air Quality*

Standard. Upton, N.Y.: Brookhaven National Laboratory, Land and Freshwater Environmental Sciences Group, 1980.

Evison, Lilian M., and A. James. "Microbiological Criteria for Tropical Water Quality." In *Water, Wastes and Health in Hot Climates*, ed. R. Feachem, M. McGarry, and D. Mara. New York: Wiley, 1977.

Fritschen, L. J., and L. W. Gay. *Environmental Instrumentation.* New York: Springer-Verlag, 1979.

Golden, Jack, and others. *Environmental Impact Data Book.* Ann Arbor, Mich.: Ann Arbor Science Publishers, Inc., 1978.

Greenwood, D. R., and others. *A Handbook of Key Federal Regulations and Criteria for Multimedia Environmental Control.* EPA-600/7-79-175. Washington, D.C.: U.S. Environmental Protection Agency, 1979.

Helliwell, P. R., and J. Bossanje. *Pollution Criteria for Estuaries.* New York: Wiley, 1975.

Hicks, Norman, and Paul Streeten. "Indicators of Development: The Search for a Basic Needs Yardstick." *World Development*, vol. 7 (1979), pp. 567–80.

Holland, Edward P., and P. L. Watson. "Measuring the Impacts of Singapore's Area License Scheme." Paper read at the World Conference on Transport Research, April 1977, Rotterdam. Processed.

Inhaber, H. *Environmental Indices.* New York: Wiley, 1976.

International Union for Conservation of Nature and Natural Resources. *Ecological Guidelines for the Use of Natural Resources in the Middle East and Southwest Asia. Proceedings of an International Meeting Held at Persepolis, Iran, 24–30 May 1975.* Gland, Switzerland, 1975.

————. *The Use of Ecological Guidelines for Development in Tropical Forest Areas of Southeast Asia. Papers and Proceedings of a Regional Meeting held in Bandung, Indonesia, 29 May to 1 June 1974.* Gland, Switzerland, 1975.

Jenkins, S. H., ed. *Design-Operation Interactions at Large Waste Water Treatment Plants.* Progress in Water Technology, vol. 8, pt. 6. Elmsford, N.Y.: Pergamon, 1978.

Johnston, D. F., ed. *Measurement of Subjective Phenomena.* Special Demographic Analyses CDS-80-3. Washington, D.C.: U.S. Bureau of the Census, 1981.

Kates, R. W. *Risk Assessment of Environmental Hazard.* New York: Wiley, 1978.

Knox, S., and D. R. Turner. "Polarographic Measurement of Manganese (II) in Estuarine Waters." *Estuarine and Coastal Marine Science*, vol. 10, no. 3 (March 1980), pp. 317–24.

Louck, O. L., and Nance McElrath. *A Position Paper on National Ecological Data Resources.* Indianapolis, Ind.: Butler University Institute of Ecology, Holcomb Research Institute, 1975.

Luken, R. A., and E. H. Pechan. *Water Pollution Control, Assessing the Impacts and Costs of Environmental Standards.* New York: Praeger, 1977.

Mabogunje, A. L., and others. *Shelter Provision in Developing Countries: The Influence of Standards and Criteria.* Scientific Committee on Problems of the Environment of the International Council of Scientific Unions, SCOPE Report 11. New York: Wiley, 1978.

McEachern, John, and Edward L. Towle. *Ecological Guidelines for Island Development.* Gland, Switzerland: International Union for Conservation of Nature and Natural Resources, 1974.

Machenthun, K. M. "Setting Standards for Waste Water Effluents—Present Status and Future Trends." In *Proceedings of a Seminar Held at Michigan University, 1977. College of Engineering.* Ann Arbor, Mich.: Ann Arbor Science Publishers, Inc., 1977.

Milbrath, L. W. "Policy-relevant Quality of Life Research." *American Academy of Political and Social Science.* Annals, vol. 444 (1979), pp. 32–55.

Munn, R. E. *Environmental Impact Assessment: Principles and Procedures.* Scientific Committee on Problems of the Environment of the International Council of Scientific Unions, SCOPE Report 5. New York: Wiley, 1979.

Noll, K. E. *Air Monitoring Survey Design.* Ann Arbor, Mich.: Ann Arbor Science Publishers, Inc., 1977.

Odum, William E. *Ecological Guidelines for Tropical Coastal Development.* Gland, Switzerland: International Union for Conservation of Nature and Natural Resources, 1976.

Organisation for Economic Co-operation and Development. *Approaches to the Development of Health Indicators.* Paris, 1976.

———. *Economic Measurement of Environmental Damage.* Washington: OECD Publications and Information Center, 1976.

———. *Measuring Social Well-Being.* Paris, 1977.

———. *Urban Environmental Indicators.* Paris, 1978.

———. *Indicators for Evaluating Transport Output.* Paris, 1979.

Organization of American States. *Environmental Quality and River Basin Development: A Model for Integrated Analysis and Planning.* Washington, D.C., 1978.

Ott, W. H. *Environmental Indices: Theory and Practice.* Ann Arbor, Mich.: Ann Arbor Science Publishers, Inc., 1978.

Perry, Roger, and Robert Young. *Handbook of Air Pollution Analysis.* New York: Halstead Press, 1978.

Pescod, M. B. "Surface Water Quality Criteria for Tropical Developing Countries." In *Water Wastes, and Health in Hot Climates,* ed. R. Feachem, M. McGarry, and D. Mara. New York: Wiley, 1977.

Poore, Duncan. *Ecological Guidelines for Development in Tropical Rain Forests.* Gland, Switzerland: International Union for Conservation of Nature and Natural Resources, 1976.

Powals, R. J., and others. *Handbook of Stack Sampling and Analysis*. Westport, Conn.: Technomic Publishing Co., 1976.

Rosen, Robert. *Fundamentals of Measurement and Representation of Natural Systems*. General Systems Research Series 1. New York: Elsevier North-Holland, Inc., 1978.

Rossi, R. J., and K. J. Gilmartin. *Handbook of Social Indicators, Sources, Characteristics, and Analysis*. New York: Garland STPM Press, 1980.

Sawaragi, Y., and H. Akashi, eds. *Environmental Systems, Planning, Design and Control*. Elmsford, N.Y.: Pergamon, 1978.

Sinden, J. A., and A. C. Worrell. *Unpriced Values: Decisions without Market Prices*. New York: Wiley, 1979.

Sors, A. I., and G. T. Goodman. "MARC-center for Environmental Assessment." *Environmental Science and Technology*, vol. 11 (1977), pp. 1061–65.

Srinivasan, T. N. "Poverty: Some Measurement Problems." *International Statistical Institute, 41st Session. Proceedings*. World Bank Reprint Series no. 77. Washington, D.C.: World Bank, 1977.

Strauss, Werner. *Measuring and Monitoring Air Pollutants*. Air Pollution Control, pt. 3. New York: Wiley, 1978.

Tunstall, D. B. "Developing Indicators of Environmental Quality: The Experience of the Council on Environmental Quality." *Social Indicators Research*, vol. 6, no. 3 (July 1979), pp. 301–47.

United Nations Educational, Scientific, and Cultural Organization. *The Use of Socioeconomic Indicators in Development Planning*. Paris, 1976.

———. *Indicators of Environmental Quality and the Quality of Life*. Paris, 1978.

United Nations Environment Programme. *Guidelines for Assessing Industrial Environmental Impact and Environmental Criteria for the Siting of Industry*. Nairobi, 1980.

U.S. Department of Commerce. National Bureau of Standards. *Procedures Used at the National Bureau of Standards to Determine Selected Trace Elements in Biological and Botanical Materials*. C 13.10:492. Washington, D.C., 1977.

U.S. Department of Energy. *Socioeconomic Impact Assessment: A Methodology Applied to Synthetic Fuels*. E 1.28:HCP/L2516-01. Washington, D.C., 1978.

U.S. Forest Service. *Forest Service Standard Specifications for Construction of Roads and Bridges*. Washington, D.C., 1979.

U.S. General Accounting Office. *Health Hazard Evaluation Program Needs Improvement*. Washington, D.C., 1978.

———. *Environmental Protection Issues Facing the Nation*. Washington, D.C., 1979.

Walabyeki-Kibirige, George. *Social Indicators in Development Planning*. Vienna: Vienna Institute for Development, 1978.

Warner, P. O. *Analysis of Air Pollutants*. New York: Wiley, 1976.

Technology Transfer and Appropriate Technology

Ahmed, Iftikhar. *Technological Change and Agrarian Structure, A Study of Bangladesh.* Geneva: International Labour Office, 1981.

Bartsch, W. H. *Employment and Technology Choice in Asian Culture.* New York: Praeger, 1977.

Bulfin, R. L., Jr., and J. R. Greenwell. *The Application of Technology in Developing Countries.* Tucson, Ariz.: University of Arizona, Office of Interdisciplinary Programs, Office of Arid Land Studies, 1976.

Canada, Fisheries and Environment Canada. *Environmentally Appropriate Technology.* 4th ed. Ottawa: Supply and Services Canada, Publishing Centre, 1977.

Clark, Wilson. "Big and/or Little? Search Is On for Right Technology." *Smithsonian,* vol. 7, no. 4 (1976), pp. 42–49.

Eckaus, Richard S. *Appropriate Technologies for Developing Countries.* Washington, D.C.: National Academy of Sciences, 1977.

Foley, Gerald. "Alternative Technology in the Third World." *Architectural Design,* vol. 46 (1976), p. 626.

Galtung, Johan. *Development, Environment and Technology: Towards a Technology for Self-Reliance.* New York: United Nations, 1978.

Gonzalez, N. L., ed. *Social and Technological Management in Dry Lands.* American Association for the Advancement of Science, Selected Symposia Series no. 10. Boulder, Colo.: Westview Press, 1978.

International Development Research Centre. *Science and Technology for Development: Case Studies on Technical Change.* Ottawa, 1980.

Jedlicka, Allen D. *Organization for Rural Development: Risk Taking and Appropriate Technology.* New York: Praeger, 1977.

———. "Technology Transfer to Subsistence Farmers: Management Process and Behavioral Technique." *Interciencia,* vol. 6, no. 4 (July–August 1981), pp. 257–60.

Nau, H. R. *Technology Transfer and U.S. Foreign Policy.* New York: Praeger, 1976.

Norman, D. W., and others. *Technical Change and the Small Farmer in Hausaland, Northern Nigeria.* Lansing, Mich.: Michigan State University Department of Agricultural Economics, 1979.

Okolie, C. C. *Legal Aspects of the International Transfer of Technology to Developing Countries.* New York: Praeger, 1975.

Ramesh, Jairam, and Charles Weiss, Jr. *Mobilizing Technology for World Development.* New York: Praeger, 1979.

Sagasti, Francisco. *Technology, Planning and Self-Reliant Development.* New York: Praeger, 1979.

Shapiro, Paul W. *Technology and Science in World Bank Operations.* Washington, D.C.: World Bank, 1980.

Singer, Hans. *Technologies for Basic Needs.* Geneva: International Labour Office, 1979.

Stewart, Frances. *International Technology Transfer: Issues and Policy Options.* Washington, D.C.: World Bank, 1979.

United Nations. *Manual for Development, Transfer and Adaptation of Appropriate Chemical Technology.* New York, 1980.

United Nations Conference on Trade and Development. *Handbook on the Acquisition of Technology by Developing Countries.* New York: United Nations, 1978.

United Nations Educational, Scientific, and Cultural Organization. *Integrated Technology Transfer.* Paris, 1979.

United Nations Industrial Development Organization. *Technologies from Developing Countries.* UNIDO Development and Transfer of Technology Series no. 7. New York: United Nations, 1978.

United Nations University. *Traditional Technology: Obstacle or Resource? Bamboo-Cement Rain-Water Collectors and Cooking Stoves.* Tokyo, 1981.

Volunteers in Technical Assistance. *Village Technology Handbook.* Mt. Rainer, Md., 1978.

Weiss, Charles, Jr. "Mobilizing Technology for Developing Countries." *Science,* vol. 203 (March 16, 1979), pp. 1083–89. World Bank Reprint Series no. 95.

Westphal, L. E. "Research on Appropriate Technology." *Industry and Development,* vol. 2 (1978), pp. 28–46. World Bank Reprint Series no. 88.

World Bank. *Appropriate Technology for Water Supply and Sanitation.* 12 vols. Washington, D.C., 1980. (See Sewerage and Sewage Treatment Plants, above, for titles of selected volumes.)

Transport

Altshuler, A. A., and others. *The Urban Transportation System: Politics and Policy Innovation.* Cambridge, Mass.: MIT Press, 1979.

American Society of Civil Engineers. *Transport for Society.* New York, 1976.

Feibel, Charles, and A. A. Walters. *Ownership and Efficiency in Urban Buses.* World Bank Staff Working Paper no. 371. Washington, D.C.: World Bank, 1980.

Hobbs, F. D. *Traffic Planning and Engineering.* Elmsford, N.Y.: Pergamon, 1977.

Hutchins, J. G. B. *Transportation and the Environment.* Boulder, Colo.: West-view Press, 1977.

Organisation for Economic Co-operation and Development. *Urban Transport and the Environment.* Paris, 1980.

Overseas Development Group. *Bangladesh Rural Transport Study: Final Report.* Dacca: Planning Commission; Norwich, England: Overseas Development Group, University of East Anglia, 1978.

Straszak, A., ed. *The Shinkansen Program: Transportation, Railway, Environmental, Regional, and National Development Issues.* Laxenburg, Austria: International Institute for Applied Systems Analysis, 1981.

"Transport and Urban Form." *Ekistics*, vol. 42, no. 248 (1976), pp. 5–11.

Transportation Research Board. *Environmental and Conservation Concerns in Transportation: Energy, Noise and Air Quality.* Transportation Research Record 648. Washington, D.C., 1977.

U.S. Department of the Interior, Fish and Wildlife Service. *The Potential Effects of Clearing and Snagging on Stream Ecosystems.* I 49.2:C58. Washington, D.C., 1958.

U.S. Department of Transportation. *Rural and Small Urban Transportation Systems.* Washington, D.C., 1981.

Wolf, C. P. *Social Impact Assessment of Transportation Planning: A Preliminary Bibliography.* Public Administration Series P. 250. Monticello, Ill.: Vance Bibliographies, 1979.

World Bank, *Urban Transport.* World Bank Sector Policy Paper. Washington, D.C., 1975.

Airports

American Society of Civil Engineers. *Airports: The Challenging Future.* New York, 1976.

Argonne National Laboratory. *Airport Vicinity Air Pollution Model: Abbreviated Version: User's Guide.* FAA-RD-78-111. Final report by L. L. Conley and D. M. Rote. Washington, D.C.: U.S. Federal Aviation Administration, September 1978.

Canada, Fisheries and Environment Canada. *Bird Hazards to Aircraft.* Ottawa: Supply and Services Canada, Publishing Centre, 1976.

Gelinas, C. G., and H. S. L. Fan. "Reducing Air Pollutant Emissions at Airports by Controlling Aircraft Ground Operations." *Journal of the Air Pollution Control Association*, vol. 29, no. 2 (February 1979), pp. 125–28.

Guski, R. "Defensive Activation toward Noise." *Journal of Sound and Vibration.* vol. 59, no. 1 (July 8, 1978), pp. 107–10.

Harris, A. S., and others. *Guidance Document on Airport Noise Control.* Cambridge, Mass.: Bolt, Beranek and Newman, Inc., 1980.

Jones, F. N. "Residence under an Airport Landing Pattern as a Factor in Teratism." *Archives of Environmental Health,* vol. 33, no. 1 (January–February 1978), pp. 10–12.

Jordan, B. C., and A. J. Broderick. "Emissions of Oxides of Nitrogen from Aircraft." *Air Pollution Control Association Journal,* vol. 29, no. 2 (February 1979), pp. 119–24.

Organisation for Economic Co-operation and Development. *Les Aeroports et L'environment.* Washington, D.C.: OECD Publications and Information Center, 1975.

Rehm, S. "Aircraft Noise and Premature Birth." *Journal of Sound and Vibration,* vol. 59, no. 1 (July 8), pp. 133–35.

Selvain, A. M. "Airborne Electrical and Microphysical Measurements in Clouds in Maritime and Urban Environments." *Atmospheric Environment,* vol. 12, no. 5 (1978), pp. 967–1101.

Tamopolsky, A. "Effects of Aircraft Noise on Mental Health." *Journal of Sound and Vibration,* vol. 59, no. 1 (July 8, 1978), pp. 89–97.

Ports and Harbors

Freemantle, M. H. "Calcium and Phosphate in the Jordan Gulf of Aqaba." *Marine Pollution Bulletin,* vol. 9, no. 3 (March 1978), pp. 79–80.

Imakita, Junichi. *A Techno-Economic Analysis of the Port Transport System.* New York: Praeger, 1978.

McCormick, M. E., ed. *Port and Ocean Engineering under Arctic Conditions.* Elmsford, N.Y.: Pergamon, 1977.

Mood, E. W. "Health Aspects of Coastal Water Pollution." In *International Workshop on Marine Pollution in the Caribbean and Adjacent Regions, Port-of-Spain, Trinidad and Tobago.* Paris: Unesco, 1977.

Organisation for Economic Co-operation and Development. *Maritime Transport.* Annual series. Paris.

Permanent International Association of Navigation Congresses. *Inland and Maritime Waterways and Ports: Design, Construction, Operation, Scotland.* 11 vols. Oxford and New York: Pergamon, 1981.

U.S. Corps of Engineers. *Shore Protection Manual.* D103.6/5:Sh7/3/977/v.1–3. Washington, D.C., 1977.

U.S. Department of Commerce, Maritime Administration. *The Effect of Federal Standards on United States Public Port Development.* C39.202:P83.4. Washington, D.C., 1978.

U.S. General Accounting Office. *The Law of the Sea Conference—Status of the Issues, 1978.* Washington, D.C., 1979.

Roads and Highways

Anand, Sudhir. "The Little-Mirrlees Appraisal of a Highway Project in Malaysia." *Journal of Transportation Economics and Policy,* vol. 10, no. 2 (September 1976), pp. 199–218.

Beenhakker, H. L., and Abderraouf Chammari. *Identification and Appraisal of Rural Roads Projects.* Washington, D.C.: World Bank, 1979.

Belal, M. "Uptake of Lead near Roads in Egypt." *Atmospheric Environment,* vol. 12, no. 6–7 (1978), pp. 1561–62.

DeVeen, J. J. *The Rural Access Roads Program.* Geneva: International Labour Office, 1980.

Headicar, P. G. "West Yorkshire Transportation Studies. Pt. 3. Analysis of Environmental Issues." *Traffic Engineering Control,* vol. 20 (February 1979).

Metcalf, J. B. *Roads and Road Research in Southeast Asia: A Personal Perspective.* Melbourne: Australia Road Research Board, 1979.

Metcalf, J. B., and P. O. Morris. *Road Research and Information: Basic Needs in Land Transport Development.* Melbourne: Australia Road Research Board, 1980.

Munby, Denys, and A. H. Watson. *Road Passenger Transport and Road Goods Transport.* Reviews of United Kingdom Statistical Sources, vol. 7. Elmsford, N.Y.: Pergamon, 1978.

Odzuck, W. "Sociological and Ecological Effects of Road Traffic on the Meadow Vegetation." *Landschaft und Stadt* (Federal Republic of Germany), vol. 10, no. 1 (1978), pp. 23–29. In German.

Oluwande, P. A. "Automobile Traffic and Air Pollution in a Developing Country: An Example of Affluence-Caused Environmental Problems." *International Journal of Environmental Studies,* vol. 11 (1977), pp. 197–203.

Organisation for Economic Co-operation and Development. *Roads and the Urban Environment.* Washington, D.C.: OECD Publications and Information Center, 1975.

———. *Construction of the Roads on Compressible Soils.* Paris, 1980.

———. *Road Research: Traffic Control in Saturated Conditions.* Report prepared by an OECD Road Research Group. Paris, 1981.

Pearsons, K.S. "The Effect of Time-Varying Traffic Noise on Speech Communication and Annoyance." *Noise Control Engineering,* vol. 10, no. 2 (May–June 1978), pp. 108–19.

Tendler, Judith. *New Directions in Rural Roads.* Washington, D.C.: U.S. Department of State, Agency for International Development, Bureau for Program and Policy Coordination, 1979.

Transportation Research Board. *Effects of Air Pollution Regulations on Highway Construction and Maintenance.* National Cooperative Highway Research Report 191. Washington, D.C., 1978.

―――. *Proceedings of the National Seminar on Asphalt Pavement.* Washington, D.C.: National Research Council, 1980.

United Nations Environment Programme. *Environmental Guidelines for the Motor Vehicle and Its Use.* Industry and Environment Guidelines Series 2. Nairobi, 1981.

Wheeler, G. L., and G. L. Rolfe. "The Relationship between Daily Traffic Volume and the Distribution of Lead in Roadside Soil and Vegetation." *Environmental Pollution,* vol. 18, no. 4 (April 1979).

Railroads

Canada, Privy Council Office. *Grain and Rail in Western Canada.* 3 vols. Ottawa: Supply and Services Canada, Publishing Centre, 1977.

Organisation for Economic Co-operation and Development. *Scope for Railway Transport in Urban Areas.* Paris, 1980.

U.S. General Accounting Office. *Problems in the Northeast Corridor Railway Improvement Project.* Washington, D.C., 1979.

U.S. Office of Technology Assessment. *An Evaluation of Railroad Safety.* Y3. T 22/2:2R 13/3. Washington, D.C., 1978.

Urban Development

Anderson, F., and others. *Environmental Improvement through Economic Incentives.* Baltimore, Md.: Johns Hopkins University Press for Resources for the Future, 1977.

Beier, George, Anthony Churchill, Michael Cohen, and Bertrand Renaud. *The Task Ahead for the Cities of the Developing Countries.* World Bank Staff Working Paper no. 209. Washington, D.C.: World Bank, 1975.

Cointreau, Sandra J. *Environmental Management of Urban Solid Wastes in Developing Countries: A Project Guide.* World Bank Technical Paper no. 5. Washington, D.C.: World Bank, June 1982.

Currie, Lauchlin. *Taming the Megalopolis.* Elmsford, N.Y.: Pergamon, 1976.

Doebele, W. A., and others. "Participation of Beneficiaries in Financing Urban Services: Valorization Charges in Bogota, Colombia." *Land Economics,* vol. 55, no. 1 (February 1979), pp. 73–92. World Bank Reprint Series no. 99.

Herbert, J. D. *Urban Development in the Third World.* New York: Praeger, 1979.

Hill, M. "A Goals Achievement Matrix for Evaluating Alternative Plans." *Journal of the American Institute of Planning,* no. 34 (1968).

Holdcraft, L. E. *The Rise and Fall of Community Development in Developing Countries, 1950–65: A Critical Analysis and an Annotated Bibliography.* East Lansing: Michigan State University, Department of Agricultural Economics, 1978.

Laconte, P., ed. *The Environment of Human Settlements, Proceedings of the World Environment and Resources Council Conference, Brussels, 1976.* 2 vols. Elmsford, N.Y.: Pergamon, 1976.

Linn, Johannes F. *Cities in the Developing World: Policies for Their Equitable and Efficient Growth.* New York: Oxford University Press, 1983.

Lynch, K. *Site Planning.* Cambridge, Mass.: MIT Press, 1962.

McGee, T. G. *The Southeast Asian City.* London: G. Bell Long, Ltd., 1967.

McHarg, J. L. *Design with Nature.* New York: Doubleday & Co., Inc., 1969.

Meier, Richard L. "A Stable Urban Ecosystem." *Science*, vol. 192 (1976), pp. 962–68.

Obudho, R. A., and S. S. El-Shakhs, eds. *Development of Urban Systems in Africa.* New York: Praeger, 1979.

Renaud, Bertrand M. *National Urbanization Policies in Developing Countries.* New York: Oxford University Press, 1982.

Rondinelli, D. A., and Kenneth Ruddle. *Urbanization and Rural Development: A Spatial Policy for Equitable Growth.* New York: Praeger, 1978.

Sant, Morgan. *Industrial Movement and Regional Development: The British Case.* Urban and Regional Planning Series no. 11. Oxford and New York: Pergamon, 1975.

Taylor, J., and D. Williams, eds. *Urban Planning Practice in Developing Countries.* Elmsford, N.Y.: Pergamon, 1981.

United Nations Department of Economic and Social Affairs, Centre for Housing, Building and Planning. *A Global Review of Human Settlements.* Elmsford, N.Y.: Pergamon, 1976.

U.S. General Accounting Office. *The Urban and Community Impact Analysis Program, If Retained, Will Need Major Improvements.* GGD-81-85. Washington, D.C., 1981.

Way, P. "Air Photo Interpretation for Land Planning." Cambridge, Mass.: Harvard University, 1968.

World Bank. *Learning by Doing: World Bank Lending for Urban Development, 1972–82.* Washington, D.C., 1983.

Utilities

Newkirk, Ross T. *Environmental Planning for Utility Corridors.* Ann Arbor, Mich.: Ann Arbor Science Publishers, Inc., 1978.

Dams

American Society of Civil Engineers. *Reservoir Flood Standards.* New York, 1975.

Davies, Ryan R., Aristedes Hall, and P. B. N. Jackson. "Some Ecological Aspects of the Cabora Bassa Dam." *Biological Conservation,* vol. 8, no. 3 (1975), pp. 189–201.

Gautam, Sid. "Dam Building No Longer Means 'Instant Progress.'" *Water and Sewage Works,* vol. 125, no. 8 (1978), pp. 30–32.

Greichus, Y. A., A. Greichus, B. D. Amman, D. J. Call, D. C. D. Hamman, and R. N. Pott. "Insecticides, Polychlorinated Biphenyls, and Metals in African Lake Ecosystems: I. Harbeespoort Dam, Transvaal and Voelvlei Dam, Cape Province, Republic of South Africa." *Archives of Environmental Contamination and Toxicology,* vol. 6, no. 2–3 (1977), pp. 371–83.

Hemens, J., D. E. Simpson, and R. J. Warwick. "Nitrogen and Phosphorus Input to the Midmar Dam, Natal." *Water S.A.,* vol. 4, no. 2 (1977), pp. 193–201.

U.S. Department of the Interior, Bureau of Reclamation. *Safety of Dams.* A Review of the Program of the U.S. Bureau of Reclamation for the Safety of Existing Dams. I27.2:D 18/13. Washington, D.C., 1978.

U.S. General Accounting Office. *Improving the Safety of Our Nation's Dams— Progress and Issues.* Washington, D.C., 1979.

Walmsley, R. D., D. F. Toerien, and D. J. Steyn. "Eutrophication of Four Transvaal Dams." *Water S.A.,* vol. 4, no. 2 (April 1978), pp. 61–75.

"Wider." *Development Forum,* vol. 4, no. 9 (1976), pp. 4–5.

Power Plants

Biswas, A. K., ed. *United Nations Water Conference, Summary and Main Documents.* Elmsford, N.Y.: Pergamon, 1978.

Blake, J. W. "Impact of Waste Heat Discharged to Estuaries When Considering Power Plant Siting." In *U.S. Environmental Protection Agency, Proceedings of a Conference.* Vol. 1. Washington, D.C.: EPA, Office of Water Planning and Standards, 1977.

Castillo, J. E. *Evaluation of Hydroelectric Energy Benefits for a Preponderantly Thermal Power System.* Technical Report, CRWR, 148. Austin, Tex.: University of Texas Center for Research in Water Resources, 1977.

Chapman, Douglas G., Dennis P. Lettermaier, Allyn H. Seymour, Gordon L. Swartzman, and Hannah E. Lawson. *Assessing the Impact of Nuclear-Power Plants on the Environment.* Annual Progress Report no. 2. NUREG-CR-0552.

Seattle, Wash.: Washington University Center for Quantitative Science in Forestry, Fisheries and Wildlife, February 1979.

Eliot, R. C. *Boiler Fuel Additives for Pollution Reduction and Energy Saving*. Park Ridge, N.J.: Noyes Data Corporation, 1978.

Fritz, E. S., and others. *Strategy for Assessing Impacts of Power Plants on Fish and Shellfish Populations*. Washington, D.C.: U.S. Fish and Wildlife Service, 1980.

Funk, J. E. "Controlling Fan Noise in and around Power Plants." *Power*, vol. 122 (September 1978), pp. 114–17.

Guile, A. E., and W. Paterson. *Electrical Power Systems*. 2d ed. In sɪ/metric units. Elmsford, N.Y.: Pergamon, 1977.

Hill, P. G. *Power Generation: Resources, Hazards, Technology and Costs*. Cambridge, Mass.: MIT Press, 1977.

Howe, J., ed. *Transfer of Nuclear Technology*. Selected papers presented at the Iran Conference, April 1977. Elmsford, N.Y.: Pergamon, 1977.

International Atomic Energy Agency. *Development of Regulatory Procedures for the Disposal of Solid Radioactive Waste in Deep Continental Formations*. Vienna, 1980.

———. *Environmental Effects of Cooling Systems*. Vienna, 1980.

———. *Waste Management and Disposal: Report of the International Nuclear Fuel Cycle Evaluation Working Group 7*. Vienna, 1980.

———. *Operating Experience with Nuclear Power Stations in Member States in 1979*. Vienna, 1981.

———. *Planning for Off-site Response to Radiation Accidents in Nuclear Facilities: Recommendations*. Safety Series no. 55. Vienna, 1981.

Noyes, Robert, ed. *Offshore and Underground Power Plants*. Park Ridge, N.J.: Noyes Data Corporation, 1977.

Organisation for Economic Co-operation and Development. *Clean Fuel Supply (Factors Affecting SO₂ Emissions in the Mid-1980's)*. Washington, D.C.: OECD Publications and Information Center, 1978.

———, Nuclear Energy Agency. *Safety of the Nuclear Fuel Cycle: A State-of-the-Art Report by a Group of Experts of the NEA Committee on the Safety of Nuclear Installations*. Paris, 1981.

Reay, D. A. *Industrial Energy Conservation, A Handbook for Engineers and Managers*. Elmsford, N.Y.: Pergamon, 1977.

Rosenblum, L., W. J. Bifano, G. F. Heim, and A. F. Ratajczak. *Photovoltaic Power Systems for Rural Areas of Developing Countries*. NASA-TM-7909. Cleveland, Ohio: National Aeronautics and Space Administration, Lewis Research Center, 1977.

Smith, Frank A., and Harold C. Hodge. "Airborne Fluorides and Man: Part 1." *CRC Critical Reviews in Environmental Control*, vol. 8, no. 4 (1978).

Sung, R., D. Strehler, and C. Thorne. *Assessment of the Effects of Chlorinated Seawater from Power Plants on Aquatic Organisms.* Final Task Report to the Environmental Protection Agency. Washington, D.C.: TRW, Inc., Redondo Beach, Calif., 1978.

U.S. Department of the Interior, Fish and Wildlife Service. *Impacts of Coal-fired Power Plants on Fish, Wildlife and Their Habitats.* I 49.2:C63. Washington, D.C., 1978.

U.S. General Accounting Office. *The Effect of Regulation on the Electric Utility Industry.* EMD-81-35. Washington, D.C., 1981.

Water Pollution Control in Developing Countries, Proceedings of the International Conference Held at Bangkok, Thailand, February 1978. Elmsford, N.Y.: Pergamon, 1978.

Woite, G. "The Potential Role of Nuclear Power in Developing Countries." *IAEA Bulletin,* vol. 17, no. 3 (1975), pp. 21–32.

Water Resources

Al-Layla, M. Anis, S. Almad, and E. J. Middlebrooks. *Water Supply Engineering Design.* Ann Arbor, Mich.: Ann Arbor Science Publishers, Inc., 1977.

Balek, Jaroslav. *Hydrology and Water Resources in Tropical Africa,* Developments in Water Science, 8. New York: Elsevier North-Holland, Inc., 1977.

Fish, H., P. M. Higgins, W. D. Schmidt, M. R. Henzen, and M. J. Pieterse. "Water Resources Quality Management Workshop." *Progress in Water Technology,* vol. 9 (1978), p. 171.

Food and Agriculture Organization. *Aquaculture Planning in Asia.* Rome, 1976.

———. *Aquaculture Planning in Latin America.* Rome, 1976.

———. *Aid for Aquaculture Development.* Rome, 1979.

Galal, S., A. A. Husseiny, J. J. Allard, J. M. Rovel, P. Treille, M. Aswed, and S. E. Hedayat. "Desalting Activities in North Africa and the Gulf States." *Desalination,* vol. 20 (1976), p. 217.

Glennie, Colin. *A Model for the Development of a Self-Help Water Supply Program.* World Bank Technical Paper no. 2. Washington, D.C.: World Bank, 1982.

Hidore, J. J. "Acceleration of Dessication and Population Trauma in Sub-Saharan Africa." *Water Resources Bulletin,* vol. 13 (1977), p. 783.

Howe, Charles W. "The Effects of Water Resource Development on Economic Growth: The Conditions for Success." *Natural Resources Journal,* vol. 16, no. 4 (1976), pp. 939–55.

International Development Research Centre. *Rural Water Supply in Developing Countries.* Ottawa, 1981.

Jorgensen, S. E. *Lake Management.* Elmsford, N.Y.: Pergamon, 1980.

Kamrany, Nake M. "The Sahel Drought: Major Development Issues." *Ekistics*, vol. 43 (1977), p. 314.

Krishnamurthy, K. V. "The Challenge of Africa's Water Development." *Natural Resources Forum*, vol. 1, no. 4 (1977), pp. 369–75.

Lauria, D. T., Donald L. Schlenger, and Roland W. Wentworth. "Models for Capacity Planning of Water Systems." *Journal of Environmental Engineering Division, ASCE*, vol. 103, no. 2 (1977), pp. 273–91.

Lord, William B., and others. *Analysis of Water Resources Planning and Decision-Making Processes and Outcomes.* NTIS-PB81-170482. Boulder, Colo.: Policy Science Associates, January 1981.

Major, D. C. *Applied Water Resource Systems Planning.* Englewood Cliffs, N.J.: Prentice-Hall, 1979.

Organisation for Economic Co-operation and Development. *Water Management Policies and Instruments.* Washington, D.C.: OECD Publications and Information Center, 1977.

Palmer, C. F. "Development of Water Tariffs in Central America." *Planning and Administration*, vol. 7, no. 2 (Autumn 1980), pp. 49–54.

Saunders, Robert J., and Jeremy J. Warford. *Village Water Supply: Economics and Policy in the Developing World.* Baltimore, Md.: Johns Hopkins University Press, 1976.

U.S. General Accounting Office. *Improved Formulation and Presentation of Water Resources Project Alternatives Provide a Basis for Better Management Decisions.* Washington, D.C., February 1978.

————. *U.S. Development Assistance to the Sahel—Progress and Problems.* Washington, D.C., 1979.

————. *U.S. Strategy Needed for Water Supply Assistance to Developing Countries.* ID-81-51. Washington, D.C., 1981.

JAMES A. LEE is the environmental adviser at the World Bank.

The most recent World Bank publications are described in the annual spring and fall lists. The latest edition is available free of charge from the Publications Sales Unit, Department B, The World Bank, Washington, D.C. 20433, U.S.A.